KITCHENER PUBLIC LIBRARY

3 9098 02199082 4

D1265508

SOCIALISM AND COMMUNISM

Political and Economic Systems

SOCIALISM AND COMMUNISM

Edited by John Murphy

Britannica
Educational Publishing

IN ASSOCIATION WITH

ROSEN
EDUCATIONAL SERVICES

Published in 2015 by Britannica Educational Publishing (a trademark of Ency-clopædia Britannica, Inc.) in association with The Rosen Publishing Group, Inc. 29 East 21st Street, New York, NY 10010

Copyright © 2015 by Encyclopædia Britannica, Inc. Britannica, Encyclopædia Britannica, and the Thistle logo are registered trademarks of Encyclopædia Britannica, Inc. All rights reserved.

Distributed exclusively by Rosen Publishing.
To see additional Britannica Educational Publishing titles, go to rosenpublishing.com.

First Edition

Britannica Educational Publishing
J.E. Luebering: Director, Core Reference Group
Anthony L. Green: Editor, Compton's by Britannica

Rosen Publishing
Hope Lourie Killcoyne: Executive Editor
John Murphy: Editor
Nelson Sá: Art Director
Brian Garvey: Designer
Cindy Reiman: Photography Manager
Karen Huang: Photo Researcher
Introduction and supplementary material by John Murphy

Cataloging-in-Publication Data

Socialism and communism/[edited by] John Murphy.—First edition.
    pages cm.—(Political and economic systems)
Includes bibliographical references and index.
ISBN 978-1-62275-335-2 (library bound)
1. Socialism—History—Juvenile literature. 2. Communism—History—Juvenile literature. I. Murphy, John, 1968–
HX36.S63 2015
335--dc23

                                                              2014004690

Manufactured in the United States of America

On the cover, p. 3: *Franz Aberham/Photographer's Choice/Getty Images*

CONTENTS

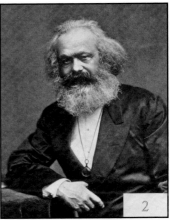

2

7

36

INTRODUCTION

Despite the fact that the political and economic systems and philosophies known as socialism and communism dominated much of the history of the twentieth century—and occasionally joined forces to oppose the common enemy that was capitalism—there is much confusion in the popular imagination about what these two philosophies share and how they differ. Karl Marx, known as the father of communism and a preeminent socialist thinker, often used the terms *communism* and *socialism* interchangeably.

Socialism predates Marx by thousands of years, according to the measure of some historians. They locate its primitive origins in biblical sources, the early Christian church, the writings of Plato and Thomas More, and the opinions of disgruntled French citizen-radicals who felt the French Revolution had not gone far enough. But it was not until the nineteenth century that socialism emerged as a coherent, broadly relevant, elaborately articulated, and globe-spanning political and economic philosophy. At this time, a worthy adversary was also emerging: industrial capitalism. In passionate, outraged, and righteous reaction to the perceived exploitations, depredations, and degradations of the Industrial Age and unfettered laissez-faire capitalism, socialism took up a diametrically opposed position. It sought to stand up for and with all the world's oppressed peoples, especially its workers, who were being crushed under the wheels of industrialization, privatized greed, and a ruling elite's attempt to monopolize wealth.

Rooted in utopian visions of a just and equal society, early socialists were committed primarily to public control and/or ownership of land, social cooperation, meaningful and stimulating work, collective labor, and reduced inequalities

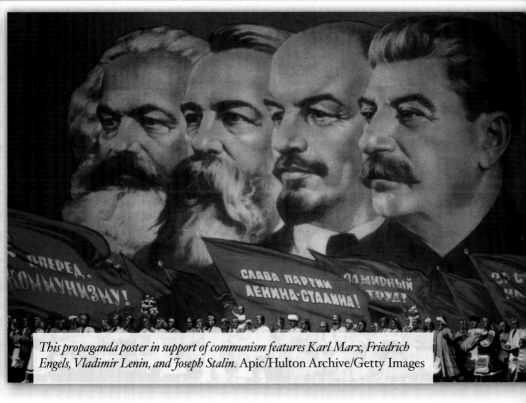

This propaganda poster in support of communism features Karl Marx, Friedrich Engels, Vladimir Lenin, and Joseph Stalin. Apic/Hulton Archive/Getty Images

of wealth. This somewhat benign utopianism gained some teeth when more radical socialist thinkers began advocating the view that society could not be transformed until the state and the ruling elites who guarded and richly benefitted from the capitalist system were overthrown. Thus, an anarchic and revolutionary spirit entered socialist philosophy, greatly radicalizing it. Socialism was no longer devoted to utopian visions of social harmony and cooperation. Instead, it called for revolutionary conflict, insurrectionist conspiracies, and paternalistic dictatorships.

Another important new element in the evolution of socialism was the placing of class struggle at the very center of history and society. The notion of class struggle was articulated by Marx and his friend and collaborator, Friedrich Engels. These two men believed that all human history was leading inevitably to a class-based warfare that would result in the violent overthrow of the upper classes by the working class. The workers would someday spontaneously rise up—at different times and places all around the world—and seize control of the land, factories, mines, transportation infrastructure, and other sources of wealth and means of production. In the final stages of revolution, a government of the people—actually a temporary dictatorship of the proletariat—would be replaced by a community of the people, fully cooperative, equitable, and self-governing.

Marx's refashioning of socialism proved to be so influential that many of its adherents began referring to themselves as Marxists. It was only after his death, however, that socialism and communism began to diverge and acquire differing meanings and distinct agendas. One wing of the movement began to question the wisdom and achievability of violent overthrow of the ruling elite, believing that socialism's aims could be achieved gradually and peacefully and through a democratic process. Radical Marxists denounced these so-called revisionists.

Among the most vociferous of these die-hard revolutionaries was Vladimir Lenin, leader of the Bolshevik, or majority, faction of the Russian Social-Democratic Workers' Party. This party triumphed in the October Revolution of 1917, filling the power vacuum left by overthrowing the tsar, Russia's former ruler, the previous February. Lenin's brand of Marxism—which was committed to anticapitalist revolution worldwide and insisted upon the allegedly temporary or transitional dictatorship of the proletariat by a governing or "vanguard" party—came to be known as Marxism-Leninism and embodied what came to be viewed as orthodox communism.

The split with the more democratically minded and moderate socialist movement was complete. Any hope for an alliance of convenience, if not of ideology, between communists and socialists in order to combat their common enemy of free-market capitalism was extinguished. Indeed the socialists, often under the banner of Social Democrats or Labour, rose to power across Western Europe through legitimate democratic means—they won free and fair elections. Once in power, they set about nationalizing industries, protecting workers' rights, establishing welfare programs, and creating more economically equitable societies. They achieved some measure of their utopian vision through compromise, pragmatism, campaigning, and a lack of bloodshed and violence. State power was won democratically, not seized by force. Society wasn't overturned or destroyed but renovated and transformed from the inside out. Elements of capitalism and free enterprise were retained to varying degrees in various nations, but social protections were installed to prevent the harshest effects of a competition-based economy. The notion of a commonwealth—of there being certain resources, industries, and forms of wealth within a nation that belonged to all its citizens—was preserved as a counterweight to private enterprise and individual wealth-building.

The outbreak of World War II led to a brief reuniting of socialists and communists in the face of the fascist threat posed by Germany, Italy, and, though officially neutral, Spain. The extent to which this was a marriage of convenience is apparent when one considers the inclusion of the arch-capitalist nation, the United States, in the Allied cause and the rapid disintegration of this tenuous alliance at the end of the war once the common cause no longer existed. The Soviet Union took advantage of the chaos and devastation of postwar Europe to establish a large sphere of influence throughout Eastern Europe. With the descent of the so-called Iron Curtain, Europe became sharply divided. Socialist Western Europe was cut off from the communist east, with Berlin—and Germany itself—being literally cut in two. World War II had ended, but the Cold War had just begun.

Communist revolution was exported or spread independently to China, other parts of Asia, Eastern Europe, and Central and South America. With Joseph Stalin's increasingly tyrannical reign in the Soviet Union and the rise of Mao Zedong in China, the "vanguard" governments of the proletariat shed any pretense to a temporary status and began to exert an overtly dictatorial and totalitarian dominance over the downtrodden people who were supposed to be ennobled and set free by communist revolution. Both leaders also stood, with undisputed, absolute power, at the helm of a single-party government of professional bureaucrats and party elites. The so-called cult of personality established by both Stalin and Mao made a sham of their pretense to be ruling on behalf of the people. They cynically used collectivism not to free their citizens from oppression and scarcity but to exert absolute control, consolidate their power, and create a fortress mentality in which the overstated specter of external threats distracted the populace from internal corruption, the enrichment of party elites, human rights abuses, and domestic tyranny.

In the meantime, socialist parties in Western Europe enjoyed success at the polls and came to dominate many of the governments. As Cold War divisions deepened and hardened, the socialists became more firmly allied with the forces of capitalism, including the great counterweight to Soviet communism: the United States. Working within a democratic system and dependent upon the support of both business and ordinary citizens, Western European socialists began to advocate a mixed or market economy, which combined private ownership and free enterprise with some government control of the economy and the institution of extensive welfare programs. More ideologically driven, "pure" socialists derided this more pragmatic model as "bureaucratic socialism."

With the Soviet Union and United States standing at ideologically opposite positions and bristling with nuclear weapons, the Cold War often threatened to get very hot indeed. What actual fighting occurred happened indirectly or by proxy in Korea, Vietnam, Cuba, and Latin America. The cost of the nuclear and conventional arms race began to wear on both nations, but the Soviet Union—with its aging and inefficient industries, sprawling and increasingly decentralized territory, and massive, hungry, and oppressed population—was far less well positioned to go the distance in a ruinously expensive standoff.

In order to address both ailing industry and an increasingly restive population, Soviet Premier Mikhail Gorbachev launched two initiatives—*glasnost* ("openness") and *perestroika* ("restructuring"). Glasnost allowed for the loosening of some political and social controls, resulting in opposition parties, multicandidate elections, and greater press freedoms. Perestroika reduced government control of the economy, strengthened the hand of local governments (thereby diminishing the role of the Communist Party and its central governance), and encouraged businesses to become self-financing rather than state-subsidized. Gorbachev's intent was not to do away with communism but to modernize it and make it viable within the context of the late twentieth century. It was hoped that both of Gorbachev's reform initiatives would help do away with one-party rule, boost productivity and efficiency, and increase the standard of living for a long-suffering populace.

In some ways, Gorbachev released a genie that Communist Party hardliners throughout the Iron Curtain could not put back in the bottle. The end result was not only the disintegration of the Iron Curtain—which quite literally fell when joyous throngs tore down the Berlin Wall and West and East Germans were reunited for the first time in almost thirty years—but also the collapse of the Soviet Union. For all intents and purposes, the Cold War was over and Marxist-Leninist communism was relegated to the dustbin of history. Most of the countries that remained nominally communist, like China, embraced market economics to a degree that would have been unthinkable a generation before, although totalitarian one-party rule remained in place. Some communist stalwarts, like Cuba and North Korea, remained, but they were increasingly isolated without the backing of the formerly ideologically orthodox powerhouses that were the Soviet Union and communist China.

Socialism and communism were once so ideologically close as to be almost indistinguishable. As terms, they were used interchangeably. Both were committed to an uncompromising vision of egalitarianism, fairness, communal effort, and social progress that stood diametrically opposed to the perceived greed, individualism, and exploitation of market capitalism. Yet both ideologies ran up against the hard realities of history and, as a result, deviated from each other and from their core principles.

The communism of Mao, Lenin, Stalin, and their successors was a cynically protracted "revolution" that, in fact, served only to preserve the conservative rule of party professionals who siphoned off the resources of the people and the land, creating inequities and suffering as great as any seen in the capitalist democracies they despised. Soviet communism collapsed under the weight of its own corruption, repression, hypocrisy, and inefficiency. China embraced the greatest excesses of freewheeling capitalism while preserving the autocratic social controls of the Mao era.

Meanwhile, socialism traded in its utopian ideals for a far more pragmatic and conciliatory compromise of sorts with free market capitalism. Hybrid systems coupled private enterprise with governmental commitment to public welfare, economic regulation, and, in some cases, limited nationalizing of industries and resources. Inequalities of wealth and status were not leveled out, but it could be argued that people were given the chance to compete fairly for greater prosperity and opportunity, while being able to rely upon a social safety net that would catch them if they fell. This was far more than a citizen of either the United States or the U.S.S.R. could hope for or expect.

This is the story of two defining political and economic ideologies of the modern era and their tangled and tortured relationship to each other and to the era's third dominant ideology: capitalism. It is a story of idealism and cynicism, hope and despair, humanity and inhumanity, revolution and repression, the social good and self-interest, philosophical passion and cold political calculation, and power and powerlessness. The entire political, economic, and social history of the industrial and postindustrial world is contained in these pages, forming an incredibly detailed and nuanced panorama of the modern era. This book will explain how we arrived at our current moment in history and illuminate the direction that the possible pathways forward may take us. It is an invaluable guide to where we've been, where we are, and where we may be going as citizens of a world still grappling with age-old questions regarding governance, equality, fairness, justice, freedom, and the rights of the individual versus those of the community. Socialism and communism attempted to answer these questions definitively and with finality. In that they failed, but in doing so, they highlighted the surpassing importance of the questions themselves and of the ordinary people whose lives and livelihoods hang in the balance.

CHAPTER 1

SOCIALISM

Socialism is a social and economic doctrine that calls for public, rather than private, ownership or control of property and natural resources. According to the socialist view, individuals do not live or work in isolation but live in cooperation with one another. Furthermore, everything that people produce is in some sense a social product, and everyone who contributes to the production of a good is entitled to a share in it. Society as a whole, therefore, should own or at least control property for the benefit of all its members.

This conviction puts socialism in opposition to capitalism, which is based on private ownership of the means of production and allows individual choices in a free market to determine how goods and services are distributed. Socialists complain that capitalism necessarily leads to unfair and exploitative concentrations of wealth and power in the hands of the relative few who emerge victorious from free market competition—people who then use their wealth and power to reinforce their dominance in society. Because such people are rich, they may choose where and how to live, and their choices in turn limit the options of the poor. As a result, terms such as *individual freedom* and *equality of opportunity* may be meaningful for capitalists but can only ring hollow for working people, who must do the capitalists' bidding if they are to survive. As socialists see it, true freedom and equality

Karl Marx (left) *and Friedrich Engels* (right) *collaborated on the writing of* The Communist Manifesto *and began a revolution in thought that continues today.* Courtesy of the trustees of the British Museum; photograph, J.R. Freeman & Co. Ltd. *(right)*, Print Collector/Hulton Archive/Getty Images *(left)*

require social control of the resources that provide the basis for prosperity in any society. Karl Marx and Friedrich Engels made this point in *Manifesto of the Communist Party* (1848), when they proclaimed that in a socialist society "the condition for the free development of each is the free development of all."

This fundamental conviction nevertheless leaves room for socialists to disagree among themselves with regard to two key points. The first concerns the extent and the kind of property that society should own or control. Some socialists have thought that almost everything except personal items, such as clothing, should be public property. This is true of the society envisioned by the English humanist Sir Thomas More, in his *Utopia* (1516). Other socialists, however, have been willing to accept or even welcome private ownership of farms, shops, and other small or medium-sized businesses.

The second disagreement concerns the way in which society is to exercise its control of property and other resources. In this case, the main camps consist of loosely defined groups of centralists and decentralists. On the centralist side are socialists who want to invest public control of property in some central authority, such as the state—or the state under the guidance of a political party, as was the case in the Soviet Union. Those in the decentralist camp believe that decisions about the use of public property and resources should be made at the local, or lowest-possible, level by the people who will be most directly affected by those decisions. This conflict has persisted throughout the history of socialism as a political movement.

Origins

The origins of socialism as a political movement lie in the Industrial Revolution. Its intellectual roots, however, reach back almost as far as recorded thought—even as far as Moses, according to one history of the subject. Socialist or communist ideas certainly played an important part in the ideas of the ancient Greek philosopher Plato, whose *Republic* depicts an austere society in which men and women of the "guardian" class share with each other not only their few material goods but also their spouses and children. Early Christian communities also practiced the sharing of goods and labour, a simple form of socialism subsequently followed in certain forms of monasticism. Several monastic orders continue these practices today.

Christianity and Platonism were combined in More's *Utopia*, which apparently recommends communal ownership as a way of controlling the sins of pride, envy, and greed. Land and houses are common property on More's imaginary island of Utopia, where everyone works for at least two years on the communal farms and people change houses every ten years so that no one develops pride of possession. Money has been abolished, and people are free to take what they need from common storehouses. All the Utopians live simply, moreover, so that they are able to meet their needs with only a few hours of work a day, leaving the rest for leisure.

More's *Utopia* is not so much a blueprint for a socialist society as it is a commentary on the failings that he perceived in the supposedly Christian societies of his day. Religious and political turmoil, however, soon inspired others to try to put utopian ideas into practice. Common ownership was one of the aims of the brief Anabaptist regime in the Westphalian city of Münster during the Protestant Reformation, and several communist or socialist sects sprang up in England in the wake of the Civil Wars (1642–51). Chief among them was the Diggers, whose members claimed that God had created the world for people to share, not to divide and exploit for private profit. When they acted on this belief by digging and planting on land that was not legally theirs, they ran afoul of Oliver Cromwell's Protectorate, which forcibly disbanded them.

Whether utopian or practical, these early visions of socialism were largely agrarian. This remained true as late as the French Revolution, when the journalist François-Noël Babeuf and other radicals complained that the Revolution had failed to fulfill the ideals of liberty, equality, and fraternity. Adherence to "the precious principle of equality," Babeuf argued, requires the abolition of private property and common enjoyment of the land and its fruits. Such beliefs

This woodcut by Ambrosius Holbein illustrates the island of Utopia as envisioned by Thomas More in the 1518 edition of Utopia. Photos.com/ Thinkstock

led to his execution for conspiring to overthrow the government. The publicity that followed his trial and death, however, made him a hero to many in the nineteenth century who reacted against the emergence of industrial capitalism.

Utopian Socialism

Conservatives who saw the settled life of agricultural society disrupted by the insistent demands of industrialism were as likely as their radical counterparts to be outraged by the self-interested competition of capitalists and the squalor of industrial cities. However, the radicals distinguished themselves by their commitment to equality and willingness to envision a future in which industrial power and capitalism were divorced. To their moral outrage at the conditions that were reducing many workers to pauperism, the radical critics of industrial capitalism added a faith in the power of people to put science and an understanding of history to work in the creation of a new and glorious society. The term *socialist* came into use about 1830 to describe these radicals, some of the most important of whom subsequently acquired the title of "utopian" socialists.

One of the first utopian socialists was the French aristocrat Claude-Henri de Saint-Simon. Saint-Simon did not call for public ownership of productive property, but he did advocate public control of property through central planning, in which scientists, industrialists, and engineers would anticipate social needs and direct the energies of society to meet them. Such a system would be more efficient than capitalism, according to Saint-Simon, and it even has the endorsement of history itself. Saint-Simon believed that history moves through a series of stages, each of which is marked by a particular arrangement of social classes and a set of dominant beliefs. Thus, feudalism, with its landed

The word utopia *was compounded by Thomas More from the Greek words* ou *("not") and* topos *("place"). This 1527 painting of More was created by Hans Holbein the Younger.* Photos.com/Thinkstock

Other Early Socialists

Other socialists in France began to agitate and organize in the 1830s and '40s; they included Louis Blanc, Louis-Auguste Blanqui, and Pierre-Joseph Proudhon. Blanc, the author of *L'Organisation du travail* (1839; *The Organization of Labour*), promoted a scheme of state-financed but worker-controlled "social workshops" that would guarantee work for everyone and lead gradually to a socialist society. Blanqui, by contrast, was a revolutionary who spent more than thirty-three years in prison for his insurrectionary activities. Socialism cannot be achieved without the conquest of state power, he argued, and this conquest must be the work of a small group of conspirators. Once in power, the revolutionaries would form a temporary dictatorship that would confiscate the property of the wealthy and establish state control of major industries.

In *Qu'est-ce que la propriété?* (1840; *What Is Property?*), Proudhon memorably declared, "Property is theft!" This assertion was not quite as bold as it appears, however, since Proudhon had in mind not property in general but property that is worked by anyone other than its owner. In contrast to a society dominated by capitalists and absentee landlords, Proudhon's ideal was a society in which everyone had an equal claim, either alone or as part of a small cooperative, to possess and use land and other resources as needed to make a living. Such a society would operate on the principle of mutualism, according to which individuals and groups would exchange products with one another on the basis of mutually satisfactory contracts. Ideally, all this would be accomplished without the interference of the state, for Proudhon was an anarchist who regarded the state as an essentially coercive institution. Yet his anarchism did not prevent him from urging Napoleon III to make free bank credit available to workers for the establishment of mutualist cooperatives—a proposal the emperor declined to adopt.

nobility and monotheistic religion, was giving way to industrialism, a complex form of society characterized by its reliance on science, reason, and the division of labour. In such circumstances, Saint-Simon argued, it makes sense to put the economic arrangements of society in the hands of its most knowledgeable and productive members so that they may direct economic production for the benefit of all.

Another early socialist, Robert Owen, was himself an industrialist. Owen first attracted attention by operating textile mills in New Lanark, Scot., that were both highly profitable and, by the standards of the day, remarkably humane: no children under age ten were employed. Owen's fundamental belief was that human nature is not fixed but formed. If people are selfish, depraved, or vicious, it is because social conditions have made them so. Change the conditions, he argued, and people will change; teach them to live and work together in harmony, and they will do so. Thus, Owen set out in 1825 to establish a model of social organization, New Harmony, on land he had purchased in the U.S. state of Indiana. This was to be a self-sufficient, cooperative community in which property was commonly owned. New Harmony failed within a few years, taking most of Owen's fortune with it, but he soon turned his attention to other efforts to promote social cooperation—trade unions and cooperative businesses, in particular.

Similar themes mark the writings of François-Marie-Charles Fourier, a French clerk whose imagination, if not his fortune, was as extravagant as Owen's. Modern society breeds selfishness, deception, and other evils, Fourier charged, because institutions such as marriage, the male-dominated family, and the competitive market confine people to repetitive labour or a limited role in life and thus frustrate the need for variety. By setting people at odds with each other in the competition for profits, the market in particular frustrates the desire for harmony. Accordingly, Fourier envisioned a form of society that would be more in keeping with human needs and desires. Such a "phalanstery," as he called it, would be a largely self-sufficient community of about 1,600 people organized according to the principle of "attractive labour," which holds that people will work voluntarily and happily if their work engages their talents and interests. All tasks become tiresome at some point, however, so each member of the phalanstery would have several occupations, moving from one to another as the person's interest waned and waxed. Fourier left room for private investment in his utopian community, but every member was to share in ownership, and inequality of wealth, though permitted, was to be limited.

The ideas of common ownership, equality, and a simple life were taken up in the visionary novel *Voyage en Icarie* (1840; *Travels in Icaria*), by the French socialist Étienne Cabet. Icaria was to be a self-sufficient community, combining industry with farming, of about one million people. In practice, however, the Icaria that Cabet founded in Illinois in the 1850s was about the size of a Fourierist phalanstery, and dissension among the Icarians prompted Cabet to depart in 1856.

Marxian Socialism

Despite their imagination and dedication to the cause of the workers, none of the early socialists met with the full approval of Karl Marx, who is unquestionably the most important theorist of socialism. In fact, Marx and his longtime friend and collaborator, Friedrich Engels, were largely responsible for attaching the label "utopian," which they intended to be derogatory, to Saint-Simon, Fourier, and Owen, whose "fantastic pictures of future society" they contrasted to their own "scientific" approach to socialism. The path to socialism proceeds not through the establishment of model communities that set examples of harmonious cooperation to the world, according to Marx and Engels, but through the clash of social classes. "The history of all hitherto existing society is the history of class struggles," they proclaimed in the *Manifesto of the Communist Party*. A scientific understanding of history shows that these struggles will culminate in the triumph of the working class and the establishment of socialism.

According to Engels, the basic elements of Marx's theory are to be found in German philosophy, French socialism, and British economics. Of these, German philosophy was surely the formative influence on Marx's thinking. Born in Trier in the German Rhineland, Marx was a philosophy student at the University of Berlin when the idealism of G.W.F. Hegel dominated German philosophy. Hegel maintained that history is the story of the unfolding or realization of "spirit"—a process that requires struggle, agony, and the overcoming of obstacles to the attainment of self-knowledge. Just as individual persons cannot realize their potential, especially the potential for freedom, if they remain forever in a childish or adolescent condition, so spirit must develop throughout history in a dialectical fashion. That is, individuals and even nations are characters in a drama that proceeds through the clash of opposing ideas and interests to a greater self-awareness and appreciation of freedom. Slavery, for example, was long taken for granted as a natural and acceptable practice, but the slave's struggle to be recognized as a person was bringing an end to slavery as master and slave came to recognize their common humanity—and thus to liberate themselves, and spirit, from a false sense of the master's superiority.

Like Hegel, Marx understood history as the story of human labour and struggle. However, whereas for Hegel history was the story of spirit's self-realization through human conflict, for Marx it was the story of struggles between classes over material or economic interests and resources. In place of

Hegel's philosophical idealism, in other words, Marx developed a materialist or economic theory of history. Before people can do anything else, he held, they must first produce what they need to survive, which is to say that they are subject to necessity. Freedom for Marx is largely a matter of overcoming necessity. Necessity compels people to labour so that they may survive, and only those who are free from this compulsion will be free to develop their talents and potential. This is why, throughout history, freedom has usually been restricted to members of the ruling class, who use their control of the land and other means of production to exploit the labour of the poor and subservient. The masters in slaveholding societies, the landowning aristocracy in feudal times, and the bourgeoisie who control the wealth in capitalist societies have all enjoyed various degrees of freedom, but they have done so at the expense of the slaves, serfs, and industrial workers, or proletarians, who have provided the necessary labour.

For Marx, capitalism is both a progressive force in history and an exploitative system that alienates capitalists and workers alike from their true humanity. It is progressive because it has made possible the industrial transformation of the world, thereby unleashing the productive power to free everyone from necessity. Yet it is exploitative in that capitalism condemns proletarians, who own nothing but their labour power, to lives of grinding labour while enabling capitalists to reap the profits. This is a volatile situation, according to Marx, and its inevitable result will be a war that will end all class divisions. Under the pressure of depressions, recessions, and competition for jobs, the workers will become conscious that they form a class, the proletariat, which is oppressed and exploited by their class enemy, the bourgeoisie. Armed with this awareness, they will overthrow the bourgeoisie in a series of spontaneous uprisings, seizing control of factories, mines, railroads, and other means of production, until they have

Other Types of Communism

There were several types of communist thought, including Christian Socialism backed by Saint-Simon, who called for a "new Christianity" that would join Christian social teachings with modern science and industry to create a society that would satisfy basic human needs.

Anarcho communism, promoted by the flamboyant Russian anarchist Mikhail Bakunin, held that religion, capitalism, and the state are forms of oppression that must be smashed if people are ever to be free. As he stated in an early essay, *The Reaction in Germany* (1842), "The passion for destruction is also a creative passion."

Fabian socialism was so called because the members of the Fabian Society admired the tactics of the Roman general Fabius Cunctator (Fabius the Delayer), who avoided pitched battles and gradually wore down Hannibal's forces. Instead of revolution, the Fabians favoured "gradualism" as the way to bring about socialism.

On the other hand, Syndicalism's hallmarks were workers' control and "direct action." Syndicalists such as Fernand Pelloutier distrusted both the state, which they regarded as an agent of capitalism, and political parties, which they thought were incapable of achieving radical change. Their aim was to replace capitalism and the state with a loose federation of local workers' groups, which they meant to bring about through direct action.

Guild socialism was an English movement that attracted a modest following in the first two decades of the twentieth century. Inspired by the medieval guild, an association of craftsmen who determined their own working conditions and activities, theorists such as Samuel G. Hobson and G.D.H. Cole advocated the public ownership of industries and their organization into guilds, each of which would be under the democratic control of its trade union.

gained control of the government and converted it into a revolutionary dictatorship of the proletariat. Under socialism or communism—Marx and Engels drew no clear or consistent distinction between the two—government itself will eventually wither away as people gradually lose the selfish attitudes inculcated by private ownership of the means of production. Freed from necessity and exploitation, people will finally live in a true community that gives "each individual the means of cultivating his gifts in all directions."

Marx maintained that the revolution by which socialism would be achieved was ordained by the logic of capitalism itself, as the capitalists' competition for profits led them to create their own "grave diggers" in the proletariat. Even the role of the revolutionary, such as Marx, was confined to that of "midwife," for revolutionaries could do no more than speed along the inevitable revolution and ease its birth pangs.

This, at least, was Marx's more or less "official" doctrine. In his writings and political activities, however, he added several qualifications. He acknowledged, for example, that socialism might supplant capitalism peacefully in England, the United States, and other countries where the proletariat was gaining the franchise. He also said that it might be possible for a semi-feudal country such as Russia to become socialist without first passing through capitalist industrialism. Moreover, Marx played an important part in the International Workingmen's Association, or First International, formed in 1864 by a group of labour leaders who were neither exclusively revolutionary nor even entirely committed to socialism. In short, Marx was not the inflexible economic determinist that he is sometimes taken to be. But he was convinced that history was on the side of socialism and the equal development of all people to be achieved under socialism would be the fulfillment of history.

Revisionism and Revolution

In 1889, on the centenary of the French Revolution, a Second International emerged from two rival socialist conventions in Paris. Intended as a revival of the International Workingmen's Association, this new organization was dominated by Marxists in general and the SPD in particular. By this time, the SPD was both officially Marxist and a force to be reckoned with in German politics. Despite Otto von Bismarck's attempts to suppress it, Wilhelm Liebknecht, August Bebel, and other leaders had transformed the SPD into a mass party.

The storming of the Bastille, depicted in this 18th-century painting, was the symbol of victory for the French people over the monarchy in the French Revolution. G. Dagli Orti/De Agostini/Getty Images

But its considerable success—the SPD won almost one-fifth of the votes cast in the parliamentary elections of 1890, for example—raised the question of whether socialism might be achieved through the ballot box, rather than through revolution. The "orthodox" position, as developed by the SPD's chief theorist, Karl Kautsky, tried to reconcile the SPD's electoral practice with Marx's revolutionary doctrine. But others had begun to think that it would be better to recognize that circumstances had changed and revise Marx's doctrine accordingly.

Foremost among the "revisionists" was Eduard Bernstein, an SPD leader who became an associate of Engels while living in England to escape Bismarck's harassment. Bernstein was also exposed to the Fabians while in England; their example encouraged him to question aspects of Marx's theory. Like others, Bernstein observed that the living and working conditions of the proletariat were not growing more desperate, as Marx had predicted, but were improving, largely as a result of trade union activity and the extension of the franchise. This led him to conclude that the revolutionary overthrow of capitalism was neither necessary nor desirable. A gradual, peaceful transformation to socialism, he argued in *Evolutionary Socialism* (1899), would be safer than the revolutionary route, with its dangerously vague and potentially tyrannical dictatorship of the proletariat.

Bernstein's writings drew a swift and hostile reaction from his SPD comrades, Kautsky in particular, and from revolutionary Marxists elsewhere. After several years of polemical war between revisionists and orthodox Marxists, the revisionists eventually triumphed within the SPD, which gradually abandoned its revolutionary pretenses. Nevertheless, some stalwarts, such as Rosa Luxemburg, remained faithful to the spirit of revolutionary Marxism.

Among the remaining orthodox Marxists was the Russian revolutionary V.I. Ulyanov, better known by his pseudonym: Lenin. As the leader of the Bolshevik, or "majority," faction of the Russian Social-Democratic Workers' Party, Lenin himself had been accused of straying from the Marxist path. The problem for Russian Marxists was that Russia in the late nineteenth century remained a semi-feudal country with barely the beginnings of industrial capitalism. To be sure, Marx had allowed that it might be possible for a country such as Russia to move directly from feudalism to socialism, but the standard position among Marxists was that capitalism was a necessary stage of economic and historical development. Otherwise, there would be neither the productive power to overcome necessity nor the revolutionary proletariat to win freedom for all, as it emancipated itself from capitalist exploitation.

This had been the standard position among Russian Marxists, too, but it was not Lenin's. Lenin had little faith in the revolutionary potential of the proletariat, arguing in *What Is to Be Done?* (1902) that the workers, left to themselves, would fight only for better wages and working conditions; therefore, they needed to be educated, enlightened, and led to revolution by a "vanguard" party of professional revolutionaries. Moreover, the authoritarian nature of the Russian government required that the vanguard party be conspiratorial, disciplined, and elitist. Lenin's Russian-Marxist rivals disputed these points, but his manipulation of the vote at a party congress enabled him to label them the Menshevik, or "minority," faction.

Lenin's commitment to revolution thus put him at odds with those who advocated a revised, evolutionary Marxism. In *Imperialism, the Highest Stage of Capitalism* (1916), Lenin argued against the revisionists, stating that the improvement in conditions enjoyed by the proletariat of Europe and the

United States was a kind of bribe made possible by the "super-profits" that their countries' capitalists were extracting from the labour and resources of the poorer parts of the world. But imperialism would also be the last stage of capitalism, for it was bound to expose the contradictions of capitalism not only in the industrial countries but also in the countries exploited by the imperialistic powers—hence, the possibility of revolution in a country that had not gone through capitalism itself.

Lenin wrote *Imperialism* during World War I, which proved to be a watershed in the history of socialism. In the years before war broke out in August 1914, most European socialists had held that the only war the proletariat should fight was the class war against the bourgeoisie. When the war began, however, socialists were forced to choose between international socialism and their countries. They generally chose the latter, though there were notable exceptions, Luxemburg and Lenin among them. Once the SPD's contingent in the Reichstag voted to issue war credits, socialists in other countries fell into line behind their own governments. The Second International lingered for a time, but to no effective purpose.

World War I also inflicted severe hardships on the Russian people, thereby contributing to the collapse of the tsarist regime and creating an opportunity for revolution, which the Bolsheviks seized in the Russian Revolution of 1917. Lenin's standing among revolutionary Marxists soared, though Luxemburg and others deplored the way in which the dictatorship of the proletariat was becoming a dictatorship of the All-Russian Communist Party, as the Bolsheviks named themselves in 1918. Still, the communists' victory gave Luxemburg and other revolutionaries hope that the Russian example would inspire socialist revolutions elsewhere.

For his part, Lenin feared that his regime could not survive without the aid of friendly—and therefore, socialist—

The interpretation by Lenin (above) of Marx's doctrine led him to become one of the most significant political leaders of the 20th century. Tass/Sovfoto

neighbours. Accordingly, he called a meeting in Moscow to establish a Third International, or Communist International (Comintern). The response from other countries was tepid, and by the time delegates convened in March 1919, prospects for a new international had been further dimmed by the failure of the Spartacus Revolt of the new Communist Party of Germany—a failure that claimed the lives of Luxemburg and Karl Liebknecht (son of Wilhelm Liebknecht), who were summarily executed by counterrevolutionary forces in 1919. Lenin pressed on with the formation of the Comintern, but it was soon apparent that it was an agent of the new Union of Soviet Socialist Republics (formally created in 1922) and not of international socialism as such. Indeed, by this time a fissure had clearly developed between communists on the one hand and socialists, or social democrats, on the other.

Socialism in the Era of World War

The division took institutional form as communist parties emerged in one country after another to challenge existing socialist parties and their common enemy: capitalism. In general, the communists were revolutionary Marxists who adhered to what came to be called Marxism-Leninism. Their socialist rivals—variously known as socialists, social democrats, and labourites—were a more diverse group, including both revisionists and non-Marxists, but they were united in their commitment to peaceful, democratic tactics. They were also less likely than communists to claim that history was moving inexorably toward the demise of capitalism and were more likely to appeal to ethical considerations. In England, for example, the reformer Richard Henry Tawney found a receptive audience within the Labour Party when he rested the case for socialism on its promotion of fellowship, the dignity of work, and the equal worth of all members of society.

On the communist side, the standard was set by the increasingly totalitarian regime of Joseph Stalin in the Soviet Union. Lenin's death in 1924 led to a power struggle between Stalin and Leon Trotsky. Stalin not only won the struggle but eventually ordered the deaths of Trotsky and other rivals—and of millions more who opposed or resisted his policies. While professing to be a revolutionary in the Marxist-Leninist tradition, Stalin concentrated his efforts on building "socialism in one country," largely through a program of forced collectivization and industrialization.

There were occasional deviations from the Marxist-Leninist line, as in the case of Antonio Gramsci, who helped found the Italian Communist Party in 1921. Gramsci resisted the tendency to reduce Marx's theory to economic terms, focusing instead on the way in which the "hegemony" of the ruling classes over schools, churches, the media, and other cultural institutions encouraged workers to acquiesce in their exploitation. But Gramsci's attempt to convince other communists of the revolutionary potential of cultural transformation was restricted by his imprisonment, from 1926 until shortly before his death in 1937, by the fascist regime of Benito Mussolini.

Fascist oppression, in fact, was a major problem for communists and socialists alike, not only in Italy but subsequently in Spain under Francisco Franco and in Germany under Adolf Hitler. Socialist parties had drawn enough votes in Germany, Britain, and France to participate in or even lead coalition governments in the 1920s and '30s. In Sweden, the Swedish Social Democratic Workers' Party won control of the government in 1932 with a promise to make their country into a "people's home" based on "equality, concern, cooperation, and helpfulness." Wherever fascists took power, however, communists and socialists were among the first to be suppressed.

Nor were there any signal victories for socialism outside Europe in the years between the world wars. Although Eugene V. Debs won nearly one million votes in the U.S. presidential election of 1920, his showing represented less than 4 percent of the votes cast and remains the electoral high point for American socialists. In India, Mahatma Gandhi attracted a mass following, but his popularity owed more to his campaign for independence from Britain than to the traces of socialism in his philosophy.

In China, another mass movement for national liberation developed at this time, though it was explicitly communist. Its leader, Mao Zedong, helped found the Chinese Communist Party (CCP) in 1921. After a disastrous beginning—the Comintern had pushed Chinese communists into an alliance with the nationalist leader Chiang Kai-shek, who attacked the communists as soon as he thought it expedient—Mao retreated to the fields and hills to rebuild the CCP. While remaining faithful to Lenin's notion of the communist party as the revolutionary vanguard, Mao proceeded to lead a guerilla movement that established its power base among the peasantry, which he regarded as a rural proletariat. In Mao's hands, moreover, the concept of nation largely replaced that of class, with China represented as a poor and oppressed proletarian nation that had to rise against the oppressing imperialist nations and their bourgeois underlings.

Postwar Socialism

World War II forged an uneasy alliance between communists and socialists—and between liberals and conservatives—in their common struggle against fascism. However, the alliance soon disintegrated as the Soviet Union established communist regimes in the Eastern European countries that it had occupied at the end of the war. The Cold War that ensued deepened the fissure between communists and other socialists, the latter seeing themselves as democrats opposed to the one-party rule of the Soviet Union and its satellites. The Labour Party, for example, won a parliamentary majority in the British elections of 1945 and subsequently established a national health care system and public control of major industries and utilities; when the party lost its majority in 1951, it peacefully relinquished the offices of government to the victorious Conservatives.

The communists also claimed to be democrats, but their notion of "people's democracy" rested on the belief that the people were not yet capable of governing themselves. Thus, Mao declared, after Chiang Kai-shek's forces were driven from mainland China in 1949, that the new People's Republic of China was to be a "people's democratic dictatorship"; that is, the CCP would rule in the interest of the people by suppressing their enemies and building socialism. Freedom of expression and political competition were bourgeois, counterrevolutionary ideas. This became the justification for one-party rule by other communist regimes in North Korea, Vietnam, Cuba, and elsewhere.

Meanwhile, the socialist parties of Europe were modifying their positions and enjoying frequent electoral success. The Scandinavian socialists set the example of "mixed economies" that combined largely private ownership with government direction of the economy and substantial welfare programs, and other socialist parties followed suit. Even the SPD, in its Bad Godesberg program of 1959, dropped its Marxist pretenses and committed itself to a "social market economy" involving "as much competition as possible—as much planning as necessary." Although some welcomed this blurring of boundaries between socialism and welfare-state liberalism as a sign of "the end of ideology," the more radical student left of the 1960s complained that there was little choice between capitalism, the "obsolete communism" of the Marxist-Leninists, and the bureaucratic socialism of Western Europe.

Elsewhere, the withdrawal of European colonial powers from Africa and the Middle East created opportunities for new forms of socialism. Terms such as *African socialism* and *Arab socialism* were frequently invoked in the 1950s and '60s, partly because the old colonial powers were identified with capitalist imperialism. In practice, these new kinds of socialism typically combined appeals to indigenous traditions, such as communal land ownership, with the Marxist-Leninist model of one-party rule for the purpose of rapid modernization. In Tanzania, for example, Julius Nyerere developed an egalitarian program of *ujamaa* (Swahili: "familyhood") that collectivized village farmlands and attempted, unsuccessfully, to achieve economic self-sufficiency—all under the guidance of a one-party state.

In Asia, by contrast, no distinctive form of socialism emerged. Aside from the communist regimes, Japan was the only country in which a socialist party gained a sizable and enduring following to the point of occasionally controlling the government or participating in a governing coalition.

Nor has there been a peculiarly Latin American contribution to socialist theory. The regime of Fidel Castro in Cuba tended to follow the Marxist-Leninist path in the 1950s and '60s, though with increasing moderation in later years, especially after the collapse of the Soviet Union in 1991. Liberation theology called on Christians to give priority to the needs of the poor, but it has not developed an explicitly socialist program. Perhaps the most distinctively Latin American expression of socialist impulses was Venezuelan Pres. Hugo Chávez's call for a "Bolivarian Revolution." Apart from the appeal to Simón Bolívar's reputation as a liberator, however, Chávez did not establish a connection between socialism and Bolívar's thoughts and deeds.

In many ways, however, the attempt by Salvador Allende to unite Marxists and other reformers in a socialist reconstruction of Chile is most representative of the direction that Latin American socialists have taken since the late twentieth century. Elected by a plurality vote in a three-way election in 1970, Allende tried to nationalize foreign corporations and redistribute land and wealth to the poor. These efforts provoked domestic and foreign opposition, which led, in the midst of economic turmoil, to a military coup and Allende's death—though whether by his or someone else's hand is not clear.

Several socialist (or socialist-leaning) leaders have followed Allende's example in winning election to office in Latin American countries. Chávez led the way in 1999 and was followed in the early twenty-first century by successful electoral campaigns by self-proclaimed socialist or distinctly left-of-centre leaders in Brazil, Chile, Argentina, Uruguay, and Bolivia. Although it would be too much to say that these leaders have shared a common program, they have tended to support increased welfare provision for the poor, nationalization of some foreign corporations, redistribution of land from large landholders to peasants, and resistance to the "neoliberal" policies of the World Bank and the International Monetary Fund.

Socialism After Communism

The most important development in the recent history of socialism is undoubtedly the collapse of communism, first in Eastern Europe in 1989 and then in the Soviet Union itself in 1991. Communist parties continued to exist, of course, and some of them remained in power—e.g., in North Korea, Vietnam, Cuba, and China. But by the late twentieth century, little of Marxism remained in the policies of the CCP, as economic reforms increasingly favoured private ownership of productive property and encouraged market competition. What did remain was the Leninist insistence on one-party rule.

Mikhail Gorbachev's attempts at *glasnost* ("openness") and *perestroika* ("restructuring"), initiated after he became general secretary of the Communist Party of the Soviet Union in 1985, signaled a move away from one-party rule and the inefficient command economy, in which wages, prices, production, and distribution were determined by bureaucrats. Gorbachev intended perestroika to increase productivity and raise living standards without going far in the direction of a market economy. But glasnost created political opportunities for those who were unhappy with communism, as the downfall of the Eastern European regimes indicated; ultimately, it prompted a reaction—an attempted coup by a group of hardline communists in 1991—that failed so swiftly and spectacularly that the Soviet Union itself disintegrated. By the end of the twentieth century, communism, although not quite dead, certainly seemed to be dying.

Beginning in the late twentieth century, the advent of what many considered a "postindustrial" economy, in which knowledge and information counted more than labour and material production, raised doubts about the relevance of socialism, which was in theory and practice primarily a response to industrial capitalism. This conviction led to much talk of a "third way"—that is, a centre-left position that would preserve the socialist commitment to equality and welfare while abandoning class-based politics and public ownership of the means of production. In 1995, the British Labour Party under Tony Blair embraced the third way by forsaking its long-standing commitment to the nationalization of basic industries; in general elections two years later, the Labour Party won a landslide victory, and Blair served as prime minister for the next ten years. Other heads of government who professed the third way in the 1990s included Pres. Bill Clinton of the United States, Chancellor Gerhard Schröder of Germany, and Prime Minister Wim Kok of the Netherlands.

Critics on the left complained that the third way reduced equality to an equal chance to compete in economies in which the rich were growing ever richer and the poor were increasingly disadvantaged. Such a position, they insisted, is hardly socialist. But even these critics seldom called for a return to a centralist form of socialism; instead, they were more likely to advocate a decentralist form of market socialism. As the name implies, market socialism blends elements of a free market economy with social ownership and control of property. Proposals have varied, but the basic idea is that businesses will compete for profits, as in capitalism, but they will be owned, or at least governed, by those who work in them. The workers in every business will choose their supervisors, control their working conditions, set the prices of their products, and decide how to share the profits—or cope with the losses—of their enterprise. Market socialism is thus a form of "workplace democracy," or "economic democracy," that enables workers not only to vote in political contests but also have a say in the economic decisions that affect them daily in their work.

If socialism has a future, it may well lie in some form of market socialism. Market socialism promises neither the utopia of the early socialists nor the brave new world that Marx and his followers envisioned as the fulfillment of history. But it does promise to promote cooperation and solidarity, rather than competitive individualism. It also aims at reducing—if not eliminating—the class divisions that foster exploitation and alienation. In these respects, this modest, decentralized version of socialism continues to sound the themes that have long inspired people to take up the cause of socialism. Even in Latin America and other places where socialists continue to call for direct, public ownership of natural resources and major industries, they nevertheless leave room for private competition for profits in the marketplace. In one way or another, socialists now seem more interested in bringing the free market under control than in eliminating it completely.

CHAPTER 2

COMMUNISM

Communism is the political and economic doctrine that aims to replace private property and a profit-based economy with public ownership and communal control of at least the major means of production (e.g., mines, mills, and factories) and natural resources of a society. Communism is thus a form of socialism—a higher and more advanced form, according to its advocates. Exactly how communism differs from socialism has long been a matter of debate, but the distinction rests largely on communists' adherence to the revolutionary socialism of Karl Marx.

Like most writers of the nineteenth century, Marx tended to use the terms *communism* and *socialism* interchangeably. In his *Critique of the Gotha Programme* (1875), however, he identified two phases of communism that would follow the predicted overthrow of capitalism. The first would be a transitional system in which the working class would control the government and economy, and yet still find it necessary to pay people according to how long, hard, or well they worked. The second would be fully realized communism—a society without class divisions or government, in which the production and distribution of goods would be based on the principle "From each according to his ability, to each according to his needs." Marx's followers, especially the Russian revolutionary Vladimir Ilich Lenin, took up this distinction.

In *State and Revolution* (1917), Lenin asserted that socialism corresponds to Marx's first phase of communist society and communism proper to the second. Lenin and the Bolshevik wing of the Russian Social-Democratic Workers' Party reinforced this distinction in 1918, the year after they seized power in Russia, by taking the name All-Russian Communist Party. Since then, communism has been largely, if not exclusively, identified with the form of political and economic organization developed in the Soviet Union and adopted subsequently in the People's Republic of China and other countries ruled by communist parties.

For much of the twentieth century, in fact, about one-third of the world's population lived under communist regimes. These regimes were characterized by the rule of a single party that tolerated no opposition and little dissent. In place of a capitalist economy, in which individuals compete for profits, moreover, party leaders established a command economy in which the state controlled property and its bureaucrats determined wages, prices, and production goals. The inefficiency of these economies played a large part in the collapse of the Soviet Union in 1991, and the remaining communist countries (except North Korea) are now allowing greater economic competition while holding fast to one-party rule. Whether they will succeed in this endeavour remains to be seen. Succeed or fail, however, communism is clearly not the world-shaking force that it was in the twentieth century.

Historical Background

Although the term *communism* did not come into use until the 1840s—it is derived from the Latin *communis*, meaning "shared" or "common"—visions of a society that may be considered communist appeared as long ago as the 4th century BCE. In the ideal state described in Plato's *Republic*, the gov-

Propter
Sion non
tacebo
Isa . 61 .

IESVS est
mea Doctrina.

Tommaso Campanella is best remembered for his socialistic work The City of
the Sun, *written while he was a prisoner of the Spanish crown (1599–1626).*
Hulton Archive/Getty Images

erning class of guardians devotes itself to serving the interests of the whole community. Because private ownership of goods would corrupt their owners by encouraging selfishness, Plato argued, the guardians must live as a large family that shares common ownership not only of material goods but also of spouses and children.

Other early visions of communism drew their inspiration from religion. The first Christians practiced a simple kind of communism—as described in Acts 4:32–37, for example—both as a form of solidarity and as a way of renouncing worldly possessions. Similar motives later inspired the formation of monastic orders in which monks took vows of poverty and promised to share their few worldly goods with each other and with the poor. The English humanist Sir Thomas More extended this monastic communism in *Utopia* (1516), which describes an imaginary society in which money is abolished and people share meals, houses, and other goods in common.

Other fictional communistic utopias followed, notably *City of the Sun* (1623), by the Italian philosopher Tommaso Campanella, as did attempts to put communist ideas into practice. Perhaps the most noteworthy (if not notorious) of the latter was the theocracy of the Anabaptists in the Westphalian city of Münster (1534–35), which ended with the military capture of the city and execution of its leaders. The English Civil Wars (1642–51) prompted the Diggers to advocate a kind of agrarian communism in which Earth would be "a common treasury," as Gerrard Winstanley envisioned in *The Law of Freedom* (1652) and other works. The vision was not shared by the Protectorate led by Oliver Cromwell, which harshly suppressed the Diggers in 1650.

It was neither a religious upheaval nor a civil war but a technological and economic revolution—the Industrial Revolution of the late eighteenth and early nineteenth centuries—that provided the impetus and inspiration for modern communism. This revolution, which achieved great gains in economic productivity at the expense of an increasingly miserable working class, encouraged Marx to think that the class struggles that dominated history were leading inevitably to a society in which prosperity would be shared by all through common ownership of the means of production.

Marxian Communism

Karl Marx was born in the German Rhineland to middle-class parents of Jewish descent who had abandoned their religion in an attempt to assimilate into an anti-Semitic society. The young Marx studied philosophy at the University of Berlin and received a doctorate from the University of Jena in 1841, but he was unable, because of his Jewish ancestry and liberal political views, to secure a teaching position. He turned to journalism, where his investigations disclosed what he perceived as systematic injustice and corruption at all levels of German society. Convinced that German—and more broadly, European—society could not be reformed from within but had to be remade from the ground up, Marx became a political radical. His views soon brought him to the attention of the police. Fearing arrest and imprisonment, he left for Paris. There, Marx renewed an acquaintance with his countryman Friedrich Engels, who became his friend and coauthor in a collaboration that was to last nearly forty years.

The son of the co-owner of a textile firm with factories in Germany and Britain, Engels was himself a capitalist who helped manage the firm's factory in Manchester. Like Marx, Engels was deeply disturbed by what he regarded as the injustices of a society divided by class. Appalled by the poverty and squalor in which ordinary workers lived and worked, he described their misery in grisly detail in *The Condition of the English Working Class* (1844).

Marx and Engels maintained that the poverty, disease, and early death that afflicted the proletariat (the industrial working class) were endemic to capitalism: they were systemic and structural problems that could be resolved only by replacing capitalism with communism. Under this alternative system, the major means of industrial production, such as mines, mills, factories, and railroads, would be publicly owned and operated for the benefit of all. Marx and Engels presented this critique of capitalism and a brief sketch of a possible future communist society in *Manifesto of the Communist Party* (1848), which they wrote at the commission of a small group of radicals called the Communist League.

Marx, meanwhile, had begun to lay the theoretical and (he believed) scientific foundations of communism, first in *The German Ideology* (written 1845–46; published 1932) and later in *Das Kapital* (1867; *Capital*). His theory has three main aspects: first, a materialist conception of history; second, a critique of capitalism and its inner workings; and third, an account of the revolutionary overthrow of capitalism and its eventual replacement by communism.

Historical Materialism

According to Marx's materialist theory, history is a series of class struggles and revolutionary upheavals, leading ultimately to freedom for all. Marx derived his views in part from the philosophy of G.W.F. Hegel, who conceived of history as the dialectical self-development of "spirit." In contrast to Hegel's philosophical idealism, however, Marx held that history is driven by the material or economic conditions that prevail in a given age. "Before men can do anything else," Marx wrote, "they must first produce the means of their subsistence." Without material production, there would be no life and thus no human activity.

According to Marx, material production requires two things: "material forces of production"—roughly, raw materials and the tools required to extract and process them—and "social relations of production"—the division of labour through which raw materials are extracted and processed. Human history is the story of both elements' changing and becoming ever more complex. In primitive societies, the material forces were few and simple—for example, grains and the stone tools used to grind them into flour. With the growth of knowledge and technology came successive upheavals, or "revolutions," in the forces and relations of production and in the complexity of both. For example, iron miners once worked with pickaxes and shovels, which they owned, but the invention of the steam shovel changed the way they extracted iron ore. Since no miner could afford to buy a steam shovel, he had to work for someone who could. Industrial capitalism, in Marx's view, is an economic system in which one class—the ruling bourgeoisie—owns the means of production, while the working class or proletariat effectively loses its independence, the worker becoming part of the means of production, a mere "appendage of the machine."

Critique of Capitalism

The second aspect of Marx's theory is his critique of capitalism. Marx held that human history had progressed through a series of stages, from ancient slave society through feudalism to capitalism. In each stage, a dominant class uses its control of the means of production to exploit the labour of a larger class of workers. But internal tensions or "contradictions" in each stage eventually lead to the overthrow and replacement of the ruling class by its successor. Thus, the bourgeoisie overthrew the aristocracy and replaced feudalism with capitalism; so, too, Marx predicted, will the proletariat overthrow the bourgeoisie and replace capital-ism with communism.

Marx acknowledged that capitalism was a historical-ly necessary stage of development that had brought about remarkable scientific and technological changes—changes that greatly increased aggregate wealth by extending hu-mankind's power over nature. The problem, Marx believed, was that this wealth—and the political power and economic opportunities that went with it—was unfairly distributed. The capitalists reap the profits while paying the workers a pittance for long hours of hard labour. Yet it is the workers who create economic value, according to Marx's labour the-ory of value, which holds that the worth of a commodity is

Van Gogh's The Potato Eaters *was influenced by Emile Zola's book* Germinal, *a social commentary on the relationship between the bourgeoisie and the working class.* De Agostini Picture Library/Getty Images

determined by the amount of labour required to produce it. Under capitalism, Marx claimed, workers are not paid fully or fairly for their labour because the capitalists siphon off surplus value, which they call profit. Thus, the bourgeois owners of the means of production amass enormous wealth, while the proletariat falls further into poverty. This wealth also enables the bourgeoisie to control the government or state, which does the bidding of the wealthy and the powerful to the detriment of the poor and the powerless.

The exploitation of one class by another remains hidden, however, by a set of ideas that Marx called ideology. "The ruling ideas of every epoch," he wrote in *The German Ideology*, "are the ideas of the ruling class." By this, Marx meant that the conventional or mainstream ideas taught in classrooms, preached from pulpits, and communicated through the mass media are ideas that serve the interests of the dominant class. In slave societies, for example, slavery was depicted as normal, natural, and just. In capitalist societies, the free market is portrayed as operating efficiently, fairly, and for the benefit of all, while alternative economic arrangements such as socialism are derided or dismissed as false or fanciful. These ideas serve to justify or legitimize the unequal distribution of economic and political power. Even exploited workers may fail to understand their true interests and accept the dominant ideology—a condition that later Marxists called "false consciousness." One particularly pernicious source of ideological obfuscation is religion, which Marx called "the opium of the people" because it purportedly dulls the critical faculties and leads workers to accept their wretched condition as part of God's plan.

Besides inequality, poverty, and false consciousness, capitalism also produces "alienation." By this, Marx meant that the worker is separated or estranged from (1) the product of his labour, which he does not own; (2) the process of production, which under factory conditions makes him "an appendage of the machine"; (3) the sense of satisfaction that he would derive from using his human capacities in unique and creative ways; and (4) other human beings, whom he sees as rivals competing for jobs and wages.

Revolution and Communism

Marx believed that capitalism is a volatile economic system that will suffer a series of ever-worsening crises—recessions and depressions—that will produce greater unemployment, lower wages, and increasing misery among the industrial proletariat. These crises will convince the proletariat that its interests as a class are implacably opposed to those of the ruling bourgeoisie. Armed with revolutionary class consciousness, the proletariat will seize the major means of production along with the institutions of state power— police, courts, prisons, and so on—and establish a socialist state that Marx called "the revolutionary dictatorship of the proletariat." The proletariat will thus rule in its own class

Friedrich Engels

Friedrich Engels (born Nov. 28, 1820, Barmen, Rhine province, Prussia [Germany]—died Aug. 5, 1895, London, Eng.) was a German socialist philosopher and the closest collaborator of Karl Marx in the foundation of modern communism. They coauthored *Manifesto of the Communist Party* (1848), and Engels edited the second and third volumes of *Das Kapital* after Marx's death.

After Marx's death (1883), Engels served as the foremost authority on Marx and Marxism. Aside from occasional writings on a variety of subjects and introductions to new editions of Marx's works, Engels completed volumes 2 and 3 of *Das Kapital* (1885 and 1894) on the basis of Marx's uncompleted manuscripts and rough notes. Engels's other two late publications are the books *Der Ursprung der Familie, des Privateigenthums und des Staats* (1884; *The Origin of the Family, Private Property and the State*) and *Ludwig Feuerbach und der Ausgang der klassischen deutschen Philosophie* (1888; *Ludwig Feuerbach and the Outcome of Classical German Philosophy*). All the while, he corresponded extensively with German social democrats and followers everywhere so as to perpetuate the image of Marx and foster some degree of conformity among the "faithful." His work was interrupted when he was stricken with cancer; he died of the disease not long after.

During his lifetime, Engels experienced, in a milder form, the same attacks and veneration that fell upon Marx. An urbane individual with the demeanour of an English gentleman, Engels customarily was a gay and witty associate with a great zest for living. He had a code of honour that responded quickly to an insult, even to the point of violence. As the hatchet man of the "partnership," he could be most offensive and ruthless—so much so that in 1848, various friends attempted unsuccessfully to persuade Marx to disavow him.

Except in the Soviet Union and other communist countries, where Engels received due recognition, posterity has generally lumped him together with Marx without adequately clarifying Engels's significant role. The attention Engels does receive is likely to be in the form of close scrutiny of his works to discover what differences existed between him and Marx. As a result, some scholars have concluded that Engels's writings and influence are responsible for certain deviations from, or distortions of, "true Marxism" as they see it. Yet scholars in general acknowledge that Marx himself apparently was unaware of any essential divergence of ideas and opinions. The Marx-Engels correspondence, which reveals a close cooperation in formulating Marxist policies, bears out that view.

interest, as the bourgeoisie did before, in order to prevent a counterrevolution by the displaced bourgeoisie. Once this threat disappears, however, the need for the state will also disappear. Thus, the interim state will wither away and be replaced by a classless communist society.

Marx's vision of communist society is remarkably (and perhaps intentionally) vague. Unlike earlier "utopian socialists," Marx did not produce detailed blueprints for a future society. Some features that he did describe, such as free education for all and a graduated income tax, are now commonplace. Other features, such as public ownership of the major means of production and distribution of goods and services according to the principle "From each according to his ability, to each according to his needs," remain as radical as they were in Marx's time. But for the most part, Marx believed that the institutions of a future communist society should be designed and decided democratically by the people living in it. It was not his task, he said, to "write recipes for the kitchens of the future." Though Marx was reluctant to write such recipes, many of his followers were not. Among them was his friend and coauthor, Friedrich Engels.

Revisionism

After Engels's death in 1895, Marx's followers split into two main camps: "revisionist" Marxists, who favoured a gradual and peaceful transition to socialism, and revolutionary Marxists, among them the leaders of the communist Russian Revolution of 1917. The foremost revisionist was Eduard Bernstein, a leader of the Social Democratic Party of Germany, who fled his homeland in 1881 to avoid arrest and imprisonment under the antisocialist laws of Chancellor Otto von Bismarck. Bernstein spent most of his exile in Britain, where he befriended Engels and later served as executor of his will. Bernstein's experiences there, including his association with the gradualist Fabian Society, led him to conclude that a peaceful parliamentary transition to socialism was possible in that country—a conclusion he defended and extended beyond Britain in his *Evolutionary Socialism* (1899).

Bernstein revised Marxian theory in four interrelated respects. First, he added an ethical dimension that had been largely lacking in Marx's thought; specifically, he held, following the German philosopher Immanuel Kant, that human beings should be treated as ends in themselves and never as means or instruments, whether by capitalists (who used workers as human machines) or by communists (who were prepared to use them as cannon fodder in the future revolution). Second, he argued that the emergence of trade unions and working-class political parties in late nineteenth-century Europe presented opportunities that required revisions in Marx's theory and therefore in Marxian political practice. Third, Bernstein noted that rising wages and better working conditions meant that—contrary to Marx's prediction of the immiseration of the proletariat—the lives of workers in advanced capitalist countries were actually improving. He traced this trend not to the kindness of capitalists but to the growing power of unions and working-class political parties. Fourth, however, he also warned of the danger of a revolutionary dictatorship of the proletariat, which was likely to become a dictatorship of "club orators and writers." On the basis of these four revisions, then, Bernstein advocated gradual, piecemeal, and peaceful reform—"evolutionary" socialism —rather than violent proletarian revolution.

Orthodox Marxists branded Bernstein a bourgeois and counterrevolutionary traitor to the cause. Chief among his communist critics was Lenin, who had devoted his life to the revolutionary transformation of Russia.

Bolshevism: Lenin's Revolutionary Communism

Russia in the early twentieth century was an unlikely setting for the proletarian revolution that Marx had predicted. Its economy was primarily agricultural, its factories were few and inefficient, and its industrial proletariat was small. Most Russians were peasants who farmed land owned by wealthy nobles. Russia, in short, was nearer feudalism than capitalism. There was, however, growing discontent in the countryside, and Lenin's Russian Social-Democratic Workers' Party saw an opportunity to harness that discontent to overthrow the autocratic tsarist regime and replace it with a radically different economic and political system.

Lenin was the chief architect of this plan. As head of the revolutionary Bolshevik faction of the party, he made two important changes to the theory and practice of communism as Marx had envisioned it—changes so significant that the party's ideology was later renamed Marxism-Leninism. The first, set out in *What Is to Be Done?* (1902), was that revolution could not and should not be made spontaneously by the proletariat, as Marx had expected, but had to be made by workers and peasants led by an elite "vanguard" party composed of radicalized middle-class intellectuals like himself. Secretive, tightly organized, and highly disciplined, the Communist Party would educate, guide, and direct the masses. This was necessary, Lenin claimed, because the masses, suffering from false consciousness and unable to discern their true interests, could not be trusted to govern themselves. Democracy was to be practiced only within the party, and even then it was to be constrained by the policy of democratic centralism. That is, full and vigorous debate would lead to a decision that would determine the party's line on an issue, whereupon the party's central leadership would close off debate and require

Though he was a seminal political figure in the 20th century, Lenin later became a symbol of oppression. In 2013 Ukrainian protesters toppled his statue during a rally against the government. AFP/Getty Images

adherence to the party line. Such strict discipline was necessary, Lenin maintained, if the party was to guide the masses to revolution and establish the socialist workers' state that would follow. In short, the revolutionary dictatorship of the proletariat had to be a dictatorship of the Communist Party in the name of the proletariat.

A second and closely related change appears in Lenin's *Imperialism, the Highest Stage of Capitalism* (1916), in which he implied that communist revolution would not begin in advanced capitalist countries such as Germany and Britain because workers there were imbued with reform-minded "trade-union consciousness" instead of revolutionary class consciousness. This, he argued, was because the most direct and brutal exploitation of workers had shifted to the colonies of imperialist nations, such as Britain. The capitalists reaped "superprofits" from the cheap raw materials and labour available in these colonies and were thus able to "bribe" workers at home with slightly higher wages, a shorter workweek, and other reforms. So contrary to Marx's expectations, communist revolution would begin in economically backward countries, such as Russia, and in the oppressed and exploited colonial countries of the capitalist periphery (later to be called the Third World).

The Russian Revolution

The Russian Revolution of 1917 came about in a way that no one, not even Lenin, had predicted. Its immediate impetus was World War I, which was taking a heavy toll on Russian soldiers at the front and peasants at home. Riots broke out in several Russian cities. When Tsar Nicholas II ordered soldiers to put them down, they refused. Nicholas abdicated, and his government was replaced by one led by Aleksandr Kerensky. Committed to continuing the war against Germany, Kerensky's provisional government was almost as unpopular as the tsar's. Lenin returned to Russia from exile in Switzerland barely in time to lead the Bolsheviks in seizing state power in October 1917. (Based on the new Gregorian calendar or "New Style" calendar established in 1582 by Pope Gregory XIII and currently in use worldwide, this revolution is now dated November, 1917. The Gregorian calendar was adopted by the Soviet Union in 1918.) He then became premier of a new government based on soviets', or workers' councils.

The Soviet government moved quickly to withdraw from the war in Europe and nationalize private industry and agriculture. In the name of the people and under the banner of War Communism, it seized mines, mills, factories, and the estates of wealthy landowners, which it redistributed to peasants. The landowners and aristocrats, aided by troops and supplies from capitalist countries, including Britain and the United States, mounted a "White" counterrevolution against the "Red" government. The Russian Civil War ended in 1920 with the victory of the Reds, but the war in Europe and the war at home left the Soviet Union in shambles, its economic productivity meagre, and its people hungry and discontented. Desperate for room to maneuver, Lenin announced in 1921 the New Economic Policy (NEP), whereby the state retained control of large industries but encouraged individual initiative, private enterprise, and the profit motive among farmers and owners of small businesses.

Stalinism

Lenin's death in 1924 left Joseph Stalin, Leon Trotsky, and Nikolay Bukharin as the leaders of the All-Russian Communist Party. Before he died, Lenin warned his party comrades to beware of Stalin's ambitions. The warning proved prophetic. Ruthless and cunning, Stalin—born Iosif Djugashvili—seemed intent on living up to his revolutionary surname (which means "man of steel"). In the late 1920s, Stalin began to consolidate his power by intimidating and discrediting his rivals. In the mid-1930s, claiming to see spies and saboteurs everywhere, he purged the party and the general populace, exiling dissidents to Siberia or summarily executing them after staged show trials. Bukharin was convicted on trumped-up charges and was executed in 1938. Trotsky, who had fled abroad, was condemned in absentia and was assassinated in Mexico in 1940 by one of Stalin's agents. Those who remained lived in fear of the NKVD (a forerunner of the KGB), Stalin's secret police.

As a variant of Marxism-Leninism, Stalinism had three key features. The first was its reliance on dialectical materialism as a way of justifying almost any course of action that Stalin wished to pursue. For example, in a report to the 16th Congress of the Communist Party in June 1930, Stalin justified the rapid growth of centralized state power as follows:

We stand for the withering away of the state. At the same time we stand for the strengthening of the...strongest state power that has ever existed....Is this "contradictory"? Yes, it is contradictory. But this contradiction...fully reflects Marx's dialectics.

But Stalin omitted mentioning that Marx believed contradictions were to be exposed and overcome, not accepted and embraced.

A second feature of Stalinism was its cult of personality. Whereas Lenin had claimed that the workers suffered from false consciousness and therefore needed a vanguard party to guide them, Stalin maintained that the Communist Party itself suffered from false consciousness (and from spies and traitors within its ranks) and therefore needed an all-wise leader—Stalin himself—to guide it. This effectively ended intraparty democracy and democratic centralism. The resulting cult of personality portrayed Stalin as a universal genius in every subject, from linguistics to genetics.

A third feature of Stalinism was the idea of "socialism in one country"—i.e., building up the industrial base and military might of the Soviet Union before exporting revolution abroad. To this end, Stalin rescinded the NEP, began the collectivization of Soviet agriculture, and embarked on a national program of rapid, forced industrialization. Specifically, he insisted that the Soviet Union had to be quickly, and, if need be, brutally transformed from a primarily agricultural nation to an advanced industrial power. During the collectivization, millions of kulaks, or prosperous peasants, were deprived of their farms and forced to labour on large collective farms. If they resisted (or were even thought likely to do so), they were shot or sent to forced labour camps in Siberia to starve or freeze to death. In the food shortages that resulted, several million people (the precise number remains unknown) starved, and many more suffered from malnutrition and disease.

In foreign policy, socialism in one country meant putting the interests of the Soviet Union ahead of the interests of the international communist movement. After World War II, as Winston Churchill famously remarked, an Iron Curtain descended across Europe as Stalin installed communist regimes in Poland, Czechoslovakia, Yugoslavia, Hungary, Romania, Albania, and Soviet-occupied East Germany as a buffer zone against an invasion from Western Europe. He also subordinated the interests and aspirations of communist parties there and elsewhere to the interests of the Communist Party of the Soviet Union (CPSU). A few dissident leaders, notably Josip Broz Tito in Yugoslavia, were rather reluctant allies; but most were pliant, perhaps out of fear of Soviet military might. Beyond Europe, the Soviet Union supported anticolonial "wars of national liberation" in Asia, Africa, and Latin America and gave economic and military support to communist regimes in North Korea, North Vietnam, and Cuba.

After Stalin's death in 1953, there was a slow liberalization within the CPSU and in Soviet society at large, though the Cold War with the West continued. Soviet Premier Nikita Khrushchev denounced Stalin's crimes in a secret speech to the 20th Party Congress in 1956. Khrushchev himself was deposed in 1964, after which a succession of Soviet leaders stifled reform and attempted to impose a modified version of Stalinism. In the 1980s, Mikhail Gorbachev's policies of *glasnost* and *perestroika* began a new liberalization of Soviet society. Yet the ghost of Stalin was not exorcized completely until the collapse of the Soviet Union and the effective demise of the CPSU in 1991.

Chinese Communism

The People's Republic of China is the only global super-power still ruled by a communist party, the Chinese Communist Party (CCP), as it has been since the communists came to power in 1949. Even so, the official Chinese version of communism—Maoism, or "Mao Zedong thought"—is a far cry from Marx's original vision. Mao Zedong, the founder of the People's Republic and China's first communist leader, claimed to have "creatively" amended Marxist theory and communist practice to suit Chinese conditions. First, he invoked Lenin's theory of imperialism to explain Chinese "backwardness" and justify a revolution in a poor agricultural society without the sizable industrial proletariat that Marx believed was generally necessary to instigate a workers' revolution. Second, Mao redefined or replaced key concepts of Marx's theory. Most notably, he replaced the Marxist concept of a proletarian "class" of industrial wage labourers exploited by the capitalist ruling class with the idea of a proletarian "nation" of agricultural peasants exploited by capitalist countries such as the United States. Mao envisioned the proletarian countries encircling the capitalist countries and waging wars of national liberation to cut off foreign sources of cheap labour and raw materials, thereby depriving the capitalist countries of the ever-expanding revenues that are the lifeblood of their economies.

Mao also planned and oversaw several industrial and agricultural initiatives that proved disastrous for the Chinese people. Among the most important of these was the Great Leap Forward (1958–60), his version of Stalin's policy of rapid, forced industrialization. Aiming to produce steel in backyard blast furnaces and manufacture other commodities in hastily erected small-scale factories, it was a spectacular failure.

Chinese Red Guards read from the little red book of "Quotations from Chairman Mao" at the beginning of the day, circa 1970. Keystone/Hulton Archive/Getty Images

As Mao consolidated his power, he became increasingly concerned with ideological purity, favouring ideologically dedicated cadres of "reds" over technical "experts" in education, engineering, factory management, and other areas. The Cultural Revolution (1966–76) attempted to enforce ideological orthodoxy, and it, too, proved disastrous. Young Red Guards attacked bureaucrats, managers, teachers, and others whose ideological purity was suspect. Widespread chaos ensued, and eventually the People's Liberation Army was called in to restore order.

Mao also aspired to being the "great helmsman" who would lead China out of poverty and into a bright communist future. His cult of personality, like Stalin's, portrayed him as larger than life and endowed with unrivaled wisdom—as found, for example, in the sayings and slogans

On June 5, 1989, a lone man blocked a line of tanks near Tiananmen Square soon after a student-led demonstration calling for political, social, and economic reforms. Several hundred protesters were killed by the end of the standoff. © AP Images

in his "Little Red Book" ("Quotations from Chairman Mao"). After Mao's death in 1976, the Chinese communist leadership began to experiment with limited free market reforms in the economy but continued to keep a tight lid on political dissent.

Non-Marxian Communism

Although Marx remains the preeminent communist theorist, there have been several varieties of non-Marxist communism. Among the most influential is anarchism, or anarcho-communism, which advocates not only communal ownership of property but also the abolition of the state. Historically important anarcho-communists include William Godwin in England, Mikhail Bakunin and Peter Kropotkin in Russia (though both spent much of their lives in exile), and Emma Goldman in the United States. In different ways, they argued that the state and private property are interdependent institutions: The state exists to protect private property, and the owners of private property protect the state. If property is to be owned communally and distributed equally, the state must be smashed once and for all. In *Statism and Anarchy* (1874), for example, Bakunin attacked Marx's view that the transitional state—the dictatorship of the proletariat— would simply wither away after it had served its purpose of preventing a bourgeois counterrevolution. No state, said Bakunin, has ever withered away, and no state ever will. To the contrary, it is in the very nature of the state to extend its control over its subjects, limiting and finally eliminating whatever liberty they once had to control their own lives. Marx's interim state would in fact be a dictatorship "over" the proletariat. In that respect, at least, Bakunin proved to be a better prophet than Marx.

CHAPTER 3

COMMUNISM IN THE SOVIET UNION

The Union of Soviet Socialist Republics (USSR), also called the Soviet Union, is a former northern Eurasian empire (1917/22–1991) stretching from the Baltic and Black seas to the Pacific Ocean and, in its final years, consisted of fifteen Soviet Socialist Republics (SSRs): Armenia, Azerbaijan, Belorussia (now Belarus), Estonia, Georgia, Kazakhstan, Kirgiziya (now Kyrgyzstan), Latvia, Lithuania, Moldavia (now Moldova), Russia, Tajikistan, Turkmenistan, Ukraine, and Uzbekistan. The capital was Moscow, then and now the capital of Russia.

The Russian Revolution

The USSR was the successor to the Russian empire of the tsars. Sometime in the middle of the nineteenth century, Russia entered a phase of internal crisis that in 1917 would culminate in revolution. Its causes were not so much economic or social as political and cultural. For the sake of stability, tsarism insisted on rigid autocracy that effectively shut out the population from participation in government. At the same time, to maintain its status as a great power, it promoted industrial development and higher education, which were inherently dynamic. The result was perpetual tension between government and society, especially its educated element, known as the intelligentsia. Of the socioeconomic causes of tsarism's ultimate collapse, the most important was rural overpopulation: tsarist Russia had the highest rate of demographic growth in Europe. In the second half of the nineteenth century, the rural population increased by more than 50 percent. Also potentially destabilizing was the refusal of the mass of Russian peasantry, living in communes, to acknowledge the principle of private property in land.

In the late nineteenth century, the political conflict pitted three protagonists: tsarism, the peasantry (with the working class, its subdivision), and the intelligentsia.

Late Tsarist Russia

The tsar was absolute and unlimited in his authority, which was subject to neither constitutional restraints nor parliamentary institutions. He ruled with the help of a bureaucratic caste, subject to no external controls and above the law, and the army, one of whose main tasks was maintaining internal order. Imperial Russia developed to a greater extent than any contemporary country a powerful and ubiquitous security police. It was a crime to question the existing system or organize for any purpose whatsoever without government permission. The system, which contained seeds of future totalitarianism, was nevertheless not rigidly enforced and was limited by the institution of private property.

The February Revolution

World War I weakened tsarism. The humiliating defeats that the Russian army suffered at the hands of the Germans, who expelled it from Poland, further lowered the prestige of the monarchy. There were also unsubstantiated rumours that Empress Alexandra, a German by origin, betrayed military secrets to the enemy.

Lenin during the Russian Revolution, 1917. Photos.com/Thinkstock

The final assault on the monarchy began in November 1916, when the head of the liberal Constitutional Democratic Party, Pavel Milyukov, during a session of the Duma, implied the government was guilty of treason. During the exceptionally severe winter of 1916–17, food and fuel deliveries to the major cities—especially the capital, Petrograd (the name given to St. Petersburg between 1914 and 1924)—continued to decline. Dissatisfaction with the government's conduct of the war, coupled with economic hardships, led in late February 1917 (early March, New Style) to an outburst of popular fury. The revolt began with a mutiny of the Petrograd garrison, staffed by superannuated reservists; from them it spread to the industrial quarters. Nicholas II, persuaded by his generals that he and his wife were the main obstacle to victory, agreed to abdicate (March 2 [March 15, New Style]). The end of tsarism brought a provisional government and a rule of "dual power," but it was ineffective, allowing revolutionary parties to emerge, each determined to bring order with its own brand of socialism.

The Bolshevik Coup

The events of February 1917 merit the name of "revolution" because they were essentially spontaneous. October 1917 (November, New Style), by contrast, was a classic coup d'état carried out by a small group of conspirators.

The Bolshevik Central Committee made the decision to seize power at a clandestine meeting held on the night of October 10 (October 23, New Style). There were considerable disagreements over the timing. Lenin wanted the coup to be carried out immediately. Leon Trotsky and most of the others preferred to convene a national Congress of Soviets, packed with Bolsheviks, and have it proclaim the overthrow of the provisional government. A compromise was struck: The coup would take place as soon as practicable, and the Congress of Soviets would ratify it.

During the night of October 24–25, Bolshevik Red Guards peacefully occupied strategic points in Petrograd. On the morning of October 25, Lenin issued a declaration in the name of the Military Revolutionary Committee, which had no authority to do so, that the provisional government was overthrown and all power was assumed by the Soviets.

The Bolshevik Dictatorship

Although Lenin and Trotsky had carried out the October coup in the name of Soviets, they intended from the beginning to concentrate all power in the hands of the ruling

Empress Alexandra

Aleksandra Fyodorovna, original name Alix, Princess (prinzessin) von Hesse-Darmstadt (born June 6, 1872, Darmstadt, Ger.—died July 16/17, 1918, Yekaterinburg, Russia), was the consort of Russian emperor Nicholas II. Her misrule while the emperor was commanding the Russian forces during World War I precipitated the collapse of the imperial government in March 1917.

A granddaughter of Queen Victoria and daughter of Louis IV, Grand Duke of Hesse-Darmstadt, Alexandra married Nicholas in 1894 and came to dominate him. She proved to be unpopular at court and turned to mysticism for solace. Through her near-fanatical acceptance of Orthodoxy and her belief in autocratic rule, she felt it her sacred duty to help reassert Nicholas's absolute power, which had been limited by reforms in 1905. In 1904, the tsarevich Alexis was born; she had previously given birth to four daughters. The tsarevich suffered from hemophilia, and Alexandra's overwhelming concern for his life led her to seek the aid of a debauched "holy man" who possessed hypnotic powers, Grigory Yefimovich Rasputin. She came to venerate Rasputin as a saint sent by God to save the throne and as a voice of the common people, whom, she believed, remained loyal to the emperor. Rasputin's influence was a public scandal, but Alexandra silenced all criticism. After Nicholas left for the front in August 1915, she arbitrarily dismissed capable ministers and replaced them with nonentities or dishonest careerists favoured by Rasputin. As a result, the administration became paralyzed and the regime discredited, and Alexandra came to be widely but erroneously believed to be a German agent. Yet she disregarded all warnings of coming changes, even the murder of Rasputin. After the October Revolution (1917), she, Nicholas, and their children were imprisoned by the Bolsheviks and were later shot to death.

Influenced by self-proclaimed holy man Grigory Rasputin, Empress Alexandra inadvertently brought an end to tsarist rule and the family she hoped to protect with Rasputin's help. Time & Life Pictures/Getty Images

organs of the Bolshevik Party. The resulting novel arrangement —the prototype of all totalitarian regimes—vested actual sovereignty in the hands of a private organization, called "the Party," which, however, exercised it indirectly through state institutions. Bolsheviks held leading posts in the state: no decisions could be taken and no laws passed without their consent. The legislative organs, centred in the Soviets, merely rubber-stamped Bolshevik orders. The state apparatus was headed by a cabinet called the Council of Peoples' Commissars (Sovnarkom), chaired by Lenin, all of whose members were drawn from the elite of the Party.

In March 1918, the Bolshevik Party was renamed the Russian Communist Party (Bolshevik) in order to distinguish it from Social Democratic parties in Russia and Europe and separate the followers of Lenin from those affiliated with

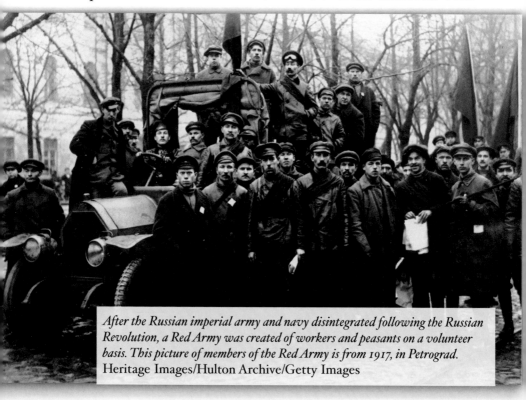

After the Russian imperial army and navy disintegrated following the Russian Revolution, a Red Army was created of workers and peasants on a volunteer basis. This picture of members of the Red Army is from 1917, in Petrograd. Heritage Images/Hulton Archive/Getty Images

the nonrevolutionary Socialist International. The party was directed by a Central Committee. To streamline work, its management was entrusted from March 1919 onward to the Secretariat, the Organizational Bureau (Orgburo), and the Political Bureau (Politburo). The Secretariat and Orgburo dealt largely with personnel matters, while the Politburo combined legislative and executive powers.

Lenin's Disillusionment

Lenin's health began to fail in 1921. It deteriorated further during the following year, when he suffered several strokes. Forced gradually to withdraw from day-to-day activity, he had the opportunity to survey his achievement. It did not please him. There is considerable evidence that if his health had allowed it, he would have carried out major reforms in the political and economic structure of the Soviet state.

One cause for concern was the growing bureaucratization of both party and state. Under the terms of the strict discipline that Lenin imposed, the ruling party became increasingly centralized, with its directorate—headed by the Politburo and the Secretariat of the Central Committee— making decisions on its own authority without consulting the party cadres. Dissent from lower organs was ignored and punished if pressed. The local branches of the party lost the right to elect their officers; these were routinely appointed by the Secretariat. The result was ossification of the Communist Party and undue concentration of power in the hands of the Moscow apparatus. The latter was increasingly dominated by Joseph Stalin, on whom Lenin relied as an efficient administrator and whom he had agreed to promote in April 1922 to serve as the party's general secretary. Stalin used his authority to appoint officials personally loyal to him and hostile to his archrival, Leon Trotsky.

The Struggle for Succession

Lenin's growing incapacitation led in 1922 to a power struggle within the party. It would culminate five years later in Trotsky's banishment and Stalin's unchallenged dictatorship.

On the face of it, Trotsky was the natural heir to Lenin, since it was Trotsky who had organized the October coup and managed the Red Army in the civil war. A superb orator and lively writer, he had an international reputation. Although far less known, Stalin was much better positioned to succeed Lenin. Intellectually unprepossessing, a dull speaker, and lacklustre writer, he operated behind the scenes. Realizing early that the centralized system of government that Lenin had created vested extraordinary power in the party machine, he avoided the spotlight and instead concentrated on building up cadres loyal to himself. Aware that his followers were squabbling and deathly afraid that the party he had built on the principle of disciplined unity would fall apart after his death, Lenin tried to interfere, but he was unsuccessful. The triumvirate, ostensibly from concern over his health, ordered him to abstain from involvement in government affairs. From December 1922 onward, Lenin lived under virtual house arrest.

On his death in January 1924, Lenin was embalmed and put on permanent display in a mausoleum in Red Square to provide superstitious peasants with a visible symbol of sainthood. By then power was in the hands of the triumvirate, which Stalin before long broke up to assume undisputed personal leadership. The party cadres, aware of the regime's unpopularity, supported him, for he promised to provide continued strong leadership, repel all democratic challenges, and maintain the privileges they had gained since November 1917.

The Stalin Era

After Lenin's death in January 1924, Stalin promoted an extravagant, quasi-Byzantine cult of the deceased leader. Archpriest of Leninism, Stalin also promoted his own cult in the following year by having the city of Tsaritsyn renamed Stalingrad (now Volgograd). His main rival, Trotsky (once Lenin's heir apparent), was now in eclipse, having been ousted by the ruling triumvirate of GrigoryZinoviev, Lev Kamenev, and Stalin. Soon afterward, Stalin joined with the rightist leaders Nikolay Bukharin and Aleksey Rykov in an alliance directed against his former co-triumvirs. Pinning his faith in the ability of the Soviet Union to establish a viable political system without waiting for the support hitherto expected from worldwide revolution, the Secretary General advocated a policy of "Socialism in one country"; this was popular with the hardheaded party managers whom he was promoting to influential positions in the middle hierarchy. His most powerful rivals were all dismissed, Bukharin and Rykov soon following Zinoviev and Kamenev into disgrace and political limbo pending execution. Stalin expelled Trotsky from the Soviet Union in 1929 and had him assassinated in Mexico in 1940.

In 1928, Stalin abandoned Lenin's quasi-capitalist New Economic Policy in favour of headlong state-organized industrialization under a succession of five-year plans. This was, in effect, a new Russian revolution more devastating in its effects than those of 1917. The dictator's blows fell most heavily on the peasantry, some twenty-five million rustic households being compelled to amalgamate in collective or state farms within a few years. Resisting desperately, the reluctant *muzhiks* were attacked by troops and OGPU (political police) units. Uncooperative peasants, termed *kulaks*, were arrested en masse, being shot, exiled, or absorbed into the rapidly expanding network of Stalinist concentration camps and worked to death under atrocious conditions. Collectivization also caused a great famine in the Ukraine. Yet Stalin continued to export the grain stocks that a less cruel leader would have rushed to the famine-stricken areas. Some ten million peasants may have perished through his policies during these years.

Crash industrialization was less disastrous in its effects, but it, too, numbered its grandiose failures, to which Stalin responded by arraigning industrial managers in a succession of show trials. Intimidated into confessing imaginary crimes, the accused served as self-denounced scapegoats for catastrophes arising from the Secretary General's policies. Yet Stalin was successful in rapidly industrializing a backward country—as was widely acknowledged by enthusiastic contemporary foreign witnesses, including Adolf Hitler and such well-known writers as H.G. Wells and George Bernard Shaw.

Among those who vainly sought to moderate Stalin's policies was his young second wife, Nadezhda Alliluyeva, whom he had married in 1919 and who committed suicide in 1932. They had two children. The son, Vasily, perished as an alcoholic after rising to unmerited high rank in the Soviet Air Force. The daughter, Svetlana, became the object of her father's alternating affection and bad temper. She emigrated after his death and later wrote memoirs that illuminate Stalin's well-camouflaged private life.

Role in World War II

During World War II Stalin emerged, after an unpromising start, as the most successful of the supreme leaders thrown up by the belligerent nations. In August 1939, after first attempting to form an anti-Hitler alliance with the Western powers, he concluded a pact with Hitler, which encouraged the German dictator to attack Poland and begin World War

II. Anxious to strengthen his western frontiers while his new but palpably treacherous German ally was still engaged in the West, Stalin annexed eastern Poland, Estonia, Latvia, Lithuania, and parts of Romania. He also attacked Finland and extorted territorial concessions. In May 1941, Stalin recognized the growing danger of German attack on the Soviet Union by appointing himself chairman of the Council of People's Commissars (head of the government); it was his first governmental office since 1923.

Stalin's prewar defensive measures were exposed as incompetent by the German blitzkrieg that surged deep into Soviet territory after Hitler's unprovoked attack on the Soviet Union in June 22, 1941. Khrushchev claimed that Stalin was shocked into temporary inactivity by the onslaught, but if so, he soon rallied and appointed himself supreme commander in chief. When the Germans menaced Moscow in the winter of 1941, he remained in the threatened capital, helping organize a great counteroffensive. The Battle of Stalingrad (in the following winter) and the Battle of Kursk (in the summer of 1943) were also won by the Soviet Army under Stalin's supreme direction, turning the tide of invasion against the retreating Germans, who capitulated in May 1945. As war leader, Stalin maintained close personal control over the Soviet battlefronts, military reserves, and war economy. At first over-inclined to intervene with inept telephoned instructions, as Hitler did, the Soviet generalissimo gradually learned to delegate military decisions.

Stalin participated in high-level Allied meetings, including those of the "Big Three" with Winston Churchill and Franklin D. Roosevelt at Tehrān (1943) and Yalta (1945). A formidable negotiator, he outwitted these foreign statesmen. His superior skill has been acclaimed by Anthony Eden, then British foreign secretary.

Stalin is pictured here with son Vasily and daughter, Svetlana. Svetlana later wrote books that detailed her father's private life. Heritage Images/Hulton Archive/Getty Images

Last Years

After the war, Stalin imposed on Eastern Europe a new kind of colonial control based on native communist regimes nominally independent but in fact subservient to himself. He thus increased the number of his subjects by about a hundred million. But in 1948, the defection of Titoist Yugoslavia from the Soviet camp struck a severe blow to world communism as a Stalin-dominated monolith. To prevent other client states from following Tito's example, Stalin instigated local show trials, manipulated like those of the Great Purge of the 1930s in Russia, in which satellite communist leaders confessed to Titoism, many being executed.

Far from continuing his wartime alliance with the United States and Great Britain, Stalin now regarded these countries—especially the United States—as the archenemies that he needed after Hitler's death. At home, the primacy of Marxist ideology was harshly reasserted. Stalin's chief ideological hatchet man, Andrey Zhdanov, a secretary of the Central Committee, began a reign of terror in the Soviet artistic and intellectual world. Foreign achievements were derided, and the primacy of Russians as inventors and pioneers in practically every field was asserted. Hopes for domestic relaxation, widely aroused in the Soviet Union during the war, were thus sadly disappointed.

Increasingly suspicious and paranoid in his later years, Stalin ordered the arrest, announced in January 1953, of certain—mostly Jewish—Kremlin doctors on charges of medically murdering various Soviet leaders, including Zhdanov. The dictator was evidently preparing to make this "Doctors' Plot" the pretext for yet another great terror menacing all his senior associates, but he died suddenly on March 5, according to the official report. So convenient was this death to his entourage that suspicions of foul play were voiced.

The Khrushchev Era

Stalin died a slow, angry, and painful death on March 5, 1953. The top leadership gathered around his bedside, but he could only move his little finger. Some were delighted, including Lavrenty Beria who earned the undying hostility of Svetlana Alliluyeva, Stalin's daughter. Others in the entourage were more circumspect. They found themselves in a predicament: how were they to choose Stalin's successor? How were they to ensure that no one acquired his awesome power? This would put their careers, and even their lives, at risk.

The Transition

Political changes included Georgy Malenkov, one of Stalin's chief lieutenants, assuming the post of senior party secretary as well as chairman of the Council of Ministers (i.e., prime minister), but his assumed post lasted only a few weeks. Khrushchev forced him to yield his top party post and thus gained the decisive margin by his control of the party machinery. In September 1953, he replaced Malenkov as first secretary and in 1955 removed Malenkov from the premiership in favour of his handpicked nominee, Marshal Nikolay A. Bulganin.

Significantly, by 1954, Khrushchev had been able to reform the Stalinist security apparatus by subordinating it to the top party leadership. Stalin's Ministry of Internal Affairs was divided into criminal police and the security services—the Committee on State Security (KGB), which in turn reported to the USSR's Council of Ministers.

In May 1955, when Khrushchev made his first trip outside the Soviet Union—to Yugoslavia with Bulganin—he began to show his flexibility. He apologized to Josip Broz Tito for Stalin's denunciation of Yugoslav communism in 1948. Later, in trips to Geneva, Afghanistan, and India, he began to exhibit a brash, extroverted personal diplomacy that was to become his trademark. Although his attacks on world capitalism were virulent and primitive, his outgoing personality and peasant humour were in sharp contrast to the image that earlier Soviet public figures had cultivated.

On February 25, 1956, during the 20th Party Congress in Moscow, Khrushchev delivered his memorable secret speech about the excesses of Stalin's one-man rule, attacking the late Soviet ruler's "intolerance, his brutality, his abuse of power." The spectacle of the first secretary of the Communist Party exposing the wrongful executions of the Great Purge of the 1930s and the excesses of Soviet police repression, after years of fearful silence, had far-reaching effects that Khrushchev himself could barely have foreseen. The resulting "thaw" in the Soviet Union saw the release of millions of political prisoners and the "rehabilitation" of many thousands more who had perished.

Khrushchev's rule was not without its dark side, including an intensified persecution of religion. Nonetheless, by smashing the repressive icon of Stalinism and the mentality of terror that had been imposed on the general population, Khrushchev inspired a new intellectual ferment and widespread hopes for greater freedom, particularly among students and intellectuals.

In foreign affairs, he widely asserted his doctrine of peaceful coexistence with the noncommunist world, which he had first enunciated in a public speech at the 20th Party Congress. In opposition to old communist writ, he stated that "war is not fatalistically inevitable." At the 21st Party Congress in 1959 he said, "We offer the capitalist countries peaceful competition." His visit to the United States in 1959, where he toured cities and farms with the ebullience of a politician running for office, was a decided success. The "spirit of Camp David" in Maryland, where he conferred with President Dwight D. Eisenhower, brought Soviet-American relations to a new high. Notwithstanding these hopeful developments, Khrushchev as a diplomat remained irascible and blunt.

Soviet success in lofting the world's first space satellite in 1957 had been followed by increased missile buildups. In 1962, Khrushchev secretly attempted to base Soviet medium-range missiles in Cuba, but these efforts were detected by the United States. During the resulting tense confrontation in October 1962, when the United States and the Soviet Union apparently stood on the brink of nuclear war, Khrushchev agreed to remove the missiles on the promise that the United States would make no further attempt to overthrow Cuba's communist government. The Soviet Union was criticized by the Chinese communists for this settlement. The Sino-Soviet split, which began in 1959, reached the stage of public denunciations in 1960. China's ideological insistence on all-out "war against the imperialists" and Mao Zedong's annoyance with Khrushchev's coexistence policies were exacerbated by Soviet refusal to assist the Chinese nuclear weapon buildup and rectify the Russo-Chinese border. The Nuclear Test-Ban Treaty reached between the Soviet Union and the United States in 1963, although generally welcomed throughout the world, intensified Chinese denunciations of Soviet "revisionism."

During Khrushchev's time in office, he had to steer constantly between, on the one hand, popular pressures toward a consumer-oriented society and agitation by intellectuals for greater freedom of expression and, on

Khruschev was likely trying to avoid the kind of famine that had swept the Soviet Union in 1922, shown in this picture from the lower Volga region. Sovfoto/Universal Images Group/Getty Images

the other, the growing fear of the Soviet bureaucracy that reform would get out of hand. The central crisis of Khrushchev's administration, however, was agriculture. An optimist, he based many plans on the bumper crops in 1956 and 1958, which fueled his repeated promises to overtake the United States in agricultural as well as in industrial production. He opened up more than 70 million acres of virgin land in Siberia and sent thousands of labourers to till them. But his plan was unsuccessful, and the Soviet Union soon again had to import wheat from Canada and the United States.

The failures in agriculture, the quarrel with China, and the humiliating resolution of the Cuban missile crisis, added to growing resentment of his own arbitrary administrative methods, were the major factors in Khrushchev's downfall. On October 14, 1964, after a palace coup orchestrated by his protégé and deputy, Leonid Brezhnev, the Central Committee accepted Khrushchev's request to retire from his position as the party's first secretary and chairman of the Council of Ministers of the Soviet Union because of "advanced age and poor health."

Last Years

For almost seven years thereafter, Khrushchev lived quietly in Moscow and at his country dacha as a "nonperson"—officially a special pensioner of the Soviet government. He was mentioned in the Soviet press occasionally and appeared in public only to vote in Soviet elections. The one break in this ordered obscurity came in 1970 with the publication of his memoirs in the United States and Europe, although not in the Soviet Union. This was the first installment of a large body of personal reminiscence that he dictated in secret during his retirement.

Almost forty-eight hours elapsed after his death before it was announced to the Soviet public. He was denied a state funeral and interment in the Kremlin wall, although he was allowed a quiet burial at Novodevichy Convent Cemetery in Moscow.

The Brezhnev Era

The new collective leadership was headed by Leonid Brezhnev, party first secretary; Aleksey Kosygin, prime minister; and Nikolay Podgorny, who became president in December 1965. The industrial and agricultural branches of the party apparat were unified, restrictions on the size of household plots and private livestock on collective farms were removed, the party apparat was informed that it would enjoy what it craved most—stability of cadres—and the central ministries reappeared as the regional councils disappeared. At the 23rd Party Congress in March–April 1966, Brezhnev became general secretary of the party—a post last held by Stalin in 1934. Khrushchev's restrictions on the tenure of office of party officials were abandoned. Brezhnev was displaying his forte, cadres.

Collective Leadership

Between 1964 and 1968, Brezhnev had to play second fiddle to Aleksey Kosygin, who took the lead in economic

Brezhnev and Soviet Culture

Brezhnev was instinctively a conservative and had little sympathy for experimentation in art and literature. Since he did not inhabit the intellectual world, he could not grasp what motivated the radicals. He preferred art and literature that lauded the Soviet system. Brezhnev published several tomes himself, but they were always ghostwritten. The Brezhnev leadership quickly revealed its intolerance. In September 1965, the writers Andrey Sinyavsky and Yuly Daniel were arrested and later sentenced to seven years' and five years' hard labour, respectively, for publishing works abroad that slandered the Soviet state. Over the following years, many other writers and their sympathizers were also arrested, imprisoned, or placed in labour camps. Dissent flourished. After the Six-Day War of 1967 between Israel and the Arab nations, attacks on Israel and Zionism took on an anti-Semitic tone. Cultural repression increased even before the invasion of Czechoslovakia in 1968. Alexandr Solzhenitsyn's unpublished manuscripts were seized and his published works withdrawn from circulation. He was expelled from the Union of Soviet Writers in 1969. In 1970, he received the Nobel Prize for Literature; this exacerbated the situation. He declined to collect his prize because he believed that he would not be allowed to return home. Also in 1970, the liberal editor of the influential monthly *Novy Mir*, Aleksandr Tvardovsky, had to resign.

The might of the state crushed overt cultural dissent, but it stimulated the development of a counterculture. Networks of like-minded individuals to discuss common interests formed and flourished. Works that could not be published in the USSR were circulated in typescript (*samizdat*) or sent abroad for publication (*tamizdat*). The arrival of the audio-cassette and later the videocassette permitted youth to enjoy the forbidden fruits of Western pop culture. The widespread teaching of foreign languages, especially English, accelerated this process. The state and the KGB probably lost control of culture in the mid-1970s. Unofficial culture became vibrant and dynamic, while official culture atrophied. The educational system was geared to producing mediocre school leavers and graduates who would not challenge the system. This stimulated many of the more able to seek out restricted and forbidden information.

reform and foreign policy. Circumstances favoured Brezhnev. The conflict with Czechoslovakia over "socialism with a human face" was his domain, since relations between ruling parties were the responsibility of the Central Committee secretariat. The turn back to Stalinism undermined Kosygin's economic reforms, and his star waned. Brezhnev increased his authority and by the early 1970s was first among equals. By the mid-1970s, he was the national leader. He pushed Podgorny aside in 1977 and donned the mantle of president. Afterward he went into physical and political decline. It took him longer than Khrushchev to become national leader, but that was because he accumulated power gradually instead of adopting the high-risk strategy of his predecessor.

Ideologically, Brezhnev was innovative. At the 22nd Party Congress in 1961, Khrushchev had launched the communist era, promising that by 1980 the foundations of communism would be laid. Brezhnev had to face reality, and he came up with "developed socialism." This meant that the road to communism was going to be longer than previously expected. It was predicted that the scientific-technical and information technology revolutions would transform the USSR. In the short term, social differentiation would increase, as the state needed to give preference to those who mastered these skills. In the long run, it was promised, everyone would benefit. There was optimism among the intelligentsia and people in the early 1970s, but this soon dissipated. Gorbachev later dismissed the Brezhnev era as one of "stagnation." This was unfair. During the first half of Brezhnev's incumbency, the USSR reached the zenith of its international power and prestige. Détente in the early 1970s was accompanied by the U.S. recognition of nuclear parity. Then it all went wrong. An economic slowdown was accompanied by increased defense spending and the disastrous decision to intervene in

Afghanistan in December 1979. By the time of Brezhnev's death in November 1982, the USSR was in headlong decline.

Nationality Policy

The Brezhnev leadership quietly pursued the goal of Russian dominance of the country. In 1971, Brezhnev spoke of the emergence of a "new historical community of people, the Soviet people." Afterward he made it clear that he would brook no opposition to the policy of eliminating differences between nations. Ukraine in 1972–73 felt the weight of this policy. The principal casualty was Pyotr Shelest, the first secretary of the Communist Party of Ukraine, who had played a leading role in the renewal of Ukrainian national assertiveness. About one thousand bureaucrats, officials, and academics were dismissed. Particularly hard hit were ideology, literature, and history. The purge added impetus to the formation of a Ukrainian dissident underground. Here, the emphasis was not to escape from Stalinism but to evolve a distinctly Ukrainian culture. Brezhnev lauded the "revolutionary energy, diligence, and deep internationalism of the Great Russian people," which had earned them the "sincere respect of the peoples" of the USSR. The expansion of education in non-Russian areas was impressive. By the 1980s, the distinctions between the developed and underdeveloped nations of the USSR, as far as access to education was concerned, had almost disappeared. The Central Asian republics had caught up and in some cases had more students per ten thousand of the population than the Russians. However, as the Muslim population grew, so did the number of young people wishing to enter university at a time when demand for graduates was declining, owing to a slowdown in the economy. Economic decline also slowed progress. By the early 1980s, despite the great expansion of tertiary education, no non-Russian republic had trained elites in all walks of life. Culture, education, and the social sciences were adequately covered, but science and technology were seriously underrepresented. As a result, industry, especially in Central Asia, was dominated by Russians and other Europeans.

The problem of language turned out to be the most acrimonious. Russian was vigorously promoted (affecting kindergartens and nurseries for the first time) as the language of learning and intercourse. Russian publications expanded, and non-Russian ones were cut back. No attempt was made to encourage the some twenty-four million Russians living outside Russia to learn the local language of their area. Only 0.2 percent of these Russians claimed mastery of the local tongue in 1989. This had disastrous consequences for Russians after the collapse of the USSR. The promotion of Russian aroused increased opposition, especially in the Baltic republics, Ukraine, and Georgia. The emphasis on Russian was clearly linked to the alarming demographic trends, where the net annual increase in the population of the USSR was almost entirely Muslim.

Native cadres in Central Asia made headway in all top party and government functions in their republics and by the late 1960s occupied more than half the posts. In the Baltic republics, locals dominated top positions. However, in the CPSU Politburo, there was a marked preference for Russians. In 1980, among the leading 150 functionaries in the CPSU Central Committee apparat, only three were non-Slav. There were also only 3 non-Slavs among the top 150 military personnel.

The Interregnum: Andropov and Chernenko

Toward the end of his life, Brezhnev lost control of the country. Regionalism became stronger as the centre faltered.

When Brezhnev died on Nov. 10, 1982, he was succeeded as party leader by Yury Andropov, although his chosen successor was Konstantin Chernenko. Andropov had been head of the KGB from 1967 to May 1982. He then slipped into the Central Committee secretariat after Mikhail Suslov, the dry and severe guardian of ideological rectitude, died. Without this move, he could not have become party leader. By June 1983, Andropov had also become president of the USSR and chairman of the defense council—all the posts that Brezhnev had filled.

Andropov was the best-informed man in the USSR and set about reforming the country. He was a cautious reformer, believing that there was nothing fundamentally wrong with the socialist system. He believed that more discipline, energy, and initiative would turn things around. Corruption, absenteeism, and alcoholism were rife and were his special concerns. The retail trade system and transportation were targeted and felt his reforming zeal. His leadership style was in sharp contrast to that of the opulent, pompous Brezhnev. He cut back privilege and met workers on the shop floor. Andropov's anti-alcohol campaign was well conceived, but it led to a sharp fall in government revenue. His industrial and agricultural policy was quite sensible but ineffective, since the economy was already in terminal decline.

Under Andropov, a group of cautious reformers rose to prominence. These included Mikhail Gorbachev, Yegor Ligachev, and Nikolay Ryzhkov. Andropov wanted Gorbachev to succeed him and added a paragraph to this effect to his report to a Central Committee plenum that did not convene until after his death on Feb. 9, 1984. Instead the seventy-two-year-old, terminally ill Konstantin Chernenko was eased into the top party post and later became president of the USSR and chairman of the defense council. The aging Politburo had plumped for a non-reformer, a throwback to Brezhnevism.

Yury Vladimirovich Andropov

Yury Vladimirovich Andropov (born June 15 [June 2, Old Style], 1914, Nagutskoye, Russia—died Feb. 9, 1984, Moscow) was head of the Soviet Union's KGB (State Security Committee) from 1967 to 1982 and his country's leader as general secretary of the Communist Party's Central Committee from November 1982 until his death fifteen months later.

The son of a railway worker, Andropov was a telegraph operator, film projectionist, and boatman on the Volga River before attending a technical college and, later, Petrozavodsk University. He became an organizer for the Young Communist League (Komsomol) in the Yaroslav region and joined the Communist Party in 1939. His superiors noticed his abilities, and he was made head of the Komsomol in the newly created Karelo-Finnish Autonomous Republic (1940–44).

The turning point in Andropov's career was his transfer to Moscow (1951), where he was assigned to the party's Secretariat staff, considered a training ground for promising young officials. As ambassador to Hungary (July 1954–March 1957), he played a major role in coordinating the Soviet invasion of that country. Andropov then returned to Moscow, rising rapidly through the communist hierarchy and, in 1967, becoming head of the KGB. Andropov's policies as head of the KGB were repressive; his tenure was noted for its suppression of political dissidents.

Andropov was elected to the Politburo, and, as Soviet leader Leonid Brezhnev's health declined, he began to position himself for succession, resigning his KGB post in 1982. Andropov was chosen by the Communist Party Central Committee to succeed Brezhnev as general secretary on November 12, scarcely two days after Brezhnev's death. He consolidated his power by becoming chairman of the Presidium of the Supreme Soviet (president) on June 16, 1983.

Ill health overtook him by August 1983, and thereafter he was never seen again in public. He accomplished little and was succeeded by a former rival, Konstantin Chernenko.

However, Gorbachev became "second" secretary, with responsibility for chairing Politburo meetings when Chernenko was away or unfit, which turned out to be quite often. But Chernenko did set a precedent: he became the first politician to succeed as party leader after having previously failed. Party privilege again grew under Chernenko. The military did not have things all its own way. The able, dynamic chief of staff, Marshal Nikolay Ogarkov, was moved sideways and replaced by Marshal Sergey Akhromeyev, another formidable soldier. Ogarkov was blamed for his aggressive promotion of the SS-20 missile program and for the shooting down of a Korean jet Flight 007, with 269 passengers and crew on board, after it had strayed into Soviet airspace in September 1983. The incident caused an international furor and increased tension between NATO and the Warsaw Pact countries.

The Gorbachev Era

Gorbachev's efforts to democratize his country's political system and decentralize its economy led to the downfall of communism and the breakup of the Soviet Union in 1991. In part because he ended the Soviet Union's postwar domination of Eastern Europe, Gorbachev was awarded the Nobel Prize for Peace in 1990.

Gorbachev's Succession

There appears to have been a tacit agreement among Politburo members that on Chernenko's death Gorbachev would take over. But some of them were having second thoughts. Grigory Romanov, Central Committee secretary for the military economy and previously party boss in Leningrad, and Viktor Grishin, Moscow party leader, both decided to try for the highest office in the land, that of party leader. Ligachev later confirmed that a power struggle had taken place and the Soviet foreign minister Andrey Gromyko, the party control commission chairman Mikhail Solomentsev, and the KGB boss Viktor Chebrikov had ensured that Gorbachev outmaneuvered Grishin. Ligachev, even though he was not at that time a member of the Politburo, later claimed he had played a significant role in Gorbachev's election through his role as Central Committee secretary in charge of organizational work. He carefully selected the Central Committee members who were invited to a hastily convened plenum on March 11, 1985, that confirmed Gorbachev as leader. About a third of the membership was not present. Ligachev became "second" secretary, since the Politburo empowered him to chair Central Committee secretariat meetings. He was also to be in control of cadres and ideology. The normal practice was for the general secretary to head the secretariat. Hence, Gorbachev started with a considerable handicap, since all personnel changes would be the subject of intense bargaining and horse trading. Gorbachev turned out to be a skillful horse trader. In April 1985, Ligachev became a full member of the Politburo and was replaced as cadres chief by Georgy Razumovsky. Gorbachev's nominee was Aleksandr Yakovlev, who became secretary for propaganda and overseer of the media. His task was to expand *glasnost* ("openness") and protect creative writers and journalists against Ligachev's ire. Gorbachev managed to make Yakovlev a full member of the Politburo by June 1987. He was a strategic ally in the battle to restructure the Soviet political and economic system. In July 1985, Romanov left the Politburo and secretariat, and Boris Yeltsin, first party secretary in Sverdlovsk, and Lev Zaikov, party boss in Leningrad province, joined. Yeltsin appears to have been an appointee of Gorbachev and Zaikov Ligachev. In July, Gorbachev managed to get Gromyko elected president and Eduard Shevardnadze appointed as foreign minister and a full member of the Politburo. In September, the octogenarian Tikhonov made way for Nikolay Ryzhkov as prime minister. At the 27th Party Congress in February–March 1986, there were wholesale changes. Yeltsin became a candidate member of the Politburo on becoming Moscow party leader. Gorbachev's brief to him was to clean up the notoriously corrupt Moscow apparat. Grishin had been known as "the Godfather." About 52 percent of the newly elected Central Committee were new appointees. The new moderate reform team was in place.

Economic and Social Reforms

When Gorbachev took office in March 1985, he was clear about his policy preferences. In a speech on Dec. 10, 1984, he spoke of the need to effect "deep transformations in the economy and the whole system of social relations," to carry through the policies of *perestroika*, the "democratization of social and economic life," and *glasnost*. He underlined the need for greater social justice, a more important role for local Soviets, and more participation by workers in the workplace. His goal was to set in motion a revolution controlled from above. He did not wish to undermine the Soviet system, only to make it more efficient. The leading role of the party and the central direction of the economy were to stay. Under Andropov, he had attended seminars by such radical scholars as Tatyana Zaslavskaya and Abel Aganbegyan. He accepted Zaslavskaya's main point that the "command-administrative system" was dragging the country down and would ruin it if not dismantled.

Initially, Gorbachev continued Andropov's reforms. He insisted on acceleration of economic growth and spoke of "perfecting" the system. Machine building was given preference as light and consumer goods took second place.

There was to be more technical innovation and worker discipline. He was enthusiastic about the anti-alcohol campaign and was dubbed the "mineral water general secretary." All this produced few positive results. He overlooked the obvious point that workers require greater incentives if they are to give their best. His policy led to a fall in the consumer goods available, and agriculture did not blossom. At the 27th Party Congress, Gorbachev spoke of the need for far-reaching reforms to get the economy going. The first clear evidence that Gorbachev and his supporters had moved to the offensive against the existing party order surfaced at the congress. The centre of contention was Boris Yeltsin, who shocked delegates by strongly criticizing the privileges of the party apparat. Among his targets were the special shops for the elite, which also had been denounced in a *Pravda* article just before the congress. Ligachev responded by vitriolically attacking the *Pravda* article and the raising of the issue in the first place. Gromyko supported him. The battle lines had been drawn. Thereafter, Ligachev would be the principal defender of the rights of the party apparat and of the existing order in general.

Glasnost was put to the test on April 26, 1986, when a reactor at the Chernobyl nuclear plant exploded. Gorbachev waited eighteen days before going on television to give an account of the worst nuclear disaster in history. Chernobyl had a profoundly negative effect on the population's thinking about nuclear power and provided a powerful stimulus to the growth of a green (environmental) movement. Afterward the regime became much more open about natural disasters, drug abuse, and crime. *Glasnost* took hold and produced much greater freedom of expression and open criticism of the political order. Gorbachev sought to win over the intelligentsia by bringing the dissident physicist Andrey Sakharov and his wife, Yelena Bonner, back to Moscow from exile in Gorky.

The intelligentsia's support was perceived to be critical if the battle with the bureaucracy was to be won.

Perestroika concentrated initially on economic reform. Enterprises were encouraged to become self-financing, cooperatives were set up by groups of people as businesses, and land could be leased to allow family farming. But the bureaucrats who ran the economy rightly feared that these activities would undermine their privileges and power. Cooperatives were heavily taxed, supplies were difficult to procure, and the public was often hostile. Lessees of land had to be very resilient to succeed.

Political Restructuring

A major problem for Gorbachev was that there was no agreement at the top as to what *perestroika*, *glasnost*, and democratization should achieve. The radical reformers, Gorbachev, Yakovlev, and Shevardnadze, were outflanked by the moderate reformers, Ligachev, Ryzhkov, and others. The problem was compounded by an apparent lack of clarity in Gorbachev's own thinking. He was never able to construct a coherent goal and the means of reaching it. His frustrations with the party apparat led him to formulate a very radical solution—to emasculate it. He wanted to exclude it from day-to-day involvement in the management of the economy and end its dominance over the state legislature and party affairs. The secretariat had been the party's brain, and all key decisions had been taken there. Gorbachev wanted to end the party officials' domination of the Soviets. He achieved this remarkable feat at the 19th Party Conference in June 1988. The party thereby lost its dominant role at the centre of the political process but gained its revenge on Gorbachev by consolidating its power at the periphery, where the weak Soviets were no match for it. Hence, there was a centrifugal flow of power from the centre to the periphery. This process had been under way since the death of Stalin, and the removal of Khrushchev had underlined the influence of local party officials. The Brezhnev era further added to the flow of power to the periphery.

Elections to the USSR Congress of People's Deputies, which replaced the USSR Supreme Soviet as the highest organ of state power, took place in March 1989. About 88 percent of the deputies were communists, but by then the Communist Party was no longer a monolithic party. The congress elected from among its members a bicameral legislature (called the Supreme Soviet), each house having 271 members. Gorbachev chaired the proceedings. Boris Yeltsin became a member of the Supreme Soviet after another deputy stood down in his favour. Yeltsin had been sacked as Moscow party leader and from his Politburo membership in November 1987 after a furious row with Ligachev. Gorbachev chose not to back him up. Thus began the titanic struggle between Gorbachev and Yeltsin that was to result in Gorbachev's political destruction. As a deputy, Yeltsin had a national platform for the first time and used it very skillfully. The main focus of his attacks was party privilege, the lack of success of *perestroika*, the need for market reforms, and personal criticism of Gorbachev's leadership.

The new pattern at the top was repeated in each republic. Congresses were elected, and Supreme Soviets emerged from them. Local Soviet elections also took place in early 1990 and led to many shocks. Communist officials, encouraged by Gorbachev to stand, were often defeated even when standing as the only candidate. In order to be elected, a deputy needed more than 50 percent of the votes cast. *Glasnost* permitted non-Russian nationalities to voice their opposition to Russian and communist domination and led to a growth of nationalism and regionalism. This was exacerbated by economic decline.

In the Baltic republics especially, many argued that they could run their economic affairs better than Moscow. Interethnic strife and conflict intensified and sometimes resulted in bloodshed. The conflict in Nagorno-Karabakh, an Armenian-dominated enclave in Azerbaijan, was the most violent and bitter. The newly elected Supreme Soviets could claim to speak for the population. This was especially true in the Baltic. Multiparty politics became legitimate in 1990, when Article 6 of the constitution, which had guaranteed a communist monopoly, was removed. Hundreds, indeed thousands, of informal associations and then parties sprang up in the receptive climate of *glasnost* and democratization. Popular fronts, most noticeably in the Baltic, united all those opposing Moscow rule and seeking independence. As these fronts dominated the Supreme Soviets, they could pass declarations of sovereignty. In March 1990, Lithuania went further and declared itself independent. In May 1990, Yeltsin became, despite Gorbachev's bitter opposition, chairman of the Russian Supreme Soviet. The following month, the Russian SFSR declared itself a sovereign state. It claimed that its laws took precedence over Soviet laws. Gorbachev ruled this invalid. This was the pattern in every republic that had declared itself sovereign. It was known as the "war of laws." As a consequence, the survival of the USSR became an issue.

Gorbachev soon tired of the "new-look" USSR Supreme Soviet and cast his net even wider in his search for a model. He eventually chose an executive presidency based on a mixture of the U.S. and French presidencies. Following U.S. custom, he needed a vice president. Unfortunately he chose Gennady Yanayev—the Kazak leader Nursultan Nazarbayev and Shevardnadze having turned down the job. The USSR Council of Ministers was abolished and replaced by a cabinet of ministers subordinate to the president. On paper Gorbachev had achieved his ambition: he was chief decision maker and indeed a constitutional dictator. His authority, or his ability to make decisions, had never been higher. However, the power that accompanies the post of president in the United States and France was not transmitted to him. His power or ability to have his decisions implemented declined daily.

The impetus for reform came from the politically active part of the Communist Party and society. However, opposition to *perestroika* was fiercest among the same group. The reformers knew that the party and state apparat were past masters at blocking reforms that they perceived to be inimical to their interests. The only way to drive through a reform was to use a battering ram. During the first three years, Gorbachev launched a series of reforms. Each time he encountered opposition from party conservatives, he retreated and sought another route to advance. According to Yakovlev, one of the architects of *perestroika* and its main theorist, the revolution from above reached a critical point at the 19th Party Conference in June 1988. There, Gorbachev was presented with a stark choice: advance and transform *perestroika* into a "genuinely popular democratic revolution, go all the way and afford society total freedom" or pull back, remain a communist reformer, and stay within the well-known milieu of the bureaucracy. Yakovlev saw various dangers facing *perestroika*: it could be suffocated by Stalinist reaction or Brezhnevite conservatism or be highjacked by officials mouthing its slogans while they redistributed power among themselves. The choice was between genuine or controlled democracy. In early 1988, Fyodor Burlatsky was a member of a small group under the chairmanship of Anatoly Lukyanov. The latter proposed a two-stage approach to the election of a Supreme Soviet. Legal authority was to be vested in local Soviets, but the relationship between the party and the Soviets was left vague. Burlatsky proposed direct elections of the Supreme Soviet, president, and vice president, but everyone opposed this except Yakovlev. Gorbachev could have effected a political revolution but, true to his low-risk strategy, chose Lukyanov's proposal. This was a fatal mistake. Had Gorbachev stood for election as president, he might have won. He would then have become the people's president. Instead he had himself elected by the USSR Congress of People's Deputies, a body dominated by communists. Unfortunately for Gorbachev, he had opened Pandora's box. Social and political forces awakened by *perestroika* could not be regulated from above. If Gorbachev would not claim them as his constituency, then others would. The Communist Party resisted the march toward democracy and lost its more radical members. They set up their own groups and challenged the party head-on. Boris Yeltsin emerged as the most likely leader of the radical constituency. His election as chairman of the Russian parliament in May 1990 proved to be a turning point for Gorbachev. Yeltsin became a pole of attraction for frustrated, radical, and especially economic reformers. Gorbachev's greatest mistakes were made in economic policy.

Economic Policy

The economic stagnation of the late Brezhnev era was the result of various factors: the exhaustion of easily available resources, especially raw materials, and the growing structural imbalance of the economy due to the distorting effects of the incentive system, which paralyzed initiative and dissuaded people from doing an honest day's work. Under *perestroika* the economy moved from stagnation to crisis, and this deepened as time passed. Hence the policies of *perestroika* must carry much of the blame for the economic catastrophe that resulted. Gorbachev admitted in 1988 that the first two years had been wasted, since he was unaware of the depth of the crisis when he took over. This is an extraordinary statement for a party leader to make. Either he had paid little attention to the underlying trends of the economy or no one at the top was aware of the real situation. The latter is probably more accurate, since the state planning commission, Gosplan, had no model of how the economy functioned. The Soviet gross national product (GNP) was almost stagnant during the first four years of *perestroika* and did not fall. Unemployment remained at about 4 percent of the labour force, almost all in the labour-surplus areas of Central Asia and the Caucasus. Open inflation remained low until 1989. Underlying trends, however, pointed to systemic failure. Shortages, endemic to all planned economies, became serious from the mid-1980s. By mid-1990, more than one thousand basic consumer goods were very seldom on sale. Rationing became widespread, with most goods being sold at the point of work. Queuing became the national pastime: a 1990 estimate put it at thirty million to forty million man-, or rather woman-, hours a year. The only thing that was not in short supply was money. This was due to a rapidly growing budget deficit, first evident in 1987. Then the Law on State Enterprises, effective from January 1988, permitted managers to increase wages to cope with the tight labour situation. These increases were far in excess of productivity growth. The State Bank lost control of monetary growth. The plan for 1990 was a growth of 10 billion rubles, but it turned out to be about 28 billion rubles. Social benefits, amounting to about a quarter of the gross family income, were always modest by international standards. However, in 1990, they increased by 21 percent as a result of the USSR Congress of People's Deputies voting to increase a whole raft of benefits, noticeably pensions. Since there were no resources to meet this extra expenditure, the budget deficit grew, as did the money supply. The kolkhoz, the comparatively free market in which peasants sold their surplus produce, is a rough guide to price trends: prices between 1985 and 1988 increased by less than 1 percent annually, but in 1989 they jumped 9.5 percent and in 1990 by 29 percent.

Responsibility for the budget deficit rested fairly and squarely on the shoulders of the Gorbachev leadership. Traditionally the budget deficit had been 2 or 3 percent of GNP. The years 1985 and 1986 changed all that. Gorbachev's desire to achieve faster growth—the policy advocated by Aganbegyan, his chief economic adviser, was acceleration—resulted in the 12th Five-Year Plan (1986–90) being returned three times to Gosplan with instructions to raise targets. In 1986, the budget deficit rose to 6 percent of GNP. The Gorbachev leadership did not mention the subject in public until 1988. By then, the deficit had risen to more than 10 percent. The result of all this was to throw the industrial sector into imbalance from 1985 onward. The Law on State Enterprises further aggravated the problem.

Between 1985 and 1987, the Gorbachev leadership increased investment and defense expenditure, while at the same time state revenue was declining owing to a fall in alcohol sales and lower prices for export goods. From 1988, the situation became dire. In 1991, the economy was facing total collapse. The government found it increasingly difficult to intervene decisively. The Law on State Enterprises reduced the power of the ministries, and simultaneously the number of officials was cut back sharply. Those who remained were overwhelmed by the workload. Since there was no effective control from Moscow, rising nationalism, ethnic strife, and regionalism fragmented the economy into dozens of mini-economies. Many republics sought independence, others sovereignty, and they all pursued policies of economic autarky. Barter was widespread. Ukraine introduced coupons, and Moscow issued ration cards.

Foreign trade suffered. Lower oil prices and economic fragmentation caused the hard currency debt to rise from

U.S. $25.6 billion at the end of 1984 to about $80 billion at the end of 1991. Imports from the West were cut back sharply between 1985 and 1987. These were almost exclusively consumer goods and not capital goods, which often could not be installed. The public vented its frustration. This led to a complete reversal, and imports from the West rose by almost 50 percent between 1987 and 1989. As a consequence, by 1989, the Soviets could no longer service their hard currency debt on time.

Recalculations of Soviet economic performance by Soviet statisticians widened the gap between the Soviet and U.S. economies. The official view was that the Soviet national income was about 64 percent of the U.S. level in 1988. Gorbachev, in a speech in October 1990, implied that the real figure was about 40 percent. Another estimate put the real level at about 46 percent in 1970, declining to 40 percent in 1987.

Gorbachev received much advice on how to solve the Soviet Union's economic crisis. There were two basic solutions: the socialist solution and the market solution. The Ryzhkov group favoured central planning, more efficient administration, and greater decision-making powers for enterprises and farms. State ownership of the means of production would continue. They called it a "regulated market economy." The radicals, led by Stanislav Shatalin, Nikolay Petrakov, and Grigory Yavlinsky, wanted a move toward a free-market economy. This involved private ownership of enterprises, land, services, and so on. It also meant the freeing of prices. Gorbachev could not make up his mind and always tried to persuade the two groups to pool their resources and arrive at a compromise. The radicals thought they had convinced Gorbachev in the autumn of 1990 to introduce a five-hundred-day program that would have implemented a market economy, but he changed his mind and sided with the conservatives. This was a fatal mistake. It left him without a viable economic policy, and the right felt that if they applied enough pressure, he would always abandon radical solutions.

One of the reasons Gorbachev shied away from the market was price liberalization. He would not risk sharp price rises because of the fear of social unrest. Despite the abundant evidence of the seriousness of the situation in 1988, the critical year, Gorbachev and other leading communists refused to draw the necessary lessons. At the 19th Party Conference in June 1988, Leonid Abalkin pointed out that the country was still suffering from stagnation. Gorbachev and others criticized him and adopted a motion claiming that the economic decline had been halted. The election of the USSR Congress of People's Deputies made it virtually impossible for the Gorbachev leadership to adopt austerity measures. The popular mood was one of spend, spend, spend. Gorbachev paid only cursory attention to the economy until late 1989. A charitable explanation for this would be that he was concentrating on political reform. A less charitable one would be that he lacked the intellectual capacity to grasp the seriousness of the economic crisis. Gorbachev was never able to construct a viable economic policy or put in place a mechanism for the implementation of economic policy.

Foreign Policy

Like Khrushchev, Gorbachev was more popular abroad than at home. He proved a brilliant diplomat and for the first time bridged the gulf between a Soviet communist leader and the Western public. He was friendly, accessible, and a skilled performer on television. It was the message the West had been waiting decades to hear. His "new political thinking" consisted of removing ideology from foreign and security policy-making and arguing that all states were interdependent. If they did not unite, the whole planet would be in danger. He proposed the elimination of all nuclear weapons by the year 2000 and the establishment of a system of comprehensive security, a military doctrine that stressed reasonable sufficiency and recognized the complexity of the modern world. He signaled a change in the USSR's attitude toward the United Nations in December 1988, when, in a speech to the UN General Assembly, he praised its role in promoting international peace and security. He announced a reduction of five hundred thousand in the Soviet armed forces over the following two years, including the reduction of the number of divisions in Europe and Asia, as well as pulling back many tanks. The Soviet General Staff, which exercised a monopoly over defense and security policy, was not altogether convinced of the wisdom of such a move. Throughout the Gorbachev era, the General Staff was more

Mikhail Gorbachev meets with U.S. president Ronald Reagan in Geneva, Switzerland, Nov. 21, 1985, during a two-day summit. AFP/Getty Images

conservative than the national leader and became bolder in its opposition as time passed. It effectively sabotaged the Conventional Forces in Europe (CFE) Treaty.

Gorbachev, ably aided by Shevardnadze, set out to end the "new Cold War" that had broken out in the late 1970s. A key reason for this was that the new leadership had come to the conclusion that the defense burden was crippling the Soviet Union.

The first Reagan-Gorbachev summit took place in Geneva in November 1985. A joint statement proposed a 50 percent reduction in the superpowers' nuclear arsenal. The next summit took place at Reykjavík, Iceland, in October 1986. The Soviets came very well prepared but demanded agreement on all their points. The discussions broke down over the Strategic Defense Initiative (SDI; a proposed U.S. system that would intercept attacking ballistic missiles), which the Americans were not willing to abandon. The third summit, held in Washington, D.C., in December 1987 was historic. It produced an agreement to eliminate a whole category of nuclear weapons: land-based intermediate- and shorter-range missiles. This was the Intermediate-Range Nuclear Forces (INF) Treaty, formalized by Reagan and Gorbachev at their final summit in Moscow in May–June 1988. Serious differences still existed, however, especially over verification of the implementation of the treaties. Reagan and Gorbachev did not discuss SDI at the Washington and Moscow summits: the Soviets had made their stand at Reykjavík and lost.

One of the agreements reached at the Geneva summit concerned the withdrawal of Soviet troops from Afghanistan. The last soldier left in February 1989. Brezhnev had blundered into Afghanistan, and the USSR had paid a heavy price in soldiers (almost fourteen thousand), materiel, and foreign hostility.

Relations between Gorbachev and Reagan's successor, George Bush, were good, and there were several summits.

These produced two historic agreements: the CFE Treaty, signed in November 1990, and the START Treaty, signed in July 1991. But opposition by the Soviet General Staff undermined the CFE Treaty, and the dissolution of the USSR in August 1991 halted progress on the START Treaty. The new relationship between the superpowers resulted in Shevardnadze voting for military action against Iraq in the UN. This was painful for Moscow because Iraq had been an ally.

Gorbachev was a hit everywhere he went in Europe. This was especially so in West Germany, where he received a rapturous welcome in 1989. In Eastern Europe, the tumultuous events of 1989 were possible because Gorbachev did not permit the intervention of the military to keep communist regimes in power. He promoted *perestroika* in the region, believing it would benefit socialism. He undermined Erich Honecker in East Germany and accelerated the collapse of that country. He was opposed to the unification of Germany but was forced in the end to accept it.

Gorbachev's visit to China in 1989 was almost a fiasco and deeply disturbed the Chinese leadership. Many Chinese were attracted to *perestroika*, but the aged leadership ruthlessly suppressed those calling for political reform.

One of the objects of Soviet foreign policy had been to strengthen socialism around the world. By 1990, it was abundantly clear that this mission had failed. The USSR's only allies were underdeveloped Third World states such as Angola, Ethiopia, and Cuba. These were all liabilities, requiring more and more aid to stay afloat.

The Attempted Coup

Rumours of a coup against Gorbachev were rife in Moscow throughout the spring and summer of 1991. The military, the KGB, and conservative communists were alarmed at the turn

of events. They wanted strong central leadership in order to keep the Soviet Union communist and together. Gorbachev had little to fear from the Communist Party. He had sharply reduced the power of the Politburo at the 28th Party Congress in June 1990 but had to concede the emergence of a Russian Communist Party. This was dominated by the party apparat and turned out to be a toothless tiger. As it eventually transpired, a coup was organized by the KGB and was timed to prevent the signing of a union treaty on August 20 that would have strengthened the republics and weakened the centre.

On Aug. 18, 1991, a delegation visited Gorbachev at his summer dacha at Foros in the Crimea. The delegation demanded Gorbachev's resignation and replacement by Gennady Yanayev, the vice president. When Gorbachev refused, he was held prisoner while the coup leaders, called the Extraordinary Commission and guided by KGB boss Vladimir Kryuchkov, declared that Gorbachev had been obliged to resign for reasons of health. As the commission tried to take over the country, Yeltsin arrived at the Russian parliament building, from where, beginning on August 19, he declared the putsch an attempt to crush Russia, called for the return of Gorbachev, and appealed for popular support. Lack of decisiveness on the part of the coup leaders led to more and more support for the Russian president. Even some soldiers and tank units turned to defend the parliament building, and some top military officers sided with Yeltsin. There were only three fatalities in Moscow before the coup collapsed on August 21.

There were many reasons why the coup should have succeeded. Many were disenchanted with the course of *perestroika*. The military was depressed about the withdrawal from Eastern Europe and the declining defense expenditure and loss of status at home. Several republican leaders,

including those in Azerbaijan, Tajikistan, Turkmenistan, and Uzbekistan, came out in support of the coup. Most others prevaricated, while the lone condemnatory voice from the beginning was that of Askar Akayev, president of the Kirghiz SSR (now Kyrgyzstan). Why then did it fail? Astonishingly, it was poorly planned and executed. The lessons of the brilliant coup of General Wojciech Jaruzelski in Poland in December 1981 were ignored. The fatal tactical error was the failure to identify and deploy loyal troops. It was assumed that orders would be obeyed. Troops had moved ruthlessly against civilians in Tbilisi, Georgia, in April 1989; in Baku, Azerbaijan, in January 1990; and in Vilnius, Lithuania, in January 1991—to name only a few instances when coercion was used. What was different this time was that troops who were overwhelmingly Russian were being ordered to move against Russians. The crucial weakness of the plotters was their inability to understand the radical political and social transformation that had occurred in the USSR since 1985. It was no longer possible to simply announce that Gorbachev had retired for "health" reasons. Yeltsin and the democrats seized the opportunity afforded by the incompetent plotters to organize very effective resistance in Moscow. Anatoly Sobchak did the same in St. Petersburg (formerly Leningrad). Probably a majority in the provinces supported the coup, but its fate was decided in the cities. There were significant divisions among top military and KGB officers. World statesmen condemned the coup and warned that all aid would be cut off.

The attempted coup destroyed Gorbachev politically. The republics rushed to be free of Moscow's control before another coup succeeded. The three Baltic republics successfully seceded from the union, as did many others. The key republic was Ukraine, politically and economically number two. It voted for independence on Dec. 1, 1991. Russia, Ukraine, and Belorussia (now renamed Belarus) on Dec. 8,

1991, in Minsk, Belarus, declared that the Soviet Union had ceased to exist and founded a loose grouping known as the Commonwealth of Independent States (CIS). On December 21 in Alma Ata (now Almaty), Kazakhstan, eleven states signed a protocol formally establishing the CIS. Of the former Soviet republics, Estonia, Latvia, Lithuania, and Georgia refused to join. Gorbachev resigned as Soviet president on December 25, and all Soviet institutions ceased to function at the end of 1991. The main benefactor was Russia. It assumed the USSR's seat on the UN Security Council, and all Soviet embassies became Russian embassies. The Soviet armed forces were placed under CIS command, but it was only a matter of time before each successor state formed its own armed forces. Russia, Ukraine, Belarus, and Kazakhstan became nuclear powers, but all except Russia declared their goal to be the destruction of their nuclear arms.

The Soviet experiment, begun in 1917, had ended in failure. The high moral goals that it had set for itself were never realized. Indeed, countless crimes had been committed in the attempt. Stalin perceived that the USSR could only be kept together by a strong central hand that was willing to use coercion. Attempts at democratization under Khrushchev began a slow unraveling of the empire. Gorbachev merely accelerated the breakup by promoting *glasnost*. He confirmed that a communist system cannot become democratic. When democracy triumphs, communism departs the stage. Economic failure was the key reason for the USSR's collapse. The socialist alternative to the market economy turned out to be an illusion.

CHAPTER 4

COMMUNISM IN THE EASTERN BLOC

Like the Soviet experiment, communism in the Eastern bloc did not survive. Its path to collapse was different from that of Russia, as Germany reeled from the failure against the Allied forces and found its country divvied up among those same Allies in the name of peace, creating dividing lines that would separate the country into two for decades and have a ripple effect on neighboring Poland and the Balkans, though none of these countries continued the communist ideology through to the twenty-first century.

Adolf Hitler reviews troops (called Wehrmacht) on the Eastern front in 1939 at the beginning of the second World War. Germany was defeated by Allied forces in 1945. Heinrich Hoffmann, Munich

Communism in East Germany

Following the German military leaders' unconditional surrender in May 1945, the country lay prostrate. The German state had ceased to exist, and sovereign authority passed to the victorious Allied powers. The physical devastation from Allied bombing campaigns and from ground battles was enormous: an estimated one-fourth of the country's housing was destroyed or damaged beyond use, and in many cities the toll exceeded 50 percent.

Allied Occupation and the Formation of the Two Germanys, 1945–49

Germany's economic infrastructure had largely collapsed as factories and transportation systems ceased to function. Rampant inflation was undermining the value of the currency, and an acute shortage of food reduced the diet of many city dwellers to the level of malnutrition. These difficulties were compounded by the presence of millions of homeless German refugees from the former eastern provinces. The end of the war came to be remembered as "zero hour," a low point from which virtually everything had to be rebuilt from the ground up.

For purposes of occupation, the Americans, British, French, and Soviets divided Germany into four zones. The American, British, and French zones together made up the western two-thirds of Germany, while the Soviet zone comprised the eastern third. Berlin, the former capital, which was surrounded by the Soviet zone, was placed under joint four-power authority but was partitioned into four sectors for administrative purposes. An Allied Control Council was to exercise overall joint authority over the country.

These arrangements did not incorporate all of prewar Germany. The Soviets unilaterally severed the German territories east of the Oder and Neisse rivers and placed these under the direct administrative authority of the Soviet Union and Poland, with the larger share going to the Poles as compensation for territory they lost to the Soviet Union. The former provinces of East Prussia, most of Pomerania, and Silesia were thus stripped from Germany. Since virtually the entire German population of some 9.5 million in these and adjacent regions was expelled westward, this amounted to a de facto annexation of one-fourth of Germany's territory as of 1937, the year before the beginning of German expansion under Hitler. The Western Allies acquiesced in these actions by the Soviets, taking consolation in the expectation that these annexations were merely temporary expedients that the final peace terms would soon supersede.

As a result of irreconcilable differences among the Allied powers, however, no peace conference was ever held. The issue of German reparations proved particularly divisive. The Soviet Union, whose population and territory had suffered terribly at the hands of the Germans, demanded large-scale material compensation. The Western Allies initially agreed to extract reparations but soon came to resent the Soviets' seizures of entire German factories as well as current production. Under the terms of inter-Allied agreements, the Soviet zone of occupation, which encompassed much of German agriculture and was less densely populated than those of the other Allies, was to supply foodstuffs to the rest of Germany in return for a share of reparations from the Western occupation zones. But when the Soviets failed to deliver the requisite food, the Western Allies found themselves forced to feed the German population in their zones at the expense of their own taxpayers. The Americans and British therefore came to favour a revival of German industry so as to enable the Germans to feed themselves, a step the Soviets opposed. When the Western powers refused in 1946 to permit the Soviets to claim further reparations from their zones, cooperation among the wartime allies deteriorated sharply. As day-by-day cooperation became more difficult, the management of the occupation zones gradually moved in different directions. Even before a formal break between East and West, opposing social, political, and economic systems had begun to emerge.

Despite their differences, the Allies agreed that all traces of Nazism had to be removed from Germany. To this end, the Allies tried at Nürnberg twenty-two Nazi leaders. The Soviets summarily removed former Nazis from office in their zone of occupation. Eventually, antifascism became a central element of East Germany's ideological arsenal. But since the East German regime denied any connection to what happened in Germany during the Nazi era, there was little incentive to examine Nazism's role in German history. The relationship of Germans to the Nazi past was more complex in West Germany. On the one hand, many former Nazis survived and gradually returned to positions of influence in business, education, and the professions, but West German intellectuals were also critically engaged with the burdens of the past, which became a central theme in the novels of Heinrich Böll, Günter Grass, and many others.

In April 1946, the Social Democratic Party leaders in the Soviet zone agreed to merge with the communists, a step denounced by the Social Democrats in the Western zones. The resulting Socialist Unity Party (SED) swept to victory with the ill-concealed aid of the Soviets in the first elections for local and regional assemblies in the Soviet zone. However, when in October 1946, elections were held under fairer conditions in Berlin, which was under four-power occupation, the SED tallied fewer than half as many votes as the Social Democratic Party, which had managed to preserve its independence in the old capital. Thereafter the SED, which increasingly fell under communist domination as Social Democrats were systematically purged from its leadership ranks, avoided free, competitive elections by forcing all other parties to join a permanent coalition under its leadership.

Nürnberg Trials

The Nürnberg (also spelled "Nuremberg") series of trials were held in Nürnberg, Germany, in 1945–46, in which former Nazi leaders were indicted and tried as war criminals by the International Military Tribunal. The indictment lodged against them contained four counts: 1) crimes against peace (i.e., the planning, initiating, and waging of wars of aggression in violation of international treaties and agreements); 2) crimes against humanity (i.e., exterminations, deportations, and genocide); 3) war crimes (i.e., violations of the laws of war); and 4) "a common plan or conspiracy to commit" the criminal acts listed in the first three counts.

After 216 court sessions, on Oct. 1, 1946, the verdict on twenty-two of the original twenty-four defendants was handed down. (Robert Ley committed suicide while in

Hermann Göring testifies from the witness box at the Nürnberg war crime trials on March 16, 1946. Keystone/Hulton Archive/Getty Images

prison, and Gustav Krupp von Bohlen und Halbach's mental and physical condition prevented his being tried.) Three of the defendants were acquitted: Hjalmar Schacht, Franz von Papen, and Hans Fritzsche. Four were sentenced to terms of imprisonment ranging from ten to twenty years: Karl Dönitz, Baldur von Schirach, Albert Speer, and Konstantin von Neurath. Three were sentenced to life imprisonment: Rudolf Hess, Walther Funk, and Erich Raeder. Twelve of the defendants were sentenced to death by hanging. Ten of them—Hans Frank, Wilhelm Frick, Julius Streicher, Alfred Rosenberg, Ernst Kaltenbrunner, Joachim von Ribbentrop, Fritz Sauckel, Alfred Jodl, Wilhelm Keitel, and Arthur Seyss-Inquart—were hanged on Oct. 16, 1946. Martin Bormann was tried and condemned to death in absentia, and Hermann Göring committed suicide before he could be executed.

The occupying powers soon approved the formation of regional governmental units called *Länder* (singular: *Land*), or states. By 1947, the *Länder* in the Western zones had freely elected parliamentary assemblies. Institutional developments followed a superficially similar pattern in the Soviet zone, but there the political process remained less than free because of the dominance of the Soviet-backed SED.

When it had become apparent by 1947 that the Soviet Union would not permit free, multiparty elections throughout the whole of Germany, the Americans and British amalgamated the German administrative organs in their occupation zones in order to foster economic recovery. The resulting unit, called Bizonia, operated through a set of German institutions located in the city of Frankfurt am Main. Its federative structure would later serve as the model for the West German state.

In the politics of Bizonia, the Social Democrats and the Christian Democrats quickly established themselves as the major political parties. The Social Democrats held to their long-standing commitment to nationalization of basic industries and extensive government control over other aspects of the economy. The Christian Democrats, after initially inclining to a vaguely conceived "Christian socialism," swung to espousal of a basically free-enterprise orientation. In March 1948, they joined with the laissez-faire Free Democrats to install as architect of Bizonia's economy Ludwig Erhard, a previously obscure economist who advocated a "social market economy," essentially a free-market economy with government regulation to prevent the formation of monopolies or cartels and a welfare state to safeguard social needs.

When repeated meetings with the Soviets failed to produce four-power cooperation, the Western occupying powers decided in the spring of 1948 to move on their own. They were particularly concerned about the deteriorating economic conditions throughout occupied Germany, which burdened their own countries and awakened fears of renewed political extremism among the Germans. The Western powers therefore decided to extend to their occupation zones American economic aid, which had been instituted elsewhere in Western Europe a year earlier under the Marshall Plan. To enhance the effectiveness of that aid, the Americans, British, and French effected a currency reform in their zones that replaced Germany's badly inflated currency (the reichsmark) with a new, hard deutsche mark, or DM. Western Germany's economy responded quickly, as goods previously unavailable for nearly worthless money came onto the market.

The Soviets responded angrily to the currency reform, which was undertaken without their approval. When the new deutsche mark was introduced into Berlin, the Soviets protested vigorously and boycotted the Allied Control

Council. Then in June 1948, they blockaded land routes from the Western zones to the Western sectors of the old capital, which were surrounded by territory occupied by the Soviet Red Army and lay about 100 miles (160 kilometers) from the nearest Western-occupied area. By sealing off the railways, highways, and canals used to deliver food and fuel, as well as the raw materials needed for the factories of Berlin's Western sectors, with a population of more than two million people, the Soviets sought to drive out their erstwhile allies and force the Western sectors to merge economically and politically with the Soviet zone that surrounded them. They were thwarted, however, when the Western powers mounted an around-the-clock airlift that supplied the West Berliners with food and fuel throughout the winter of 1948–49. In May 1949, the Soviets relented and lifted the blockade.

Formation of the Federal Republic of Germany

Instead of halting progress toward the political integration of the Western zones, as the Soviets apparently intended, the Berlin blockade accelerated it. In April 1949, the French began to merge their zone into Bizonia, which became Trizonia. That September, a Parliamentary Council of sixty-five members chosen by the parliaments of the *Länder* began drafting a constitution for a West German government. Twenty-seven seats each in this council were held by the Social Democrats and the Christian Democrats, five by the Free Democrats, and the rest by smaller parties, including two by the communists. The Council completed its work in the spring of 1949, and the Federal Republic of Germany (Bundesrepublik Deutschland), commonly known as West Germany, came into being in May 1949 after all the *Länder* except Bavaria had ratified the Grundgesetz (Basic Law), as the constitution was called to underline the provisional nature of the new state. Indeed, this document specified that it was designed only for temporary use until a constitution had been freely adopted by the German people as a whole.

The Basic Law was approved by the Western Allied military governors with certain reservations, notably the exclusion of West Berlin, which had been proposed as the federation's 12th *Land*. The eleven-constituent *Länder* of West Germany, then, were Bavaria, Bremen, Hamburg, Hessen, Lower Saxony, North Rhine–Westphalia, Rhineland-Palatinate, Schleswig-Holstein, Baden, Württemberg-Baden, and Württemberg-Hohenzollern (the last three were merged in 1952 to form Baden-Württemberg, and in 1957 Saarland became the 10th *Land*).

By the terms of the Basic Law, the Federal Republic of Germany was established with its provisional capital in the small city of Bonn. The West German state took shape as a federal form of parliamentary democracy. An extensive bill of rights guaranteed the civil and political freedoms of the citizenry. In keeping with German traditions, many spheres of governmental authority were reserved for the individual *Länder*. The key locus of power at the federal level lay in the lower legislative chamber, the Bundestag, elections for which had to take place at least every four years. The deputies were chosen by a voting procedure known as "personalized proportionality," which combined proportional representation with single-seat constituencies. In order to minimize the proliferation of smaller political parties that had helped discredit democracy in the Weimar Republic, a party had to win a minimum of 5 percent of the overall vote to gain representation in the Bundestag. The *Länder* were represented in the upper legislative chamber, the Bundesrat, whose members were designated by the governments of the *Länder*, their number varying according to the states' populations. The chancellor, elected by the Bundestag, headed the government. However, in response to the misuse of presidential power in the Weimar Republic, the constitution greatly reduced the powers of the president, who was chosen indirectly by a federal convention. The final key institution of the Federal Republic was the Federal Constitutional Court. Independent of both the legislative and executive branches, it successfully introduced into German practice for the first time the American principle of judicial review of legislation. Its seat was established in the city of Karlsruhe.

Initially, West Germany was not a sovereign state. Its powers were circumscribed by an Occupation Statute drawn up by the American, British, and French governments in 1949. That document reserved to those powers ultimate authority over such matters as foreign relations, foreign trade, the level of industrial production, and all questions relating to military security. Only with the permission of the Western occupation powers could the Federal Republic legislate or otherwise take action in those spheres. Alterations in the Basic Law required the unanimous consent of the three Western powers, and they reserved veto power over any legislation they deemed unconstitutional or at variance with occupation policies. In the event of an emergency that endangered the new West German government, the Western Allies retained the right to resume their full authority as occupying powers.

Formation of the German Democratic Republic

When it became clear that a West German government would be established, a so-called election for a People's Congress was held in the Soviet occupation zone in May 1949. But instead of choosing among candidates, voters were allowed only the choice of approving or rejecting—usually in less-than-secret circumstances—"unity lists" of candidates drawn from all parties, as well as representatives of mass organizations controlled by the communist-dominated SED. Two additional parties, a Democratic Farmers' Party and a National Democratic Party, designed to attract support from farmers and from former Nazis, respectively, were added with the blessing of the SED. By ensuring that communists predominated in these unity lists, the SED determined in advance the composition of the new People's Congress. According to the official results, about two-thirds of the voters approved the unity lists. In subsequent elections, favourable margins in excess of 99 percent were routinely announced.

In October 1949, following the formation of the Federal Republic, a constitution ratified by the People's Congress went into effect in the Soviet zone, which became the German Democratic Republic (Deutsche Demokratische Republik), commonly known as East Germany, with its capital in the Soviet sector of Berlin. The People's Congress was renamed the People's Chamber, and this body, together with a second chamber composed of officials of the five *Länder* of the Soviet zone (which were abolished in 1952 in favour of centralized authority), designated the communist Wilhelm Pieck of the SED as president of the German Democratic Republic on Oct. 11, 1949. The next day, the People's Chamber installed the former Social Democrat Otto Grotewohl as premier at the head of a cabinet that was nominally responsible to the chamber. Although the German Democratic Republic was constitutionally a parliamentary democracy, decisive power actually lay with the SED and its boss, the veteran communist functionary Walter Ulbricht, who held only the obscure position of deputy premier in the government. In East Germany, as in the Soviet Union, the government served merely as the agent of an all-powerful communist-controlled party, which was in turn ruled from above by a self-selecting Politburo.

Political Consolidation and Economic Growth, 1949–69

The government that emerged from the Federal Republic's first general election in August 1949 represented a coalition of the Christian Democrats with the Free Democrats. Konrad Adenauer of the Christian Democratic Union, a veteran Roman Catholic politician from the Rhineland, was elected the country's first chancellor by a narrow margin in the Bundestag. Because of his advanced age of seventy-three, Adenauer was expected by many to serve only as an interim officeholder, but in fact he retained the chancellorship for fourteen years. Theodor Heuss of the Free Democratic Party was elected as West Germany's first president. As economics minister in the Adenauer cabinet, Ludwig Erhard launched the Federal Republic on a phenomenally successful course of revival as a social market economy. His policies left the means of production mainly in private hands and allowed market mechanisms to set price and wage levels. The government promoted social justice with measures designed to ensure an equitable distribution of wealth generated by the pursuit of profit. Under these policies, industrial output rapidly recovered, living standards steadily rose, the government soon abolished all rationing, and West Germany became renowned for its *Wirtschaftswunder*, or "economic miracle."

One of the most urgent internal problems for Adenauer's first administration was the resettlement of refugees. By 1950, West Germany had become the new home of 4.5 million Germans from the territory east of the Oder-Neisse line; 3.4 million ethnic Germans from Czechoslovakia, prewar Poland, and other Eastern European countries; and 1.5 million from East Germany. The presence of these refugees put a heavy social burden on West Germany, but their assimilation proved surprisingly easy. Many of the refugees were skilled, enterprising, and adaptable, and their labour proved an important contributor to West Germany's economic recovery.

In East Germany, the SED regime concentrated on building a viable economy in a territory that lacked rich natural resources, was less than half the size of the Federal Republic, and had a population (seventeen million) only one-third as large. The regime used its centralized control over a planned economy to invest heavily in the construction of basic industries at the expense of the production of consumer goods. Moreover, war reparations required that much productive capacity be diverted to Soviet needs. Despite an impressive rate of industrial growth, the standard of living remained low, lagging far behind that of West Germany. Even food was a problem, as thousands of farmers fled to West Germany each year rather than give in to mounting pressure to merge their land (which many had only recently obtained through the postwar agrarian reform) into the collective farms favoured by the communist regime. Food rationing had to be continued long after it had ended in West Germany. The resulting material hardships, along with relentless ideological indoctrination, repression of dissent, and harassment of churches by a militantly atheistic regime, prompted many thousands of East Germans to flee to West Germany every year. In 1952, East Germany sealed its borders with West Germany, but East Germans continued to leave through Berlin, where free movement still prevailed between the Soviet and Western sectors of the city.

In West Germany, Adenauer followed a resolute policy of linking the new state closely with the Western democracies, even at the cost of perpetuating Germany's division for the time being. In 1951, the chancellor succeeded in gaining membership for West Germany in the European Coal and Steel Community, which later served as the core of the European Economic Community, the precursor of the European Union. In that same year, the Americans, British, and French agreed to a revision of the Occupation Statute that substantially increased the internal authority of the Federal Republic. Skillfully exploiting the Western fears of a communist assault on Europe, which had been awakened by the Korean War, Adenauer gained further concessions from the Western occupying powers in return for his agreement to rearm West Germany within the context of a Western European defense system. In 1955, West Germany became a full member of the North Atlantic Treaty Organization (NATO) and gained sovereignty over its foreign relations as the Occupation Statute expired.

With West Germany's impressive economic recovery continuing, the voters confirmed the policies of the Adenauer government. In 1953, the coalition of the Christian and Free Democrats increased its previously thin majority. In 1957, the chancellor's party achieved the first and only absolute majority ever recorded by a German party in a free general election. The FDP, which had left the government in 1956 over policy disputes, remained in opposition, along with the SPD.

In 1961, the flow of refugees to West Germany through Berlin increased dramatically, bringing the total number of East Germans who had fled since the war to some three million. On Aug. 13, 1961, the East German government surprised the world by sealing off West Berlin from East Berlin and the surrounding areas of East Germany, first with barbed wire and later by constructing a concrete wall through the middle of the city and around the periphery of West Berlin. East Germans could no longer go to the West through the tightly guarded crossing points without official permission, which was rarely granted. East Germans who sought to escape by climbing over the wall risked being shot by East German guards under orders to kill, if need be, to prevent the crime of "flight from the republic." By thus imprisoning

Communist soldiers build up the Berlin Wall between East and West Berlin even higher than before, in October 1961. Robert Lackenbach/Time & Life Pictures/Getty Images

the population, the SED regime stabilized the economy of East Germany, which eventually became the most prosperous of the Soviet bloc but which nevertheless continued to lag behind that of West Germany in both the quantity and quality of its consumer goods. Under party boss Ulbricht, the East German government also tightened the repressive policies of what had become a totalitarian communist dictatorship. Upon the death of President Pieck in 1960, Ulbricht had assumed the powers of the presidency as head of a newly created Council of State. In 1968, he imposed a new constitution on East Germany that sharply curtailed civil and political rights.

Ostpolitik and Reconciliation, 1969–89

When the SPD scored impressive gains in the election of 1969 and its candidate, Gustav Heinemann, also captured the presidency, West Germany underwent its first full-scale change of government. After twenty years of CDU-CSU domination, the SPD captured the chancellorship for Willy Brandt in coalition with the FDP, whose leader, Walter Scheel, became foreign minister. This so-called social-liberal coalition carried through a number of domestic reforms, but its principal impact was on the Federal Republic's relations with East Germany and the communist-ruled countries of Eastern Europe. While confirming West Germany's commitment to the Western alliance, the new government embarked upon a bold new "eastern policy," or *Ostpolitik*.

Previously, West Germany had refused to recognize even the existence of the East German government. And by the terms of the Hallstein Doctrine (named for one of Adenauer's key foreign-policy aides, Walter Hallstein), the Bonn authorities had refused to maintain diplomatic relations with all those countries (other than the Soviet Union) that recognized the German Democratic Republic. Now the Brandt-Scheel cabinet reversed these policies by opening direct negotiations with East Germany in 1970 to normalize relations between the two German states.

In 1970, the government entered into treaties with the Soviet Union and Poland that required Bonn to recognize the Oder-Neisse line as Germany's eastern boundary. After the Soviet Union joined in 1971 with the Americans, British, and French in a Four Power Agreement that regularized Berlin's status and opened the way for an easing of the West Berliners' lot, the Brandt-Scheel cabinet and East Germany in 1972 concluded the Basic Treaty, which regularized the relations of the two German states. By its terms each side recognized, and agreed to respect, the other's authority and independence. Each foreswore any title to represent the other internationally, which meant West Germany's abandonment of its long-standing claim to be the sole legitimate spokesman of the German people. The two agreed to exchange "permanent missions," which meant that their relations stopped short of full diplomatic recognition.

The new *Ostpolitik* met with bitter resistance within West Germany from the Christian Democrats, who denounced it as a surrender on many points that should await settlement by a peace treaty, including the status of the eastern territories that were severed from Germany in 1945. The Christian Democrats especially objected to the appearance that West Germany had given legitimacy to a dictatorial East Germany that refused to allow free elections, maintained the Berlin Wall, and ordered its border guards to shoot fleeing citizens. The Christian Democrats therefore pledged not to ratify the Basic Treaty if they regained power in the election of November 1972. The voters endorsed the Brandt government's *Ostpolitik*, however, by making the SPD the largest party in the Bundestag (for the first time) and by strengthening their coalition partner, the FDP. The Basic Treaty was signed at the end of 1972, and in the following year both German states gained admission to the United Nations.

West Germany's original overtures toward East Germany had met with resistance from Ulbricht, but the path for negotiations was cleared by a withdrawal of Soviet support that led to Ulbricht's replacement by another communist functionary, Erich Honecker, as East German leader in 1971. In his last years, Ulbricht had experimented with a decentralization of economic decision making, but under Honecker East Germany reverted to Soviet-style centralized planning.

East Germany benefited greatly from the Basic Treaty. Once Bonn had accorded East Germany recognition, the

Western democracies followed suit so that the East German state at last enjoyed the international acceptance that it had long sought. The benefits of international recognition were offset by the dangers posed to the dictatorial East German government by increased contact with democratic West Germany as a result of the Basic Treaty's easing of restrictions on visits by West Germans to East Germany. In an effort to deal with the subversive effects of such contacts, the East German government repeatedly sought to reduce the influx of West German visitors by raising the fees it charged for visas. It classified some two million of its citizens as "bearers of secrets" and forbade them personal contact with Westerners. To stifle dissent at home, the government tightened its already repressive ideological controls on artists and intellectuals, imprisoning some and stripping others of their citizenship and banishing them to West Germany. To emphasize the distinctness of the German Democratic Republic, an amended constitution was adopted in 1974 that minimized the use of the word *German* and stressed the socialist nature of the East German state and its irrevocable links with the Soviet Union.

Faced with mounting dissent at home, Honecker's East German government sought to enhance its claims to legitimacy by seeking further recognition from West Germany. It was therefore buoyed when Chancellor Helmut Schmidt paid an often-postponed official visit to East Germany in December 1981. At that time, Schmidt ignored Honecker's demand that Bonn treat East Germans as foreigners and cease to bestow West German citizenship automatically on those who fled to the West. Nevertheless, after Schmidt's visit East Germany began making it easier for its citizens to visit West Germany. By 1986, nearly 250,000 East Germans were visiting West Germany each year. As only one family member at a time was permitted to go, virtually all returned home. The East German government also began granting some of its dissatisfied citizens permission to emigrate to the West, an opportunity utilized each year in the 1980s by a few tens of thousands who managed to surmount formidable bureaucratic obstacles. These concessions were reciprocated by West Germany's guarantee of several large Western bank loans to East Germany. In 1987, the East German government realized a long-held ambition when, after many postponements, Honecker was at last received in Bonn by Chancellor Helmut Kohl with full state honours, seemingly confirming West Germany's acceptance of the permanence of the East German state.

But behind the Honecker government's facade of stability, East Germany was losing its legitimacy in the eyes of the overwhelming majority of its citizenry. Particularly among younger East Germans, the new opportunities for travel to West Germany produced discontent rather than satisfaction. There they experienced a much more advanced, consumer-oriented society that provided its citizens with an abundance of far-higher-quality goods than were available at home.

The Reunification of Germany

The swift and unexpected downfall of the German Democratic Republic was triggered by the decay of the other communist regimes in Eastern Europe and the Soviet Union. The liberalizing reforms of President Mikhail Gorbachev in the Soviet Union appalled the Honecker regime, which in desperation was by 1988 forbidding the circulation within East Germany of Soviet publications that it viewed as dangerously subversive. The Berlin Wall was in effect breached in the summer of 1989, when a reformist Hungarian government began allowing East Germans to escape to the West through Hungary's newly opened border with Austria. By the fall, thousands of East Germans had followed this route, while thousands of

The Berlin Wall

The Berlin Wall came to symbolize the Cold War's division of East from West Germany and of Eastern from Western Europe. About 5,000 East Germans managed to cross the Berlin Wall (by various means) and reach West Berlin safely, while another 5,000 were captured by East German authorities in the attempt and 191 more were killed during the actual crossing of the wall.

East Germany's hardline communist leadership was forced from power in October 1989 during the wave of democratization that swept through Eastern Europe. On November 9, the East German government opened the country's borders with West Germany (including West Berlin), and openings were made in the Berlin Wall through which East Germans could travel freely to the West. The wall henceforth ceased to function as a political barrier between East and West Germany.

others sought asylum in the West German embassies in Prague and Warsaw, demanding that they be allowed to immigrate to West Germany. At the end of September, Hans-Dietrich Genscher, still West Germany's foreign minister, arranged for their passage to West Germany, but another wave of refugees from East Germany soon took their place. Mass demonstrations in the streets of Leipzig and other East German cities defied the authorities and demanded reforms.

In an effort to halt the deterioration of its position, the SED Politburo deposed Honecker in mid-October and replaced him with another hardline communist, Egon Krenz. Under Krenz the Politburo sought to eliminate the embarrassment occasioned by the flow of refugees to the West through Hungary, Czechoslovakia, and Poland. On the evening of November 9, Günter Schabowski, a communist functionary, mistakenly announced at a televised news conference that the government would allow East Germans unlimited passage to West Germany, effective "immediately." While the government had in fact meant to require East Germans to apply for exit visas during normal working hours, this was widely interpreted as a decision to open the Berlin Wall that evening, so crowds gathered and demanded to pass into West Berlin. Unprepared, the border guards let them go. In a night of revelry, tens of thousands of East Germans poured through the crossing points in the wall and celebrated their new freedom with rejoicing West Berliners.

The opening of the Berlin Wall proved fatal for the German Democratic Republic. Ever-larger demonstrations demanded a voice in government for the people, and in mid-November Krenz was replaced by a reform-minded communist, Hans Modrow, who promised free, multiparty elections. When the balloting took place in March 1990, the SED, now renamed the Party of Democratic Socialism (PDS), suffered a crushing defeat. The eastern counterpart of Kohl's CDU, which had pledged a speedy reunification of Germany, emerged as the largest political party in East Germany's first democratically elected People's Chamber. A new East German government headed by Lothar de Maizière, a longtime member of the eastern Christian Democratic Union and backed initially by a broad coalition, including the eastern counterparts of the Social Democrats and Free Democrats, began negotiations for a treaty of unification. A surging tide of refugees from East to West Germany that threatened to cripple East Germany added urgency to those negotiations. In July, that tide was somewhat stemmed by a monetary union of the two Germanys that gave East Germans the hard currency of the Federal Republic.

The final barrier to reunification fell in July 1990, when Chancellor Helmut Kohl prevailed upon Gorbachev to drop

The Berlin Wall came down on Nov. 9, 1989. In January 1990, West Berliners (pictured) *were still celebrating the opening of the 28-mile barrier.* The Washington Post/Getty Images

his objections to a unified Germany within the NATO alliance in return for sizable (West) German financial aid to the Soviet Union. A unification treaty was ratified by the Bundestag and the People's Chamber in September and went into effect on Oct. 3, 1990. The German Democratic Republic joined the Federal Republic as five additional *Länder*, and the two parts of divided Berlin became one *Land*. (The five new *Länder* were Brandenburg, Mecklenburg–West Pomerania, Saxony, Saxony-Anhalt, and Thuringia.)

The lingering economic gap between the east and west was just one of several difficulties attending unification. Not surprisingly, many easterners resented what they took to be western arrogance and insensitivity. The terms *Wessi* ("westerner") and *Ossi* ("easterner") came to imply different approaches to the world: the former competitive and aggressive, the product of what Germans call the West's "elbow society"; the latter passive and indolent, the product of the stifling security of the communist regime. The PDS became the political voice of eastern discontents, with strong if localized support in some of the new *Länder*. Moreover, the neofascist German People's Union (Deutsche Volksunion), led by millionaire publisher Gerhard Frey, garnered significant support among Eastern Germany's mass of unemployed workers. In addition to the resentment and disillusionment over unification that many easterners and some westerners felt, there was also the problem of coming to terms with the legacies left by forty years of dictatorship. East Germany had developed a large and effective security apparatus (the Stasi), which employed a wide network of professional and amateur informants. As the files of this organization began to be made public, Eastern Germans discovered that many of their most prominent citizens, as well as some of their friends, neighbours, and even family members, had been on the Stasi payroll. Coming to terms with these revelations—

legally, politically, and personally—added to the tension of the post-unification decade.

Communist Poland

The post–World War II Polish republic, renamed in 1952 the Polish People's Republic, occupied an area some 20 percent smaller than prewar Poland, and its population of almost thirty million rose to nearly thirty-nine million in the following four decades. The Holocaust, together with the expulsion of several million Germans and population transfers with the USSR, left Poland virtually homogeneous in its ethnic composition. The expulsion of the Germans was approved by the Potsdam Conference, but the final decision regarding the new German-Polish border along the Oder-Neisse Line was left to a future peace conference. The USSR cleverly capitalized on its status as the sole guarantor of this border, which gave Poland a long seacoast, with such harbours as Szczecin and Gdańsk, and such natural resources as coal and zinc in Silesia.

Despite the potential for wealth established by the redrawn borders, the fact remained that the war had devastated Poland. Warsaw, Wrocław, and Gdańsk lay in ruins, and social conditions bordered on chaos. Huge migrations, mainly to the ex-German "western territories," added to the instability. Fighting against the remnants of the Ukrainian Liberation Army was followed by the mass relocation of the Ukrainians (Operation Vistula) in 1947. Persecutions of the AK and political opponents (the National Party was outlawed) by the communists led to armed clashes that continued for several years. It was under these conditions that a Jewish pogrom occurred in Kielce in June 1946, claiming more than forty lives.

Bolesław Bierut, who was formally nonpartisan but in fact was an old communist, assumed the presidency. In a cabinet headed by a socialist and dominated by communists and fellow travelers, Stanisław Mikołajczyk became deputy prime minister. He successfully re-created a genuine Polish Peasant Party (PSL; Polskie Stronnictwo Ludowe, later also called the Polish People's Party), which was larger than the PPR and its socialist and democratic satellite parties. Supported by all enemies of communism, Mikołajczyk sought to challenge the PPR in the "free and unfettered" elections stipulated by the Yalta accords. His opponents included the ruthless secretary-general of the PPR, Władysław Gomułka, a "home communist," and the men in charge of security (Jakub Berman) and of the economy (Hilary Minc), who had returned from Russia.

The Sovietization of Poland, accompanied by terror, included the nationalization of industry and the expropriation of privately owned land parcels larger than 125 acres (50 hectares). Yet in some areas (namely, matters concerning the church and foreign policy), the communists trod lightly during this transition period. The test of strength between Mikołajczyk and the PPR first occurred during the referendum of 1946—the results of which, favourable to Mikołajczyk, were falsified—and then in the general elections of 1947, which were hardly "free and unfettered." Mikołajczyk, fearing for his life, fled the country. The victorious communists completed their monopoly of power in 1948 by absorbing the increasingly dependent PPS to become the Polish United Workers' Party (PUWP).

Over the next few years, the Bierut regime in Poland closely followed the Stalinist model in politics (adopting the Soviet-style 1952 constitution), economics (emphasizing heavy industry and collectivization of agriculture), military affairs (appointing the Soviet Marshal Konstantin Rokossovsky as commander of Polish forces and adhering to the Warsaw Pact of 1955), foreign policy (joining the Communist Information

Bureau, the agency of international communism), culture, and the rule of the secret police. Political terror in Poland, however, did not include, as elsewhere, show trials of fallen party leaders. Gomułka, denounced as a "Titoist" and imprisoned in 1951, was spared such a trial. Moreover, the primate of Poland, Stefan Wyszyński, could still negotiate a modus vivendi in 1950, though, as the pressure on the church increased, he was arrested in September 1953 (by which time he had been named a cardinal).

The death of Joseph Stalin in March 1953 opened a period of struggle for succession and change in the USSR that had repercussions throughout the Soviet bloc. The interlude of liberalization that followed culminated in the Soviet leader Nikita Khrushchev's denunciation of Stalinism at the 20th Party Congress in February 1956. With the sudden death of Bierut, anti-Stalinists in Poland raised their heads; a violently suppressed workers' strike in Poznań in June 1956 shook the whole country. Gomułka, who believed in a "Polish road to socialism," became a candidate for the leadership of the party. What appeared as his confrontation with Khrushchev and other top Soviet leaders who descended on Warsaw in October and threatened intervention made Gomułka popular throughout Poland. In reality, the Polish leader convinced Khrushchev of his devotion to communism and of the need for a reformist approach to strengthen its doctrine.

Important changes followed, among them Polish-Soviet accords on trade and military cooperation (Rokossovsky and most Soviet officers left the country), a significant reduction of political terror, an end to forced collectivization, the release of Cardinal Wyszyński (followed by some concessions in the religious sphere), and increased contacts with the West, including freer travel. Gomułka's objective, however, was to bridge the gap between the people and the party, thereby legitimizing the latter. Hence, the period of reform known as "Polish October" did not prove to be the beginning of an evolution of communism that revisionists at home and politically motivated émigrés had hoped for.

Within a decade economic reform slowed down, the activity of the church was circumscribed, and intellectuals were subjected to pressures. Demonstrations by students in favour of intellectual freedom led to reprisals in March 1968 that brought to an end the so-called "little stabilization" that Gomułka had succeeded in achieving. Ever more autocratic in his behaviour, Gomułka became involved in an "anti-Zionist" campaign that resulted in purges within the party, administration, and army. Thousands of people of Jewish origin emigrated.

Also in 1968, Polish troops joined the Soviet-led intervention in Czechoslovakia. In 1970, Gomułka registered a foreign-policy success by signing a treaty with West Germany that involved a recognition of the Oder-Neisse border. In December 1970, however, major strikes in the shipyards at Gdańsk, Gdynia, and Szczecin, provoked by price increases, led to bloody clashes with police and troops in which many were killed. Gomułka had to step down and was replaced as first secretary by the more pragmatic head of the party in Silesia, Edward Gierek.

The Gierek decade (1970–80) began with ambitious attempts to modernize the country's economy and raise living standards. Exploiting East-West détente, he attracted large foreign loans and investments. Initial successes, however, turned sour as the world oil crisis and mismanagement of the economy produced huge budget deficits, which Gierek tried to cover through increased borrowing. The policy of consumerism failed to strengthen the system, and new price increases in 1976 led to workers' riots in Ursus and Radom, which once again were brutally suppressed.

Pope John Paul II

Karol Józef Wojtyła (born May 18, 1920, Wadowice, Poland—died April 2, 2005, Vatican City; beatified May 1, 2011; feast day October 22) was the bishop of Rome and head of the Roman Catholic Church (1978–2005). He was the first non-Italian pope in 455 years and the first from a Slavic country. His pontificate of more than twenty-six years was the third longest in history. As part of his effort to promote greater understanding between nations and between religions, he undertook numerous trips abroad, traveling far greater distances than had all other popes combined, and he extended his influence beyond the church by campaigning against political oppression and criticizing the materialism of the West. He also issued several unprecedented apologies to groups that historically had been wronged by Catholics, most notably Jews and Muslims. His unabashed Polish nationalism and his emphasis on nonviolent political activism aided the Solidarity movement in communist Poland in the 1980s and ultimately contributed to the peaceful dissolution of the Soviet Union in 1991.

A Workers' Defense Committee (KOR) arose and sought to bridge the gap between the intelligentsia, which had been isolated in 1968, and the workers, who had received no support in 1970. The names of such dissidents as Jacek Kuroń and Adam Michnik became internationally known. Other committees appeared that claimed the legality of their activity and protested reprisals as being contrary to the 1975 Helsinki Accords. The PUWP responded with measures of selective intimidation.

In 1978, the election of Karol Cardinal Wojtyła, the archbishop of Kraków, as Pope John Paul II gave the Poles a father figure and a new inspiration. The coalition of workers and intellectuals, operating largely under the protective umbrella of the church, was in fact building a civil society. The pope's visit to Poland in 1979 endowed that society with national, patriotic, and ethical dimensions. A strike at the Gdańsk shipyard led by a charismatic electrician, Lech Wałęsa, forced an accord with the government on Aug. 31, 1980. Out of the strike emerged the almost ten-million-strong Independent Self-Governing Trade Union Solidarity (Solidarność), which the government was forced to recognize. Here was an unprecedented working-class revolution directed against a "socialist" state, an example to other peoples of the Soviet bloc.

A huge movement that sought not to govern but to ensure freedom through a "self-limiting revolution," Solidarity could not have been homogeneous. The opponents of communism ranged from those who opposed the system as contrary to liberty and democracy to those who saw it as inimical to national and Christian values and to those who felt that it had not lived up to its socioeconomic promises. These three attitudes all resurfaced after the fall of communism and explain a good deal about the developments in Poland in the 1990s.

Gierek did not politically survive the birth of Solidarity, and he was replaced by Stanisław Kania, who was followed by General Wojciech Jaruzelski. By the autumn of 1981, Jaruzelski held the offices of premier, first secretary of the party, and commander in chief. His decision to attempt to break Solidarity through the introduction of martial law in December 1981 may well have stemmed from a conviction that the constant tug of war between Solidarity and the government was leading the country toward anarchy, which had to be ended by Polish or Soviet hands. It is likely that he could not conceive of any Poland except a communist one.

Martial law effectively broke Solidarity by paralyzing the country and imprisoning virtually all of the movement's leadership, Wałęsa included. It did not, however, destroy the movement. After the lifting of martial law in

1983, the government, despite its best attempts, could not establish its legitimacy. Severe economic problems worsened the political deadlock. In 1984 a popular priest, Jerzy Popieluszko, was murdered by the secret police, but for the first time in such a case, state agents were arrested and charged with the crime.

In 1985, when Mikhail Gorbachev came to power as the leader of the Soviet Union, his policies of reform started a process that eventually led to the collapse of communism in Eastern Europe and the disintegration of the USSR. The Jaruzelski regime realized that broad reforms were unavoidable and a revived Solidarity had to be part of them. The roundtable negotiations under the auspices of the church—Józef Cardinal Glemp succeeded Wyszyński as primate—resulted in a "negotiated revolution." Solidarity was restored and participated in partly free elections in June 1989 that brought it a sweeping victory.

Communism in the Balkans

After World War II, Albania and Yugoslavia almost immediately fell to the communists, who owed their victory to their strength within the resistance movements and to the disengagement of the Western powers from the region. In Romania and Bulgaria, the communists moved more cautiously and slowly than in Albania and Yugoslavia. But by the end of 1947, they had gradually eliminated all opponents from the army, noncommunist trade unions, civil service, and other political parties.

Questions of Federation

It seemed that, for the first time in many generations, the Balkans would be united, and once again it was an external force—this time, Soviet communism—that was the dominant influence. The more optimistic of the communists hoped that this new, ideologically homogeneous Balkan region would also be one that was more clearly defined. In the north, it would include Romania and the Roman Catholic areas of Yugoslavia but not Catholic Austria. In this way, the old dividing lines between Catholic and Orthodox Europe, between the former Habsburg and Ottoman lands, would be discarded. There were still frontier disputes with Austria over Carinthia (Kärnten) and, more seriously, with Italy over Trieste. But the communist optimists—owing to the resoluteness of Josip Broz Tito—hoped to incorporate Trieste. They also hoped that communists would be successful in the Greek Civil War and thereby enable Greece to be integrated into the new Balkans.

These dreams were dashed, however, as were dreams that ideological conformity would produce political unity. Although a broad Balkan federation was more seriously discussed than at any previous time, it failed to materialize. The dominant internal force in the region was Tito's Yugoslavia, which viewed Balkan federalization as a process in which new units would be added to the six republics that constituted the new, federal South Slav state. The Bulgarians refused to accept this, instead anticipating that such a federation would be the coming together of two equal partners, Yugoslavia and Bulgaria—or three partners, if Romania could be included. Most Albanians, too, had reservations about being absorbed into a Belgrade-dominated federation. Predictably, however, an external factor—Stalin—was decisive in the eventual outcome. By 1947, he had decided that Tito was becoming too powerful within the communist empire and that he should not be allowed too great an extension of his influence. Moscow vetoed Balkan federation, and in 1948, Yugoslavia was expelled from the Soviet communist camp.

Establishing the Power of the Party

Yugoslavia's expulsion from the Soviet bloc did not lead it to abandon communism. Initially, Tito held fast to his interpretation of Marxism-Leninism, and thus a unity of policy was preserved. All the Balkan states, except Greece, pushed down the path of agricultural collectivization, rapid urbanization, and industrialization. Also, despite doctrinal differences between Belgrade and the pro-Soviet leaders in the other capitals, there was a general uniformity of political and social practices. The communist takeovers had seen the elimination, usually by the most brutal of methods, of the communists' political opponents. Once communist power had been established, party control was imposed over every aspect of life through the existing mechanisms of the political police, through a *nomenklatura* system that gave local party leaders a stranglehold on all important or rewarding jobs, and through mass social organizations such as trade unions, Soviet friendship societies, and women's and youth groups—all of which were ultimately controlled by the communists. Within a brief period there were few adult citizens whose lives were not ultimately dependent on the goodwill of the party.

An integral part of the consolidation of communist authority was a series of purges that first affected the party itself and then spread to encompass the whole society in a mesh of terror and intimidation. In Albania, Bulgaria, and Romania, those who suffered were likely to be dubbed "national deviationists" or "Titoists." In Yugoslavia, the targets of reaction were branded "Cominformists," as those who wished to subordinate national sovereignty to the wider interests of the international communist movement run from Moscow were known, or "nationalists," the label ascribed to those who opposed the subordination of Serbian, Croatian, or Macedonian nationalism to Tito's ideal of "brotherhood and unity." In all cases, the purges served to intimidate both the party and the population at large into inactivity while collectivization and industrialization precipitated widespread social change and tension. Among those particularly at risk during the purges were individuals who had connections with organizations outside the communist bloc. Protestant churches suffered heavily, as did the Roman Catholic Church when it was not too entrenched an institution to tackle. Societies such as the Boy Scouts, the Rotarians, and even the Esperantists, which had maintained contact with similar organizations in the West, were condemned and disbanded, with their leading members usually imprisoned or placed in forced-labour camps. All this meant that the Balkans, again with the exception of Greece, were more isolated from the West than at any other time since the height of Ottoman power in the sixteenth century.

Pulling Back from Moscow

Isolation from the West was coupled with increasing Soviet influence. The Soviet Union sent thousands of advisers to work on construction projects and in the armies, civil services, railways, parties, and—above all—secret police forces of the Balkan states in its sphere of influence. The Soviet model was copied in education, culture, the military, and all other aspects of public life. In Bulgaria, two individual letters were dropped from the Bulgarian alphabet to make it appear more like Russian. In Romania, there were furious though hardly convincing efforts to show that Romanian was a Slavic language, and in Bessarabia (which had been reincorporated into the Moldavian SSR), the Romanian language was now printed in Cyrillic. The national economies were not only refashioned on the Soviet model but also subordinated to Soviet needs. This subordination was particularly true for Bulgaria and Romania, which, as defeated powers in World

War II, were forced to sign disadvantageous trade agreements with the Soviet Union and had to agree to the creation of so-called joint-stock companies.

Despite such initial ideological unity, the Balkans rapidly reverted to their customary divisions. Even before the split of 1948, the Yugoslavs, though remaining rigidly loyal to Marxist-Leninist ideas, had balked at many aspects of the Soviets' patronizing and domineering behaviour. They had successfully resisted attempts by Stalin to set up joint-stock companies, and they were perplexed by the Soviet demand to place its agents in a country and a party that had proved themselves loyal to Stalin, the Soviet Union, and socialism. Even after 1948, Tito continued to insist that he had broken with the Cominform but not with socialism. Although Yugoslavia soon accepted American aid, its Stalinist economic and police policies were not diluted until the early 1950s. After that, with his introduction of "socialist self-management" and his leadership in the nonaligned movement, Tito sought to plot a middle way between the two opposing poles of the Cold War, though his basic commitment to socialism was never in doubt.

Albania was next to leave the Soviet fold. Albanian nationalism had already reacted unfavourably to Yugoslav plans for union, and, after the Soviet leader Nikita Khrushchev's rapprochement with Tito in 1955, the Albanian party leader Enver Hoxha became disillusioned with Moscow as well. Beginning in 1961, Albania found support from the Kremlin's new rival, China.

Romania broke loose in the early 1960s. Soviet plans to introduce a division of labour in the socialist economies through the Council for Mutual Economic Assistance (commonly known as Comecon) would have made good many of the faults of Stalinism, which had produced autarkic economies in each Balkan state, but they also would have required Romania's economy to remain predominantly agricultural and thereby would have slowed social evolution and progress toward full communism. Romania therefore switched to a more nationally oriented policy that was well received by the majority of its skeptical population and provided the regime with much-needed legitimacy. Thereafter, Romania could not forgo its nationally oriented policies, but once again commitment to socialism was never in doubt. Unlike Albania, Romania remained a member (albeit a maverick one) of the Warsaw Pact, a Soviet-led military alliance formed in 1955.

These deviations from the Soviet line made Bulgaria the sole Balkan country to maintain loyalty to and conformity with Soviet policies. Yet the Soviets could tolerate this situation because the Balkan Peninsula was declining in strategic importance. The major land confrontation with the West would now take place, it was assumed, in Germany, while the delivery systems of modern long-range weapons diminished the significance of the Dardanelles as a naval asset.

After World War II, Greece followed a very different historical path from all of its Balkan neighbours. As a result of the 1944 understanding between Churchill and Stalin and the 1949 defeat of the communist forces in the Greek Civil War by the Greek government, which enjoyed significant support from Great Britain and later the United States, Greece was the only Balkan country that did not fall under communist control. With the exception of a seven-year military dictatorship (1967–74), Greece remained a capitalist and democratic state, an outpost of Western Europe in the Balkans. It became a member of the North Atlantic Treaty Organization (NATO) in 1952 and joined the European Economic Community (later the European Union within the European Community) in 1981.

Economic Collapse and Nationalist Resurgence

Although the communist Balkan states differed in many respects, there were similarities. When the regimes had settled into place, nepotism appeared in Albania, Bulgaria, and Romania. After Hoxha's death in 1985, his widow continued to exercise considerable influence. Bulgarian leader Todor Zhivkov gave his daughter control of cultural affairs and, at the end of his years in power, was attempting to move his son up the party ladder. In Romania, Nicolae Ceauşescu and his wife placed at least forty relatives in prominent party and state posts.

Nationalism also came to dominate the affairs of all states. Initially, many observers thought that the advent of communist party rule had at last solved the issue of nationalism. In Romania, a new autonomous region was created for the Hungarians, and in Bulgaria, minorities enjoyed unprecedented freedom in education, publishing, and culture. In Yugoslavia, cooperation between the constituent republics was smooth and effective, and Serb-Croat relations were never closer than immediately after the signature in 1954 of the Novi Sad agreement, by which the writers' unions of the two republics (organizations that could not act without official approval) agreed to cooperate in literary and linguistic matters.

The new cooperation created a misleading image. Resentments and hostilities were concealed rather than removed. In Yugoslavia, internal harmony flowed more from the fear of Cominform intervention than from the burying of old hatchets. In 1946, the Albanian population of Yugoslavia was designated a "national minority," rather than one of Yugoslavia's constituent nations. In addition, they were not granted their own republic, and they generally found themselves living in either the Autonomous Region of Kosovo and Metohija or the Republic of Macedonia.

By the 1960s, other difficulties had become apparent. For example, in the immediate postwar years the Bulgarian communists had acknowledged the existence of a Macedonian minority in their country and had even been prepared to cede parts of Bulgaria to a separate Macedonia that would be part of a broader Balkan confederation. However, after the split between Tito and Stalin, there was an immediate reversal in Sofia, so that by the early 1960s severe penalties were imposed on anyone making a public display of Macedonian identity. In 1989, approximately three hundred thousand Turks were forced to leave Bulgaria and settle in Turkey. Many Roma (Gypsies) left with them.

In Romania, the Hungarian autonomous region was gerrymandered out of existence in 1960, the Hungarian Revolution of 1956 providing Bucharest's leaders with an excellent excuse to increase central control over this minority. For other minorities, there were increasing restrictions, and they were in any case becoming more aware that official toleration had been extended to them primarily to make indoctrination more effective. Bulgarian Turks, for example, could easily obtain the works of Marx or Stalin in Turkish but not the Qur'ān.

The nationalist issue was complicated by economic factors. By the mid-1960s, it was clear that the economic system was in need of reform. This was in part because the first stage of socialist construction, based on extensive development and the building of a heavy industrial base, was nearing completion. The next would be based more on technological innovation and the satisfaction of consumer needs. In 1965, the Yugoslavs went ahead with a radical reform program that was intended to move the economy toward "market socialism" by allowing the private ownership of small businesses, abolishing many price controls, and requiring larger enterprises to compete more directly with one another and with foreign companies. Meanwhile, the Romanians sought ways to make themselves less dependent on the rest of the Soviet bloc, and the Bulgarians initiated a number of changes, only to be frightened off by the conservative climate that followed the suppression of the Prague Spring—a period of liberal social and economic reforms—in 1968. Other reform programs followed in the late 1970s and early '80s.

The salient feature of all the major reform initiatives throughout the Balkans was that they failed. Promises of increased standards of living could not be kept, which fatally compromised the prevailing Marxist-Leninist ideology. By the mid-1960s, there were few adherents to the old ideology, but the power structure remained, and those who benefited from it were determined to maintain it. Needing to find an alternative means to legitimacy, they instead chose nationalism. In foreign affairs each state emphasized its individual approach, while in domestic policy pressures on minorities were intensified—with Bulgaria forcing Roma, Pomaks (Bulgarian-speaking Muslims), and Turks to adopt Bulgarian names and the Romanian government subjecting Hungarian and German speakers to ever-greater assimilationist pressures.

The use of nationalism as a legitimizing factor in the communist state was possible only where that state was a true nation-state, such as in Albania, Bulgaria, and Romania. In Yugoslavia, however, attempts to create a sense of Yugoslav identity had only limited success. In all Eastern European states, the communist takeovers had brought to power individuals who were not only ideologically committed but also uncharacteristically young and therefore not well educated. After twenty years of communist domination, a much better educated generation had emerged only to find that most of the rewarding and influential jobs were occupied by people who, though less qualified than they, had twenty more years to serve before retirement. In all states, this was a source of tension and one more reason for the regimes to seek enhanced legitimization. But in Yugoslavia—especially Slovenia, Croatia, and Bosnia and Herzegovina—tension was made worse by the fact that the first generation of rulers recruited during the Partisan struggle contained a disproportionate number of Serbs. By the 1960s, the fear of Soviet pressure, which had been a unifying force in Yugoslavia immediately after the split of 1948, was no longer felt, and it was revived only momentarily in August 1968 by the Soviet invasion of Czechoslovakia. Moreover, reforms in the 1960s had allowed Yugoslavs to travel abroad, and many had gone to work in Western Europe. These people returned not only with German marks and American dollars but also with greater expectations of freedom, national as well as individual—expectations that could only be heightened by moves toward liberalization and decentralization in the new Yugoslav constitution of 1963. At the same time, with an increasing inflow of hard currency, the northern republics grew resentful of the obligation to lodge most of this money in the federal bank in Belgrade. Such centrifugal pressures could not go unnoticed for long, and indeed, by 1968, the Croatian party had become dominated by nationalist communists—who were then purged by Tito.

Yugoslav devolutionists were granted concessions in the 1974 constitution, which gave the party of each constituent element of the federation much greater authority in its own area. For the most part, interference from without was prevented, and in this way the Yugoslav republics became fiefdoms ruled by native barons in much the same way that the other Balkan states were ruled by their national parties. This compartmentalization became a fundamental feature of Yugoslav stability for the next decade. It was in his rejection of this convention by revoking the autonomy of Kosovo in 1989 that the Serbian party leader Slobodan Milošević upset Yugoslavia's already fragile peace. (By the turn of the twenty-first century, he had definitively destroyed the idea of Yugoslavism.)

The transition from authoritarianism to democracy in the Balkans was punctuated in many areas, particularly in Yugoslavia, with civil war. By December 1990, both Croatia and Slovenia had voted for autonomy, and the Serb minority in Croatia had sought to unite with Serbia. That same month, Serbians elected the fiery nationalist and ex-communist Milošević president, and he launched a campaign aimed at unifying the Serbs for the first time since the great migration into the Habsburg empire at the end of the seventeenth century. Croatia and Slovenia both declared their independence on June 25, 1991; the republics of Macedonia and Bosnia and Herzegovina soon followed. As fighting erupted over disputed territories of mixed population, the presidents of the six republics—Serbia, Croatia, Bosnia and Herzegovina, Slovenia, Macedonia, and Montenegro—failed to revive the loose confederation. To stem the conflict, the United Nations (UN) dispatched some fifteen thousand peacekeepers (mostly British and French) and devised a plan that would have divided Bosnia and Herzegovina and Croatia into a crazy quilt of cantons based on local ethnic majorities. However, the plan pleased no one, and fighting escalated amid atrocities and evidence of "ethnic cleansing" by the Serbs.

By the mid-1990s, Slovenia was independent and at peace, and the Republic of Macedonia, protected by a small international force, was admitted to the UN under the name the Former Yugoslav Republic of Macedonia at the insistence of Greece, which claimed a monopoly on the use of the term *Macedonia*. Croatia controlled almost all its putative territory, including the Dalmatian coast. What remained of Yugoslavia included Serbia, Montenegro, and portions of Bosnia and Herzegovina inhabited or claimed by Bosnian Serbs, including a corridor stretching almost to the Adriatic Sea. The would-be state of Bosnia was strangled within this noose as the fighting between Serbs, Bosnian Serbs, Bosniaks (Muslims), and Croats shifted from Sarajevo to Goražde to Bihać. Each time a truce seemed near, fighting broke out anew, until the Dayton Accords of 1995 created a loosely federalized Bosnia and Herzegovina divided roughly between the Federation of Bosnia and Herzegovina (a decentralized federation of Croats and Bosniaks) and the Republika Srpska (Bosnian Serb Republic). In Kosovo in February 1998, widespread fighting erupted between Serbs and ethnic Albanians when Milošević ordered troops into the province to regain territory controlled by the Kosovo Liberation Army. To bring about Serbia's withdrawal, the North Atlantic Treaty Organization launched a bombing campaign the following year against Serbia, forcing Milošević to accept a peace plan jointly sponsored by Russia, the European Union (EU), and the United States. In 2000, Milošević was defeated in presidential elections by Vojislav Koštunica and was later arrested and extradited to The Hague to stand trial for war crimes.

The new Yugoslavia, now composed of only Serbia and Montenegro, attempted to rebuild its shattered society and economy, while the independent states of Bosnia and Herzegovina, Croatia, Macedonia, and Slovenia sought closer ties with the countries of the EU. However, secessionists in Montenegro soon pushed for independence from the new Yugoslavia against the wishes of the international community, which feared that further political instability might rekindle the destructive forces that were unleashed in the early 1990s. In 2002, the EU brokered an agreement between the leaders of Yugoslavia, Serbia, and Montenegro that called for the formation of a loose federation, called

Serbia and Montenegro, which would have a single federal policy on defense, foreign affairs, and trade but would grant each republic autonomy in most other policy areas and enable either republic to hold a referendum on independence after three years. The agreement was ratified by the federal parliament and the Serbian and Montenegrin assemblies in 2003, effectively erasing Yugoslavia from the map. Three years later, after Montenegrins approved a referendum on independence, Serbia and Montenegro disbanded the federation and became independent republics.

Meanwhile, the future status of Kosovo remained uncertain. The ethnic Albanian majority there desired independence, but Serbia emphatically opposed it. Kosovo formally seceded from Serbia in February 2008. The United States and most members of the EU supported the move, but Serbia and Russia refused to recognize Kosovar independence.

Outside Yugoslavia, secession from a large federation also brought independence, as the Moldavian Soviet Socialist Republic became Moldova, the majority of whose inhabitants were ethnic Romanians. This did not bring union with Romania, however, which would have angered Moldova's own minorities—particularly the Russians. In Romania itself, an ingrained fear of the security police produced a short and intense civil war. A similar development in Albania, where terror and deprivation had been as great, was only just avoided. Only in Bulgaria—where, for ethnic Bulgarians at least, the last years of communist rule had been relatively benign—was a peaceful transition achieved.

The various Balkan states thus found different paths out of socialism but faced similar problems when they emerged. The vast subsidized and hugely inefficient heavy industrial plants in which communist propagandists had taken such pride were now virtually useless. Their products, many of which had previously been sold in the "soft" Soviet and

Eastern European markets for "soft" currencies, were too low in quality and too high in price to survive in a competitive market. Widespread unemployment was the not-surprising consequence. Furthermore, the old communist-inspired industries left another and potentially even more dangerous legacy: environmental pollution on a prodigious scale.

In all post-communist states except Serbia, the solutions to economic problems were expected to be found in a market economy and in eventual association with the EU. International agencies such as the World Bank and the International Monetary Fund promised financial help for the new Balkan regimes but required an economic transformation, as the states were expected to privatize their industries and agriculture, remove government subsidies, and restrain public expenditure. The social costs of these adjustments were enormous. Restricting public expenditure meant limiting social security funds just when unemployment and inflation were taking their heaviest toll. In this context, constructing an open, pluralist system that tolerated minority groups was a daunting task.

There were other challenges as well. As in the past, the Balkans had little more to export than food, raw materials, and agricultural products—the very items against which the EU's tariffs discriminated most sharply. But even less promising was the obvious alternative: membership in a Black Sea zone sponsored by Turkey. Such an association would align the Balkan states with a less-developed area; it would divide them from the rest of Europe; and, most uncomfortable of all, it would turn the peninsula back toward Istanbul. Ever since the Slavs settled in the Balkans, they had attempted to restrict the power of that great city on the Bosporus, yet no sooner had they emerged from Byzantine rule than the Ottomans appeared and reestablished Eastern domination of the peninsula. From the end of the eighteenth century,

centrifugal forces spearheaded by Balkan Christian nationalism gained greater strength, but the weakness of this movement was its inability to resolve differences between its own
different nationalities. Domination first by central European
fascism and then by Russian socialism followed, and, when
these powers collapsed in turn, the Balkan peoples faced the
same dangers that had plagued them throughout the period
they had occupied the peninsula.

At the close of the first decade of the twenty-first
century, the prospects for peace, stability, and economic
prosperity for the peoples of the Balkans had improved
significantly. NATO and, more important, the EU
expanded their influence in the area by offering membership to an increasing number of Balkan states. The successful continuation of this process holds out hope that
notions of "primitive Balkan mentalities" and "age-old Balkan hatreds" would soon be consigned to the dustbin of
history.

CHAPTER 5

COMMUNISM IN CHINA

Just as Russia overthrew its monarchy, China's Nationalist Party, also called Kuomintang, was originally a revolutionary league working for the overthrow of the Chinese monarchy. The Nationalists became a political party in the first year of the Chinese republic (1912). The party participated in the first Chinese parliament, which was soon dissolved by a coup d'etat (1913). This defeat moved its leader, Sun Yat-sen, to organize it more tightly, first (1914) on the model of a Chinese secret society and later (1923–24) under Soviet guidance on that of the Bolshevik party. The Nationalist Party owed its early successes largely to Soviet aid and advice and to close collaboration with the Chinese communists (1924–27). The Paris Peace Treaty, the meeting that inaugurated the international settlement after World War I, sparked unrest in the new Chinese republic. It set the country down a path that locked in communist ideology, leaving it the lone global superpower still ruled by a communist party, the Chinese Communist Party (CCP), in the twenty-first century.

Riots and Protests

On May 4, 1919, patriotic students in Beijing protested the decision at the Paris Peace Conference that Japan should retain defeated Germany's rights and possessions in Shandong. Many students were arrested in the rioting that followed. Waves of protest spread throughout the major cities of China. Merchants closed their shops, banks suspended business, and workers went on strike to pressure the government. Finally, the government was forced to release the arrested students, dismiss some officials charged with being tools of Japan, and refuse to sign the Treaty of Versailles. This outburst helped spread the iconoclastic and reformist ideas of the intellectual movement, which became known as the May Fourth Movement. By the early 1920s, China was launched on a new revolutionary path.

(From left to right) *David Lloyd George, Vittorio Orlando, Georges Clemenceau, and Woodrow Wilson, known as the "Big Four," signed the Treaty of Versailles in 1919 that ended World War I, though some, including China, refused to sign.* National Archives, Washington, D.C.

The Chinese Communist Party

The CCP grew directly from the May Fourth Movement. Its leaders and early members were professors and students who came to believe that China needed a social revolution and who began to see Soviet Russia as a model. Chinese students in Japan and France had earlier studied socialist doctrines and the ideas of Karl Marx, but the Russian Revolution of 1917 stimulated a fresh interest in keeping with the enthusiasm of the period for radical ideologies. Li Dazhao, the librarian of Peking University, and Chen Duxiu were the CCP's cofounders.

The CCP spent the next two years recruiting, publicizing Marxism and the need for a national revolution directed against foreign imperialism and Chinese militarism, and organizing unions among railway and factory workers. A Dutch communist named Handricus Sneevliet, who used the Cominterm name Maring in China, was instrumental in bringing the KMT and CCP together in a national revolutionary movement. A number of young men were sent to Russia for training. Among the CCP members were many students who had worked and studied in France, where they had gained experience in the French labour movement and with the French Communist Party; Zhou Enlai was one of these. Other recruits were students influenced by the Japanese socialist movement. By 1923, the party had some three hundred members, with perhaps three thousand to four thousand in the ancillary Socialist Youth League.

Communist-Nationalist Cooperation

By then, however, the CCP was in serious difficulty. The railway unions had been brutally suppressed, and there were few places in China where it was safe to be a known communist.

In June 1923, the Third Congress of the CCP met in Guang-zhou, where Sun Yat-sen provided a sanctuary. After long debate, this congress accepted the Comintern strategy pressed by Maring—that communists should join the KMT and make it the centre of the national revolutionary move-ment. Sun had rejected a multiparty alliance but had agreed to admit communists to his party, and several, including Chen Duxiu and Li Dazhao, had already joined the KMT. Even though communists would enter the other party as individuals, the CCP was determined to maintain its separate identity and autonomy and to attempt to control the labour union movement. The Comintern strategy called for a period of steering the Nationalist movement and building a base among the Chinese masses, followed by a second stage—a socialist revolution in which the proletariat would seize power from the capitalist class.

By mid-1923, the Soviets had decided to renew the effort to establish diplomatic relations with the Beijing government. Lev M. Karakhan, the deputy commissar for foreign affairs, was chosen as plenipotentiary for the negotiations. In addition to negotiating a treaty of mutual recognition, Karakhan was to try to regain for the Soviet Union control of the Chinese Eastern Railway. On the revolutionary front, the Soviets had decided to financially assist Sun in Guangzhou and send a team of military men to help train an army in Guangdong. By June, five young Soviet officers were in Beijing for language training. More importantly, the Soviet leaders selected an old Bolshevik, Mikhail M. Borodin, as their principal adviser to Sun Yat-sen. The Soviet leaders also decided to replace Maring with Voytinsky as principal adviser to the CCP, which had its headquarters in Shanghai. Thereafter, three men—Karakhan in Beijing, Borodin in Guangzhou, and Grigory Voytinsky in Shanghai—were the field directors of the Soviet effort to bring China into the anti-imperialist camp of "world revolution."

The offensive was aimed primarily at the positions in China of Great Britain, Japan, and the United States.

Reactions to Warlords and Foreigners

These countries, too, were moving toward a new, postwar relationship with China. At the Washington Conference (November 1921–February 1922), China put forth a ten-point proposal for relations between it and the other powers, which, after negotiations, became four points: to respect the sovereignty, independence, and territorial and administrative integrity of China; to give China the opportunity to develop a stable government; to maintain the principle of equal opportunity in China for the commerce and industry of all countries; and to refrain from taking advantage of conditions in China to seek exclusive privileges detrimental to the rights of friendly countries. The treaty was signed as the Nine-Power Pact on February 6. Two other Chinese proposals, tariff autonomy and abolishing extraterritoriality, were not included in the pact but were assigned to a committee for further study. In the meantime, separate negotiations between China and Japan produced a treaty in which Japan agreed to return the former German holdings in Shandong to China—although under conditions that left Japan with valuable privileges in the province.

For a few years thereafter, Great Britain, Japan, the United States, and France attempted to adjust their conflicting interests in China, cooperated in assisting the Beijing government, and generally refrained from aiding particular Chinese factions in the recurrent power struggles. But China was in turmoil, with regional militarism in full tide. Furthermore, a movement against the Unequal Treaties began to take shape.

With China in turmoil, Christian missionaries operated many schools, hospitals, and other philanthropic enterprises in China. Pictured is French missionary Father Jacquino with refugee children in 1937. Watanabe/Time & Life Pictures/Getty Images

The Nationalist Government from 1928 to 1937

The most serious immediate problem facing the new government was the continuing military separatism. The government had no authority over the vast area of western China, and even regions in eastern China were under the rule of independent regimes that had lately been part of the Nationalist coalition. After an unsuccessful attempt at negotiations, Chiang Kai-shek, commander of the revolutionary army, launched a series of civil wars against his former allies. By 1930, one militarist regime after another had been reduced to provincial proportions, and Nanjing's influence was spreading. Explained in material terms, Chiang owed his success to the great financial resources of his base in Jiangsu and Zhejiang and to foreign arms. Quick recognition by the foreign powers brought the Nationalist government the revenues collected by the efficient Maritime Customs Service; when the powers granted China the right to fix its own tariff schedules, that revenue increased.

The Nationalist government during its first few years in power had some success in reasserting China's sovereignty. Several concession areas were returned to Chinese control, and the foreign powers assented to China's resumption of tariff autonomy. Yet these were merely token gains; the Unequal Treaties were scarcely breached. The country was in a nationalistic mood, determined to roll back foreign economic and political penetration. Manchuria was a huge and rich area of China in which Japan had extensive economic privileges, possessing part of the Liaodong Peninsula as a leasehold and controlling much of southern Manchuria's economy through the South Manchurian Railway. The Chinese began to develop Huludao, in Liaodong, as a port to rival Dairen (Dalian) and to plan railways to compete with Japanese lines.

Zhang Xueliang (Chang Hsüeh-liang), Zhang Zuolin's son and successor as ruler of Manchuria, was drawing closer to Nanjing and sympathized with the Nationalists' desire to rid China of foreign privilege.

For Japan, Manchuria was regarded as vital. Many Japanese had acquired a sense of mission that Japan should lead Asia against the West. The Great Depression had hurt Japanese business, and there was deep social unrest. Such factors influenced many army officers—especially officers of the Kwantung Army, which protected Japan's leasehold in the Liaodong Peninsula and the South Manchurian Railway—to regard Manchuria as the area where Japan's power must be consolidated.

Japanese Aggression

In September 1931, a group of officers in the Kwantung Army set in motion a plot (beginning with the Mukden Incident) to compel the Japanese government to extend its power in Manchuria. The Japanese government was drawn step by step into the conquest of Manchuria and the creation of a regime known as Manchukuo. China was unable to prevent Japan from seizing this vital area. In 1934, after long negotiations, Japan acquired the Soviet interest in the Chinese Eastern Railway, thus eliminating the last legal trace of the Soviet sphere of influence there. During 1932–35, Japan seized more territory bordering on Manchuria. In 1935, it attempted to detach Hebei and the Chahar region of Inner Mongolia from Nanjing's control and threatened Shanxi, Shandong, and the Suiyuan region of Inner Mongolia. The National Government's policy was to trade space for time in which to build military power and unify the country. Its slogan "Unity before resistance" was directed principally against the Chinese communists.

The Sino-Japanese War

On July 7, 1937, the Marco Polo Bridge Incident, a minor clash between Japanese and Chinese troops near Beiping (Beijing's name under the Nationalist government), finally led the two countries into war. The Japanese government tried for several weeks to settle the incident locally, but China's mood was highly nationalistic, and public opinion clamoured for resistance to further aggression. In late July, new fighting broke out. The Japanese quickly took Beiping and captured Tianjin. On August 13, savage fighting broke out in Shanghai. By now the prestige of both nations was committed, and they were locked in a war.

The Pacific War (which in China became known as the War of Resistance Against Japanese Aggression) ended on

Chinese Nationalist soldiers during the battle for the city of Xuzhou on Dec. 4, 1948. © AP Images

Aug. 14 (Aug. 15 in China), 1945, and the formal Japanese surrender came on September 2. China rejoiced. Yet the country faced enormously difficult problems of reunification and reconstruction and a future clouded by the dark prospect of civil war.

Civil War (1945–49)

In a little more than four years after Japan's surrender, the CCP and the People's Liberation Army (PLA; the name by which communist forces were now known) conquered mainland China, and on Oct. 1, 1949, the People's Republic of China was established, with its capital at Beijing (the city's former name restored). The factors that brought this about were many and complex and subject to widely varying interpretation, but the basic fact was a communist military triumph growing out of a profound and popularly based revolution. The process may be perceived in three phases: 1) from August 1945 to the end of 1946, the Nationalists and communists raced to take over Japanese-held territories, built up their forces, and fought many limited engagements while still conducting negotiations for a peaceful settlement; 2) during 1947 and the first half of 1948, after initial Nationalist success, the strategic balance turned in favour of the communists; and 3) the communists won a series of smashing victories beginning in the latter part of 1948 that led to the establishment of the People's Republic.

A Race for Territory

As soon as Japan's impending surrender was known, the commander of the communist armies, Zhu De, ordered his troops, on August 11, to move into Japanese-held territory and take over Japanese arms, despite Chiang Kai-shek's order that they stand where they were. The United States aided the Chinese government by flying many divisions from the southwest to occupy the main eastern cities, such as Beiping, Tianjin, Shanghai, and the prewar capital, Nanjing. The U.S. Navy moved Chinese troops from southern China to other coastal cities and landed fifty-three thousand marines at Tianjin and Qingdao to assist in disarming and repatriating Japanese troops but also serve as a counterweight to the Soviet army in southern Manchuria. Furthermore, U.S. Gen. Douglas MacArthur ordered all Japanese forces in China proper to surrender their arms only to forces of the Nationalist government. They obeyed and thereby were occasionally engaged against Chinese communist forces.

Immediately after the surrender, the communists sent political cadres and troops into Manchuria. This had been planned long in advance. Gen. Lin Biao became commander of the forces (the Northeast Democratic Allied Army), which incorporated puppet troops of the former Japanese Manchukuo regime and began to recruit volunteers. It got most of its arms from Japanese stocks taken over by the Soviets.

Manchuria was a vast area with a population of forty million, the greatest concentration of heavy industry and railways in China, and enormous reserves of coal, iron, and many other minerals. The Soviet Union had promised the Nationalist government that it would withdraw its occupying armies within ninety days of Japan's surrender and return the region to China. The government was determined to control Manchuria, which was vital to China's future as a world power. However, Lin Biao's army attempted to block the entry of Nationalist troops by destroying rail lines and seizing areas around ports of entry. Soon the two sides were locked in a fierce struggle for the corridors into Manchuria, although negotiations were under way in Chongqing between Mao Zedong and Chiang for a peaceful settlement. The Soviet army avoided direct involvement in the struggle, but it dismantled much industrial machinery and shipped it to the Soviet Union together with hundreds of thousands of Japanese prisoners of war. By the end of 1945, the Nationalists had positioned some of their best U.S.-trained armies in southern Manchuria as far north as Mukden (present-day Shenyang), a strategic rail centre to which Nationalist troops were transported by air. The government's hold was precarious, however, because the communist Eighteenth Army Group and the New Fourth Army had regrouped in northern China, abandoning areas south of the Yangtze after a weak bid to take Shanghai. By the end of 1945, communist forces were spread across a band of provinces from the northwest to the sea. They had a grip on great sections of all the railway lines north of the Longhai line, which were vital supply lines for Nationalist armies in the Tianjin-Beiping area and in Manchuria. The Nationalist government held vast territories in the south and west and had reestablished its authority in the rich provinces of the lower Yangtze Valley and in a few important cities in northern China. It had also assumed civil control on Taiwan.

Attempts to End the War

Peace negotiations continued in Chongqing between Nationalist and communist officials after Japan's surrender. An agreement reached on Oct. 10, 1945, called for the convening of a multiparty Political Consultative Council to plan a liberalized postwar government and draft a constitution for submission to a national congress. Still, the sides were far apart over the character of the new government, control over the areas liberated by the communists, and the size and degree of autonomy of the communist armies in a national military system. Patrick J. Hurley resigned his ambassadorship on November 26, and the next day U.S. Pres. Harry S. Truman appointed Gen. George C. Marshall as his special representative, with the specific mission of trying to bring about political unification and the cessation of hostilities in China.

Marshall arrived in China on December 23. The Nationalist government proposed the formation of a committee of three, with Marshall as chairman, to end the fighting. This committee, with Generals Chang Chun (Zhang Qun) and Zhou Enlai as the Nationalist and communist representatives, respectively, met on Jan. 7, 1946. The two agreed on January 10 that Chiang and Mao would issue orders to cease hostilities and halt troop movements as of January 13 midnight, with the exception of government troop movements south of the Yangtze and into and within Manchuria to restore Chinese sovereignty. The agreement also called for the establishment in Beiping of an executive headquarters, equally represented by both sides, to supervise the cease-fire.

This agreement provided a favourable atmosphere for meetings in Chongqing of the Political Consultative Council, composed of representatives of the KMT, the CCP, the Democratic League, the Young China Party, and nonparty delegates. For the remainder of January, the council issued a series of agreed recommendations regarding governmental reorganization, peaceful national reconstruction, military reductions, creation of a national assembly, and drafting of a constitution. President Chiang pledged that the government would carry out these recommendations, and the political parties stated their intention to abide by them. The next step was meetings of a military subcommittee, with Marshall as adviser, to discuss troop reductions and amalgamation of forces into a single national army.

Early 1946 was the high point of conciliation. It soon became clear, however, that implementing the various recommendations and agreements was being opposed by conservatives in the KMT, who feared these measures would dilute their party's control of the government, and by Nationalist generals, who objected to reducing the size of their armies. The communists attempted to prevent the extension of Nationalist military control in Manchuria. On March 17–18, a communist army attacked and captured a strategic junction between Mukden and Changchun, the former Manchukuo capital; on April 18, communists captured Changchun from a small Nationalist garrison directly following the Soviet withdrawal. On that day, Marshall returned to China after a trip to Washington and resumed his efforts to stop the spreading civil war.

Resumption of Fighting

Each side seemed convinced that it could win by war what it could not achieve by negotiation: dominance over the other. Despite the efforts of Chinese moderates and General Marshall, fighting resumed in July in Manchuria, and in northern China the Nationalists attempted massive drives in Jiangsu and Shandong to break the communist grip on the railways. The communists launched a propaganda campaign against the United States, playing upon the nationalistic theme of liberation. They were hostile because of the extensive U.S. military and financial assistance to the KMT at the very time that Marshall was mediating. The Nationalist government had become increasingly intransigent, confident of continued U.S. help. To exert pressure and to try to keep the United States out of the civil war, Marshall imposed in August an embargo on further shipment of U.S. arms to China. By the end of the year, however, he realized that his efforts had failed.

In January 1947, he left China, issuing a statement denouncing the intransigents on both sides. All negotiations ended in March; the die was cast for war.

In the latter half of 1946, government forces made significant gains in northern China and Manchuria, capturing 165 towns from the enemy. Buoyed by these victories, the government convened a multiparty National Assembly on November 15, despite a boycott by the CCP and Democratic League. The delegates adopted a new constitution, which was promulgated on New Year's Day, 1947. The constitution reaffirmed Sun Yat-sen's Three Principles of the People as the basic philosophy of the state; called for the fivefold division of powers among the executive, legislative, judicial, control, and examination *yuan* ("governmental bodies"); and established the people's four rights of initiation, referendum, election, and recall. The way was prepared for election of both central and local officials, upon which the period of Nationalist tutelage would end.

The Nationalist government struggled with grave economic problems. Inflation continued unabated, caused principally by government financing of military and other operations through the printing press: approximately 65 percent of the budget was met by currency expansion and only 10 percent by taxes. Government spending was uncontrolled; funds were dissipated in maintaining large and unproductive garrison forces. Much tax revenue failed to reach the treasury because of malpractices throughout the bureaucracy. Inflation inhibited exports and enhanced the demand for imports. The government had to import large amounts of grain and cotton, but in the months immediately after Japan's surrender, it also permitted the import of luxury goods without effective restrictions. As an antiinflationary measure, it sold gold on the open market. These policies permitted a large gold and U.S. currency reserve, estimated at $900 million at the end of the war, to be cut in half by the end of 1946. Foreign trade was hampered by excessive regulation and corrupt practices.

The spiraling effects of inflation were somewhat curbed by large amounts of supplies imported by the United Nations Relief and Rehabilitation Administration, chiefly food and clothing, a wide variety of capital goods, and materials for the rehabilitation of agriculture, industry, and transportation. In August 1946, the United States sold to China civilian-type army and navy surplus property at less than 20 percent of its estimated procurement cost. In spite of these and other forms of aid, the costs of civil war kept the budget continuously out of balance. Speculation, hoarding of goods, and black market operations as hedges against inflation continued unabated. The constant depreciation in the value of paper currency undermined morale in all classes who depended on salaries, including troops, officers, and civilian officials.

By contrast, it appears that the communists in their areas, which were mostly rural, practiced a Spartan style of life close to the common people. Morale remained high in the army and was continuously bolstered by indoctrination and effective propaganda. As they had during the war years, communist troops tried in many ways to win support of the masses. In newly occupied areas, social policy was at first reformist rather than revolutionary.

In Manchuria, Lin Biao was forging a formidable army of veteran cadres from northern China and natives of Manchuria, now well equipped with Japanese weapons. By 1947, the communists' Northeast Democratic Allied Army controlled all of Manchuria north of the Sungari (Songhua) River, the east, and much of the countryside in the Nationalist stronghold in the south. There, the Nationalists had most of their best-trained and best-equipped divisions, but the troops had been conscripted or recruited in China's southwest, and they garrisoned cities and railways in a distant land. Beginning in January 1947, Lin Biao launched a series of small offensives. By July, the Nationalists had lost half of their territory in Manchuria and much materiel; desertions and casualties, caused by indecisive Nationalist leadership and declining troop morale, reduced their forces by half. Lin Biao was not yet strong enough to take Manchuria, but he had the Nationalist armies hemmed up in a few major cities and with only a tenuous hold on the railways leading southward.

The Decisive Year, 1948

The year 1948 was the turning point in the civil war. In central China, communist armies of five hundred thousand troops proved their ability to fight major battles on the plains and capture, though not always hold, important towns on the Longhai line, such as Luoyang and Kaifeng. In northern China, they encircled Taiyuan, the capital of Shanxi; took most of Chahar and Jehol, provinces on Manchuria's western flank; and recaptured Yan'an, which had been lost in March 1947. The decisive battles were fought in Shandong and Manchuria, where the forces of Chen Yi and Liu Bocheng and those under Lin Biao crushed the government's best armies. For the government, it was a year of military and economic disasters.

In Shandong, despite the departure of Chen Yi's forces, communist guerrillas gradually reduced the government's hold on the railway from Qingdao to Jinan; they penned up about sixty thousand government troops in the latter city, an important railway junction. Instead of withdrawing that garrison southward to Suzhou, the government left it, for political reasons, to stand and fight. Then Chen Yi's forces returned to Shandong and overwhelmed the dispirited Jinan garrison on September 24. This opened the way for a communist attack on Suzhou, the historic northern shield for Nanjing and a vital railway centre.

Beginning in December 1947, a communist offensive severed all railway connections into Mukden and isolated the Nationalist garrisons in Manchuria. The government armies went on the defensive in besieged cities, partly out of fear that demoralized divisions would defect in the field. Instead of withdrawing from Manchuria before it was too late, the government tried unsuccessfully to reinforce its armies and supply the garrisons by air. With the fall of Jinan, Lin Biao launched his final offensive. He now had an army of six hundred thousand, nearly twice the Nationalist force in Manchuria. He first attacked Jinzhou, the government's supply base on the railway between Jinan and Mukden; it fell on October 17. Changchun fell three days later. The great garrison at Mukden then tried to retake Jinzhou and Changchun and open the railway line to the port of Yingkou on Liaodong Bay. In a series of battles, Lin Biao's columns defeated this cream of the Nationalist forces. By early November, the Nationalists had lost some four hundred thousand troops as casualties, captives, or defectors.

The government's military operations in the first part of 1948 produced ever-larger budget deficits through the loss of tax receipts, dislocation of transportation and productive facilities, and increased military expenditures. Inflation was out of control. In August, the government introduced a new currency, the gold yuan, to replace the old notes at the rate of 3,000,000:1, promising drastic reforms to curtail expenditures and increase revenue. Domestic prices and foreign-exchange rates were pegged, with severe penalties threatened for black market operations. The people were required to sell their gold, silver, and foreign currency to the government at the pegged rate; large numbers did so in a desperate effort to halt the inflation. In Shanghai and some other places, the government used draconian methods to enforce its decrees against speculators, but it apparently could not control its own expenditures or stop the printing presses. Furthermore, the government's efforts to fix prices of food and commodities brought about an almost complete stagnation of economic activity, except for illicit buying and selling at prices far above the fixed levels. Some army officers and government officials were themselves engaged in smuggling, speculation, and other forms of corruption. Then came the loss of Jinan and the knowledge of the threat in Manchuria. During October, the final effort to halt inflation collapsed, with shattering effect to morale in Nationalist-held cities. Prices started rocketing upward once more.

Communist Victory

Between early November 1948 and early January 1949, the two sides battled for control of Suzhou. Zhu De concentrated six hundred thousand troops under Chen Yi, Liu Bocheng, and Chen Geng near that strategic centre, which was defended by Nationalist forces of similar size. Both armies were well equipped, but the Nationalists had a superiority in armour and were unopposed in the air. Yet poor morale, inept command, and a defensive psychology brought another disaster to the Nationalist government. One after another, its armies were surrounded and defeated in the field. When the sixty-five-day battle was over on January 10, the Nationalists had lost some five hundred thousand men and their equipment. The capital at Nanjing would soon lie exposed.

With Manchuria and most of the eastern region south to the Yangtze in communist hands, the fate of Tianjin and Beiping was sealed. The railway corridor between Tianjin and Zhangjiakou was hopelessly isolated. Tianjin fell on January 15 after a brief siege, and Beiping surrendered on the 23rd, allowing a peaceful turnover of China's historic capital and centre of culture.

Thus, during the last half of 1948, the communist armies had gained control over Manchuria and northeastern China nearly to the Yangtze, except for pockets of resistance. They had a numerical superiority and had captured such huge stocks of rifles, artillery, and armour that they were better equipped than the Nationalists.

Great political shifts occurred in 1949. Chiang Kai-shek retired temporarily in January, turning over to the vice president, Gen. Li Tsung-jen (Li Zongren), the problem of holding the government together and trying to negotiate a peace with Mao Zedong. Li's peace negotiations (February–April) proved hopeless. The Nationalists were not prepared to surrender; they still claimed to govern more than half of China and still had a large army. General Li tried to secure U.S. support in the peace negotiations and in the military defense of southern China, but the U.S. government, attempting to extricate itself from its entanglement with the collapsing forces of the Nationalist government, pursued a policy of noninvolvement.

When peace negotiations broke down, communist armies crossed the Yangtze virtually unopposed; the Nationalist government abandoned its indefensible capital on April 23 and moved to Guangzhou. In succession, communist forces occupied Nanjing (April 24), Hankou (May 16–17), and Shanghai (May 25). The Nationalists' last hope lay in the south and west, but Xi'an, a longtime Nationalist bastion and the gateway to the northwest, had fallen to Gen. Peng Dehuai on May 20. During the last half of 1949, powerful communist armies succeeded in taking the provinces of southern and western China. By the end of the year, only the islands of Hainan, Taiwan, and a few other offshore positions were still in Nationalist hands, and only scattered pockets of resistance remained on the mainland. The defeated Nationalist government reestablished itself on Taiwan, to which Chiang had withdrawn early in the year, taking most of the government's gold reserves and the Nationalist air force and navy. On October 1, with most of the mainland held by the PLA, Mao proclaimed the establishment in Beijing of the government of the People's Republic of China.

Establishment of the People's Republic

The communist victory in 1949 brought to power a peasant party that had learned its techniques in the countryside but had adopted Marxist ideology and believed in class struggle and rapid industrial development. Extensive experience in running base areas and waging war before 1949 had given the Chinese Communist Party (CCP) deeply ingrained operational habits and proclivities. The long civil war that created the new nation, however, had been one of peasants triumphing over urban dwellers and had involved the destruction of the old ruling classes. In addition, the party leaders recognized that they had no experience in overseeing the transitions to socialism and industrialism that would occur in China's huge urban centres. For this, they turned to the only government with such experience: the Soviet Union. Western hostility against the People's Republic of China, sharpened by the Korean War, contributed to the intensity of the ensuing Sino-Soviet relationship.

When the CCP proclaimed the People's Republic, most Chinese understood that the new leadership would be preoccupied with industrialization. A priority goal of the communist political system was to raise China to the status of a great power. While pursuing this goal, the "centre of gravity" of communist policy shifted from the countryside to the city, but Chairman Mao Zedong insisted that the revolutionary vision forged in the rural struggle would continue to guide the party.

In a series of speeches in 1949, Chairman Mao stated that his aim was to create a socialist society and, eventually, world communism. These objectives, he said, required transforming consumer cities into producer cities to set the basis on which "the people's political power could be consolidated." He advocated forming a four-class coalition of elements of the urban middle class—the petty bourgeoisie and the national bourgeoisie—with workers and peasants, under the leadership of the CCP. The people's state would exercise a dictatorship "for the oppression of antagonistic classes" made up of opponents of the regime.

The authoritative legal statement of this "people's democratic dictatorship" was given in the 1949 Organic Law for the Chinese People's Political Consultative Conference, and at its first session the conference adopted a Common Program that formally sanctioned the organization of state power under the coalition. Following the communist victory, a widespread urge to return to normality helped the new leadership restore the economy. Police and party cadres in each locality, backed up by army units, began to crack down on criminal activities associated with economic breakdown. Soon it was possible to speak of longer-term developmental plans.

The cost of restoring order and building up integrated political institutions at all levels throughout the country proved important in setting China's course for the next two decades. Revolutionary priorities had to be made consonant with other needs. Land reform did proceed in the countryside: Landlords were virtually eliminated as a class; land was redistributed; and, after some false starts, China's countryside was placed on the path toward collectivization. In the cities, however, a temporary accommodation was reached with noncommunist elements. Many former bureaucrats and capitalists were retained in positions of authority in factories, businesses, schools, and governmental organizations. The leadership recognized that such compromises endangered their aim of perpetuating revolutionary values in an industrializing society, yet out of necessity they accepted the lower priority for communist revolutionary goals and a higher place for organizational control and enforced public order.

Once in power, communist cadres could no longer condone what they had once sponsored, and inevitably they adopted a more rigid and bureaucratic attitude toward popular participation in politics. Many communists, however, considered these changes a betrayal of the revolution. Their responses gradually became more intense, and the issue eventually began to divide the once cohesive revolutionary elite. That development became a central focus of China's political history from 1949.

Mao Zedong

Mao Zedong (Wade-Giles Romanization: Mao Tse-tung [born Dec. 26, 1893, Shaoshan, Hunan province, China—died Sept. 9, 1976, Beijing]), was a principal Chinese Marxist theorist, soldier, and statesman who led his nation's communist revolution. Leader of the Chinese Communist Party from 1935, he was chairman (chief of state) of the People's Republic of China from 1949 to 1959 and chairman of the party until his death.

When China emerged from a half century of revolution as the world's most populous nation and launched itself on a path of economic development and social change, Mao Zedong occupied a critical place in the story of the country's resurgence. To be sure, he did not play a dominant role throughout the whole struggle. In the early years of the

Chinese Communist Party, he was a secondary figure, though by no means a negligible one, and even after the 1940s (except perhaps during the Cultural Revolution) the crucial decisions were not his alone. Nevertheless, looking at the whole period from the foundation of the Chinese Communist Party in 1921 to Mao's death in 1976, one can fairly regard Mao Zedong as the principal architect of the new China.

Early Years

Born in the village of Shaoshan in Hunan province, Mao was the son of a former peasant who had become affluent as a farmer and grain dealer. He grew up in an environment in which education was valued only as training for keeping records and accounts. From the age of eight, he attended his native village's primary school, where he acquired a basic knowledge of the Confucian Classics. At thirteen, he was forced to begin working full-time on his family's farm. Rebelling against paternal authority (which included an arranged marriage that was forced on him and that he never acknowledged or consummated), Mao left his family to study at a higher primary school in a neighbouring county and then at a secondary school in the provincial capital, Changsha. There, he came

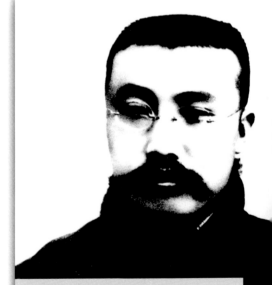

Professor Li Dazhao of Peking University met with Russian communists in 1920 and later helped organize the Socialist Youth League, cofounded the Communist Party, and mentored Mao Zedong. Sovfoto/Universal Images Group/Getty Images

in contact with new ideas from the West, as formulated by such political and cultural reformers as Liang Qichao and the Nationalist revolutionary Sun Yat-sen. Scarcely had he begun studying revolutionary ideas when a real revolution took place before his very eyes. On Oct. 10, 1911, fighting against the Qing Dynasty broke out in Wuchang, and within two weeks the revolt had spread to Changsha.

Enlisting in a unit of the revolutionary army in Hunan, Mao spent six months as a soldier. While he probably had not yet clearly grasped the idea that, as he later put it, "political power grows out of the barrel of a gun," his first brief military experience at least confirmed his boyhood admiration of military leaders and exploits. In primary school days, his heroes had included not only the great warrior-emperors of the Chinese past but Napoleon and George Washington as well.

The spring of 1912 saw the birth of the new Chinese republic and the end of Mao's military service. For a year he drifted from one thing to another, trying, in turn, a police school, law school, and business school; he studied history in a secondary school and then spent some months reading many of the classic works of the Western liberal tradition in the provincial library. This period of groping, rather than indicating any lack of decision in Mao's character, was a reflection of China's situation at the time. The abolition of the official civil service examination system in 1905 and the piecemeal introduction of Western learning in so-called modern schools had left young people in a state of uncertainty as to what type of training, Chinese or Western, could best prepare them for a career or for service to their country.

Mao eventually graduated from the First Provincial Normal School in Changsha in 1918. While officially an institution of secondary level rather than of higher education, the normal school offered a high standard of instruction in Chinese history, literature, and philosophy as well as in Western ideas. While at the school, Mao also acquired his first experience in political activity by helping establish several student organizations. The most important of these was the New People's Study Society, founded in the winter of 1917–18, many of whose members were later to join the Communist Party.

From the normal school in Changsha, Mao went to Peking University, China's leading intellectual centre. The half year he spent there working as a librarian's assistant was of disproportionate importance in shaping his future career, for it was then that he came under the influence of the two men who were to be the principal figures in the foundation of the Chinese Communist Party: Li Dazhao and Chen Duxiu. Moreover, he found himself at Peking University precisely during the months leading up to the May Fourth Movement of 1919, which was to a considerable extent the fountainhead of all the changes that were to take place in China in the ensuing half century.

In a limited sense, May Fourth Movement is the name given to the student demonstrations protesting against the Paris Peace Conference's decision to hand over former German concessions in Shandong province to Japan instead of returning them to China. But the term also evokes a period of rapid political and cultural change, beginning in 1915, that resulted in the Chinese radicals' abandonment of Western liberalism for Marxism-Leninism as the answer to China's problems and the subsequent founding of the Chinese Communist Party in 1921. The shift from the difficult and esoteric classical written language to a far more accessible vehicle of literary expression patterned on colloquial speech also took place during this period. At the same time, a new and very young generation moved to the centre of the political stage. To be sure, the demonstration on May 4 was launched by Chen Duxiu, but the students soon realized that they themselves were the main actors. In an editorial published in July 1919, Mao wrote:

"The world is ours, the nation is ours, society is ours. If we do not speak, who will speak? If we do not act, who will act?"

From then onward, his generation never ceased to regard itself as responsible for the nation's fate, and, indeed, its members remained in power, both in Beijing and in Taipei, until the 1970s.

The Transition to Socialism

The period 1953–57, corresponding to the First Five-Year Plan, was the beginning of China's rapid industrialization, and it is still regarded as having been enormously successful. A strong central governmental apparatus proved able to channel scarce resources into the rapid development of heavy industry. Despite some serious policy issues and problems, the communist leadership seemed to have the overall situation well in hand. Public order improved, and many saw a stronger China taking form. The march to socialism seemed to go along reasonably well with the dictates of industrial development. The determination and fundamental optimism of the communist leaders appeared justified, especially in view of the decades of invasion, disintegration, self-doubt, and humiliation that had been the lot of the Chinese people before 1949.

The First Five-Year Plan was explicitly modeled on Soviet experience, and the Soviet Union provided both material aid and extensive technical advice on its planning and execution. During 1952–54, the Chinese established a central planning apparatus and a set of central ministries and other government institutions that were close copies of their Soviet counterparts. Those actions were officially ratified by the first meeting of the National People's Congress in September 1954, which formally established the Central People's Government and adopted the first constitution of the People's Republic of China. The plan adopted Stalinist economic priorities. In a country where more than four-fifths of the population lived in rural areas, about four-fifths of all government investment was channeled into the urban economy. The vast majority of this investment went to heavy industry, leaving agriculture relatively starved for resources. The plan provided for substantial income differentials to motivate the labour force in the state sector, and it established a "top down" system in which a highly centralized government apparatus exercised detailed control over economic policy through enormous ministries in Beijing. Those developments differed substantially from the priorities and proclivities of the Chinese communist movement in the decades before 1949. Nevertheless, the First Five-Year Plan was linked with the transition of China's rural and urban economy to collective forms.

Political Developments

The socialist transformation of agriculture, industry, and commerce thus went relatively smoothly. Nevertheless, such changes could not take place without considerable tensions. Many peasants streamed into the cities in 1956–57 to escape the new cooperatives and seek employment in the rapidly expanding state-run factories, where government policy kept wages rising rapidly. China's urban population mushroomed from 77 million in 1953 to 99.5 million by 1957.

Several problems also became increasingly pressing. First, CCP leaders found that the agricultural sector was not growing fast enough to provide additional capital for its own development and to feed the workers of the cities. Until then, agricultural policy had attempted to wring large production increases out of changes in organization and land ownership, with little capital investment. By 1956–57, that policy was shown to be inadequate.

Second, Soviet assistance had been made available to China as loans, not grants. After 1956, China had to repay more each year than it borrowed in new funds. Thus, the Chinese could no longer count on Moscow for net capital accumulation in its industrialization drive.

Third, the vastly expanded governmental responsibility for managing the country's urban firms and commerce required far more experts than before. For this, the leadership tried to resolve the increasingly severe strains that had characterized the relationship between the country's intellectuals (including technical specialists) and the CCP.

The leadership's policies up to that point had been ambivalent toward the intelligentsia. On the one hand, it had required their services and prestige; but on the other, it had suspected that many were untrustworthy, coming from urban and bourgeois backgrounds and often having close family and other personal ties with the KMT. After 1949, and particularly during the first part of the Korean War, the Central Committee launched a major campaign to reeducate teachers and scientists and discredit Western-oriented scholarship. In 1951, the emphasis shifted from general campaigns to self-reform. In 1955, it shifted once again to an intensive thought-reform movement, following the purge of Hu Feng, until then the party's leading spokesman on art and literature. This latter movement coincided with the denunciation of a scholarly study of the *Dream of the Red Chamber* (*Hongloumeng*), an eighteenth-century novel of tragic love and declining fortunes in a Chinese family. Literature without a clear class moral received blistering criticism, as did any hint that the party should not command art and literature—a theme identified with the ousted Hu Feng—and "Hu Feng elements" were exposed among intellectuals in schools, factories, and cooperatives.

The intensity of these attacks slackened in early 1956. Party leaders publicly discussed the role of intellectuals in the new tasks of national construction and adopted the line "Let a hundred flowers blossom, a hundred schools of thought contend." Because intellectuals in China included high school graduates as well as those with college or advanced professional training, the policy affected a vast number of people. The "hundred flowers" line explicitly encouraged "free-ranging" discussion and inquiry, with the explicit assumption that this would prove the superiority of Marxism-Leninism and speed the conversion of intellectuals to communism. Their response to the party's invitation for free discussion and criticism was gradual and cautious. Instead of embracing Marxism, moreover, many used the opportunity to translate and discuss Western works and ideas and blithely debated "reactionary" doctrines at the very moment Hungarian intellectuals were triggering a wave of anticommunist sentiment in Budapest.

Following this initial phase of the Hundred Flowers Campaign, Mao Zedong issued what was perhaps his most famous post-1949 speech, "On the Correct Handling of Contradictions Among the People" (Feb. 27, 1957). Its essential message was ambiguous. He stressed the importance of resolving "nonantagonistic contradictions" by methods of persuasion, but he stated that "democratic" methods of resolution would have to be consistent with centralism and discipline. He left it unclear when a contradiction might become an "antagonistic" and no-holds-barred struggle. The final authoritative version of his speech contained explicit limits on the conduct of debate that had been absent in the original. According to that version, the party would judge words and actions to be correct only if they united the populace; were beneficial to socialism; strengthened the state dictatorship; consolidated organizations, especially the party; and generally helped strengthen international communism. In addition, these textual manipulations led to an unresolved controversy concerning the initial intent of Mao's speech.

The leadership's explanation was that Mao had set out to trap the dangerous elements among the intellectuals by encouraging their criticism of the party and government. An alternative view was that the leaders used the metaphor of the trap to rationalize their reaction to the unanticipated criticism, popular demonstrations, and general antiparty sentiments expressed in the late spring, when the term *hundred flowers* gained international currency. Whatever the correct explanation for these significant textual changes, the communist leaders had encouraged free criticism of the party and its programs, and they had then turned on their critics as rightists and counterrevolutionaries. In June, noncommunists who had thrown caution to the wind reaped the full fury of retaliation in an anti-rightist campaign. The intellectuals who had responded to Mao's call for open criticism were the first victims, but the movement quickly spread beyond that group to engulf many specialists in the government bureaucracy and state-run firms. By the fall, the fury of the campaign began to turn toward the countryside, and those—especially among the rural cadres who had remained unenthusiastic about the "high tide" of agricultural change—came under fire and were removed. The spreading anti-rightist campaign then inspired fear in those who wanted a slower, more pragmatic approach to development and shifted the initiative to others who, like Mao, believed that the solutions to China's core problems lay in a major break with the incrementalist Soviet strategy and in a bold new set of distinctly Chinese ideas.

International events dovetailed with that basic thrust by the winter of 1957–58.

New Directions in National Policy, 1958–61

The pressures behind the dramatic inauguration in 1958 of "Three Red Banners"—i.e., the general line of socialist construction, the Great Leap Forward, and the rural people's communes—are still not fully known. Undoubtedly, a complex mixture of forces came into play. Mao personally felt increasingly uncomfortable with the alliance with the Soviet Union and with the social and political ramifications of the Soviet model of development. On ideological grounds, and because it shifted policy away from his personal political strengths, Mao disliked the Soviet system of centralized control by large government ministries, substantial social stratification, and strong urban bias. In addition, the Soviet model assumed that agricultural surplus need only be captured by the government and made to serve urban development. This was true for the Soviet Union in the late 1920s, when the model was developed, but the situation in China was different. Chinese policy had to devise a way first to create an agricultural surplus and then take a large part of it to serve urban growth. The Soviet model also rested on implicit assumptions about the energy and transportation sectors that were not compatible with the Chinese realities of the 1950s.

The general line of socialist construction and the Great Leap Forward were announced at the second session of the Eighth Party Congress (May 1958), which concentrated as much on political slogans as on specific objectives. Special emphasis was placed on political guidance by party cadres of the country's scientists and technicians, who were viewed as potentially dangerous unless they would become fully "Red and expert." The progressive indoctrination of experts would be paralleled by introductory technical training for cadres, thereby in theory transforming the entire elite into political-technical generalists. The Congress of 1958 called for a bold form of ideological leadership that could unleash a "leap forward" in technical innovation and economic output. To link the new generalist leaders and the masses, emphasis fell on sending cadres to the lower levels (*xiafang*) for firsthand experience and manual labour and for practical political indoctrination.

The Great Leap Forward involved an enormous amount of experimentation. It had no detailed blueprint, but there were some underlying strategic principles. There was a general reliance on a combination of ideological and organizational techniques to overcome seemingly insuperable obstacles that was focused on the countryside and that drew from policies of the 1930s and '40s. The basic idea was to convert the massive labour surplus in China's hinterlands into a huge production force through a radical reorganization of rural production. The search for the best organizational form to achieve this result led in August 1958 to popularization of the "people's commune," a huge rural unit that pooled the labour of tens of thousands of peasants from different villages in order to increase agricultural production, engage in local industrial production, enhance the availability of rural schooling, and organize a local militia force in accordance with Mao's preferred national military strategy of combining the deterrence of an atomic bomb with guerrilla warfare.

Mao believed that through these radical organizational changes, combined with adequate political mobilization techniques, the Chinese countryside could be made to provide the resources both for its own development and for the continuing rapid development of the heavy industrial sector in the cities. Through this strategy of "walking on two legs," China could obtain the simultaneous development of industry and agriculture and, within the urban sector, of both large- and small-scale industry. If it worked, this would resolve the dilemma of an agricultural bottleneck that had seemed to loom large on the horizon as of 1957. It would, however, involve a major departure from the Soviet model, which would predictably lead to increased tensions between Beijing and Moscow.

Readjustment and Reaction, 1961–65

Mao was in fact deeply troubled as he contemplated China's situation during 1961–65. He perceived the Soviet socialist revolution in the years after Stalin's death in 1953 to have degenerated into "social imperialism." Mao evidently had been shocked by these developments in the Soviet Union, and the revelation made him look at events in China from a new vantage point. Mao became convinced that China, too, was headed down the road toward revisionism. He used class struggle and ideological campaigns, as well as concrete policies in various areas, to try to prevent and reverse this slide into revolutionary purgatory. Mao's nightmare about revisionism played an increasing role in structuring politics in the mid-1960s.

Mao was not the only leader who harboured doubts about the trends in the recovery effort of 1961–65. Others gathered around him and tried to use their closeness to Mao as a vehicle for enhancing their political power. The key individuals involved were Mao's political assistant of many years, Chen Boda, who was an expert in the realm of ideology; Mao's wife, Jiang Qing, who had strong policy views in the cultural sphere; Kang Sheng, whose strength lay both in his understanding of Soviet ideology and in his mastery of Soviet-style secret police techniques; and Lin Biao, who headed the military and tried to make it an ideal type of Maoist organization that combined effectiveness with ideological purity. Each of these people in turn had personal networks and resources to bring to a coalition. While their goals and interests did not entirely coincide, they all could unite on two efforts: enhancing Mao's power and upsetting Mao's relations with Liu Shaoqi (then the likely successor to Mao), Deng Xiaoping, and most of the remainder of the party leadership.

Mao took a number of initiatives in domestic and foreign policy during the period. At a major Central Committee plenum in September 1962, he insisted that "class struggle" remain high on the Chinese agenda, even as enormous efforts continued to be made to revive the economy. He also called for a campaign of "socialist education," aimed primarily at reviving the demoralized party apparatus in the countryside. By 1964, he began to press hard to make the Chinese educational system less elitist by organizing "part-work, part-study" schools that would provide more vocational training. Throughout this period, foreign observers noted what appeared to be some tension between a continuing thread of radicalism in China's propaganda and a strong pragmatic streak in the country's actual domestic policies.

The most important set of measures Mao took concerned the People's Liberation Army (PLA), which he and Lin Biao tried to make into a model organization. Events on the Sino-Indian border in the fall of 1962 helped the PLA reestablish discipline and its image. From 1959 to 1962, both India and China, initially as a by-product of the uprising in Tibet, resorted to military force along their disputed border. On Oct. 12, 1962, a week before the Chinese moved troops into disputed border territories, Indian Prime Minister Jawaharlal Nehru stated that the army was to free all Indian territory of "Chinese intruders." In the conflict that followed,

Beijing's regiments defeated Indian forces in the border region, penetrating well beyond it. The Chinese then withdrew from most of the invaded area and established a demilitarized zone on either side of the line of control. Most significantly, the leadership seized on the army's victory and began to experiment with the possibility of using army heroes as the ideal types for popular emulation.

Increasingly preoccupied with indoctrinating its heirs and harking back to revolutionary days, Beijing's leaders closest in outlook to Mao Zedong and Lin Biao viewed the soldier-communist as the most suitable candidate for the second- and third-generation leadership. Army uniformity and discipline, it was seen, could transcend the divided classes, and all army men could be made to comply with the rigorous political standards set by Mao's leadership.

In the summer of 1964, Mao wrote a document titled "On Khrushchev's Phony Communism and Its Historical Lessons for the World," which summarized most of Mao's doctrinal principles on contradiction, class struggle, and political structure and operation. This summary provided the basis for the reeducation ("revolutionization") of all youth hoping to succeed to the revolutionary cause. This high tide of revolutionization lasted until early August, when U.S. air strikes on North Vietnam raised the spectre of war on China's southern border. A yearlong debate followed on the wisdom of conducting disruptive political campaigns during times of external threat.

This period of time has come to be interpreted as one of major decision within China. One ingredient of the debate was whether to prepare rapidly for conventional war against the United States or continue the revolutionization of Chinese society, which in Mao's view had fundamental, long-term importance for China's security. Those who argued for a postponement of the internal political struggle supported more conventional strategies for economic development and took seriously Soviet calls for "united action" in Vietnam and the establishment of closer Sino-Soviet ties. Their position, it was later alleged, received the backing of the general staff. With the dispatch of about fifty thousand logistic personnel to Vietnam after February 1965, factional lines began to divide the military forces according to ideological or national security preferences.

Meanwhile, some members tried to restore rigid domestic controls. Where Mao in May 1963 had called for an upsurge in revolutionary struggle, by the following September other leaders were circumscribing the area of cadre initiative and permitting a free-market system and private ownership of rural plots to flourish. A stifling of the revolutionary upsurge was supposedly evident in regulations of June 1964 for the organization of poor and lower-middle-peasant associations, and by early 1965, Mao could point to bureaucratic tendencies throughout the rural areas. In a famous document on problems arising in the course of the socialist education campaign, usually referred to as the "Twenty-Three Articles," Mao in January 1965 stated for the first time that the principal enemy was to be found within the party, and he once more proclaimed the urgency of class struggle and mass-line politics.

It was in that period of emphasis on self-reliant struggle that China acquired nuclear weapons. Although the Soviet Union supported Chinese nuclear aims for a time, that effort was taken over completely by the Chinese after June 1959. By 1964, the costs of the program had forced a substantial reduction in other defense costs. China's first atomic explosion (Oct. 16, 1964) affected the debate by appearing to support Mao's contention that domestic revolutionization would in no way jeopardize long-term power aspirations and defense capabilities.

Mao's military thinking, a product of his own civil war experiences and an essential component of his ideology, stressed the importance of military strength through sheer numbers ("people's war") during the transition to nuclear status. He felt that preparation for such a war could turn China's weaknesses into military assets and reduce its vulnerability. Mao's view of people's war belittled the might of modern advanced weapons as "paper tigers" but recognized that China's strategic inferiority subjected it to dangers largely beyond its control. His reasoning thus made a virtue out of necessity in the short run, when China would have to depend on its superior numbers and the morale of its people to defeat any invader. In the long run, however, he held that China would have to have nuclear weapons to deprive the superpowers of their blackmail potential and deter their aggression against smaller states.

Lin Biao repeated Mao's position on people's war, further arguing that popular insurrections against noncommunist governments could succeed only if they took place without substantial foreign assistance. To the extent that indigenous rebels came to depend on outside support, inevitably their bonds with the local populace would be weakened. When this happened, the rebellion would wither for lack of support. On the other hand, the hardships imposed by relying on indigenous resources would stimulate the comradeship and ingenuity of the insurgents. Equally important, Lin's statement also indicated a high-level decision for China to remain on the defensive.

Lin's speech coincided with yet another secret working conference of the Central Committee, in which the Maoist group reissued its call for cultural revolutionization, this time convinced that the effort of 1964 had been deliberately sabotaged by senior party and military officials. Initiated by Mao Zedong and Lin Biao, the purge first struck dissident army leaders, especially the chief of staff; as the power struggle began, China turned its back on the war in Vietnam and other external affairs. The September meeting may be taken as a clear harbinger of what came to be known as the "Great Proletarian Cultural Revolution."

The Cultural Revolution, 1966–76

As the clash over issues in the autumn of 1965 became polarized, the army initially provided the battleground. The issues concerned differences over policy directions and their implications for the organization of power and the qualifications of senior officials to lead. Much of the struggle went on behind the scenes; in public, it took the form of personal vilification and ritualized exposés of divergent worldviews or, inevitably, "two lines" of policy. Lin Biao, in calling for the creative study and application of Mao's thought in November and at a meeting of military commissars the following January, consistently placed the army's mission in the context of the national ideological and power struggle. In these critical months, the base of operations for Mao and Lin was the large eastern Chinese city of Shanghai, and newspapers published in that city, especially the *Liberation Army Daily*, carried the public attacks on the targets selected.

During 1967, Mao called on the PLA under Lin Biao to step in on behalf of the Maoist Red Guards, but this politico-military task produced more division within the military than unified support for radical youths. Tensions surfaced in the summer, when Chen Zaidao, a military commander in the key city of Wuhan, arrested two key radical CCP leaders. Faced with possible widespread revolt among local military commanders, Mao tilted toward reestablishing some order.

In 1968, Mao decided to rebuild the CCP and bring things under greater control. The military dispatched officers and soldiers to take over schools, factories, and government agencies. The army simultaneously forced millions of urban Red Guards to move to the hinterlands to live, thereby removing the most disruptive force from the cities. These drastic measures reflected Mao's disillusionment with the Red Guards' inability to overcome factional differences. The Soviet invasion of Czechoslovakia in August 1968, which greatly heightened China's fears for its security, gave these measures added urgency.

China After the Death of Mao

Perhaps never before in human history had a political leader unleashed such massive forces against the system that he had created. The resulting damage to that system was profound,

Fireworks go off over the National Stadium during the opening ceremony for the Olympic Games in Beijing, August 8, 2008. © AP Images

and the goals that Mao Zedong sought to achieve ultimately remained elusive. The agenda he left behind for his successors was extraordinarily challenging.

International Relations

The collapse of communism in Eastern Europe beginning in mid-1989 and the subsequent disintegration of the Soviet Union deeply disturbed China's leaders. While hardliners used these developments to warn about the dangers of reform, Deng Xiaoping and Jiang Zemin were able to minimize such backsliding and move China closer to becoming a major world power. The country's admission into the World Trade Organization in 2001 was considered a significant step in its further integration into the global economy. Added to that was the international prestige that accompanied Beijing's selection to host the 2008 Summer Olympic Games. The Games, which included events held in six other Chinese cities, were generally considered a great success. Two years later, the country staged the highly successful Expo 2010 Shanghai China world exposition, which showcased what was by then one of the world's largest and most technologically advanced metropolises.

CHAPTER 6

COMMUNISM IN SOUTHEAST ASIA

Southeast Asia moved from colonialism by the West to colonialism at the hands of the Japanese during the Pacific War. Following the war, Southeast Asia was finally in a position to rule its own countries, though it struggled to find footing as they all decolonized rapidly. As independent states, they formed systems based on the Western capitalist model.

Patterns of a Colonial Age

Except in Java and much of the Philippines, Southeast Asia was mainly under Western colonial rule for the nineteenth and the beginning of the twentieth centuries. The arrival of the Japanese armed forces in Southeast Asia in 1941-42 did not, however, occasion independence. A few leaders perhaps had been naive enough to think that it might—and some others clearly admired the Japanese and found it acceptable to work with them. But on the whole, the attitude of intellectuals was one of caution and, very quickly, realization that they were now confronted with another, perhaps more formidable and ferocious, version of colonial rule. The Japanese had no plans to radicalize or in any way destabilize Southeast Asia, which, after all, was slated to become part of a Tokyo-centred Greater East Asia Co-prosperity Sphere. In the short term, they sought to win the war, and in the long run they hoped to modernize the region on a Japanese model. Continuity served these purposes best, and in Indochina, the Japanese even allowed the French to continue to rule in return for their cooperation. Little wonder that, before long, Southeast Asians began to observe that despite "Asia for the Asians" propaganda, the new and old colonial rulers had more in common with each other than either had with the indigenous peoples.

Still, for two distinct reasons the period does represent a break from the past. First, the Japanese attempted to mobilize indigenous populations to support the war effort and encourage modern, cooperative behaviour on a mass scale; such a thing had never been attempted by Western colonial governments. Virtually all of the mobilization efforts, however, were based on Japanese models, and the new rulers were frustrated to discover that Southeast Asians did not behave in the same fashion as Japanese. Frequently the result was disorder, corruption, and, by the end of the war, a seething hatred of the Japanese. It was also the case that, both because the war was going against them and because the response to other approaches was unenthusiastic, the Japanese were compelled before long to utilize local nationalism in their mobilization campaigns, again something quite impossible under European rule. The consequences were to benefit local rather then Japanese causes and, ironically, contribute handsomely to the building of anti-Japanese sentiment.

A second difference between Western and Japanese colonialism was in the opportunities the occupation provided the new educated elite. The Japanese were wary of these people because of their Western orientation but also favoured them because they represented the most modern element in indigenous society, the best partner for the present, and the best hope for the future. Often dismissed as "pseudo-intellectuals" by the Western colonial governments and prevented from obtaining any real stake in the state, the new intellectuals under the Japanese were accorded positions of real (though not unlimited or unsupervised) authority. Nor could Southeast Asians who found themselves in these positions easily fault the policies that they now accepted responsibility for carrying out or at least supporting, since many of these policies were in fact—if not always in spirit—similar to ones they had endorsed in earlier decades. In short, the Western-educated elite emerged from the Japanese occupation stronger in various ways than they had ever been. By August 1945, they stood poised to inherit (or, given the variety of political conditions at the end of the war, to struggle among themselves over inheriting) the mantle of leadership over their own countries.

Southeast Asia was changed in an evolutionary, rather than revolutionary, way by the Japanese occupation. Although returning Europeans and even some Southeast Asians themselves complained that Japanese fascism had deeply influenced the region's societies, there is not much evidence that this was the case. Japanese rule, indeed, had destroyed whatever remained of the mystique of Western supremacy, but the war also had ruined any chances that it might be replaced with a Japanese mystique. There was clearly little clinging to Japanese concepts except where they could be thoroughly indigenized. Even the collaboration issue, so important to Europeans and their thinking about the immediate postwar era, failed to move Southeast Asians for long. And, if the general population appeared less docile in 1945 than four years earlier, the reason lay more in the temporary removal of authority at the war's end than in the tutelage of the Japanese.

Struggle for Independence

The swift conclusion of the war in the Pacific made it impossible for the former colonial masters to return to Southeast Asia for several weeks, in some areas for months. During the interim, the Japanese were obliged by the Allies to keep the peace, but real power passed into the hands of Southeast Asian leaders, some of whom declared independence and attempted with varying degrees of success to establish government struc- tures. For the first time since the establishment of colonial rule, firearms in large numbers were controlled by Southeast Asians. Such was the groundwork for the establishment of new, independent states.

Prewar nationalism had been most highly developed in Vietnam and Indonesia, and the colonial powers there were least inclined to see the new realities created by the war, perhaps because of the large numbers of resident French and Dutch and because of extensive investments. The result in both countries was an armed struggle in which the Western power was eventually defeated and independence secured. The Indonesian revolution, for all its internal complexities, was won in little more than four years with a combination of military struggle and civilian diplomacy. The revolution of the Vietnamese, who had defeated the French by 1954, continued much longer because of an internal political struggle and because of the role that Vietnam came to play in global geopolitics, which ultimately led to the involvement of other external powers, among them the United States. In both cases, however, independence was sealed in blood, and a mythologized revolution came to serve as a powerful, unifying nationalist symbol. In the rest of Southeast Asia, the achievement of independence was, if not entirely peaceful, at least less violent. Malaysia and the Philippines suffered "emergencies" (as armed insurgencies were euphemistically called), and Burma, too, endured sporadic internal military conflict. For better or worse, these conflicts were no substitutes for a genuine revolutionary experience.

Whether by revolution or otherwise, decolonization proceeded rapidly in Southeast Asia. The newly independent

An Indonesian army drill during the 1960s, when hostilities over Malaysia were at a peak. Three Lions/Hulton Archive/Getty Images

states all aspired toward democratic systems more or less on the Western model, despite the lack of democratic preparation and the impress of nationalist sentiment. None expressed a desire to return to precolonial forms of government, and, although some Western observers professed to see in such leaders as Indonesia's Sukarno Southeast Asian societies returning to traditional behaviour, their judgment was based more on ephemeral signs than on real evidence. For one thing, societies as a whole had been too much altered in the late nineteenth and early twentieth centuries to make it clear what "tradition" really was. For another, the new leadership retained the commitment to modernization that it had developed earlier. They looked forward to a new world, not an old one. The difficulty, however, was that there was as yet little consensus on the precise shape this new world should take, and colonial rule had left indigenous societies with virtually no experience in debating and reaching firm decisions on such important matters. It is hardly surprising that one result of this lack of experience was a great deal of political and intellectual conflict. Often forgotten, however, is another result: an outpouring of new ideas and creativity, particularly in literature. This signaled the beginning of a kind of cultural renaissance, the dimensions and significance of which are still insufficiently understood.

Defining New States and Societies

The first two decades of independence constituted a period of trial and error for states and societies attempting to re-define themselves in contemporary form. During this time, religious and ethnic challenges to the states essentially failed to split them, and (except in the states of former Indochina) both communism and Western parliamentary democracy were rejected. Indonesia, the largest and potentially most powerful nation in the region, provided the most spectacular examples of such developments, ending in the tragic events of 1965–66, when between five hundred thousand and one million lives may have been lost in a conflict between the Indonesian Communist Party and its opponents. Even Malaysia, long the darling of Western observers for its apparent success as a showcase of democracy and capitalist growth, was badly shaken by violence between Malays and Chinese in 1969. The turmoil often led Southeast Asia to be viewed as inherently unstable politically, but from a longer perspective—and taking into account both the region's great diversity and the arbitrary fashion in which boundaries had been set by colonial powers—this perhaps has been a shortsighted conclusion.

The new era that began in the mid-1960s had three main characteristics. First, the military rose as a force in government, not only in Vietnam, Burma, and Indonesia, but also in the Philippines and—quietly—in Malaysia. The military establishments viewed themselves as actual or potential saviours of national unity and as disciplined, effective champions of modernization; at least initially, they frequently had considerable support from the populace. Second, during this period renewed attention was given by all Southeast Asian nations to the question of unifying (secular and national) values and ideology. Thailand, Indonesia, and Vietnam had been first in this area in the 1940s and '50s, but the others followed. Even Singapore and Brunei developed ideologies, with the express purpose of defining a national character for their people. Finally, virtually all Southeast Asian states abandoned the effort of utilizing foreign models of government and society—capitalist or communist—and turned to the task of working out a synthesis better suited to their needs and values. Each country arrived at its own solution, with varying degrees of success. By the 1980s, what generally had emerged were quasi-military bourgeois regimes willing to live along modified democratic lines—i.e., with what in Western eyes appeared to be comparatively high levels of restriction of personal, political, and intellectual freedom. Whatever their precise political character, these were conservative governments. Even Vietnam, the most revolutionary-minded among them, could not stomach the far-reaching and murderous revolution of the Khmer Rouge in Cambodia in the mid-1970s and by the end of the decade had moved to crush it.

Tempting as it may be to conclude that greater doses of authoritarian rule (some of it seemingly harking back directly to colonial times) merely stabilized Southeast Asia and permitted the region to get on with the business of economic development, this approach was not successful everywhere. In Burma (called Myanmar since 1989), the military's semi-isolationist, crypto-socialist development schemes came to disaster in the 1980s, revealing the repressive nature of the regime and bringing the country to the brink of civil war by the end of the decade. In the Philippines, the assault by President Ferdinand Marcos and his associates on the old ruling elite class brought a similar result, in addition to a spectacular level of corruption and the looting of the national treasury. In Vietnam, where the final achievement of independence in 1975 brought bitter disappointment to many and left the country decades behind the rest of the region in economic development, public and internal Communist Party unrest forced an aging generation of leaders to resign and left the course for the future in doubt as never before.

The states generally thought to be most successful to date—Thailand, Indonesia, Malaysia, and especially Singapore—have followed policies generally regarded as moderate and pragmatic. All are regarded as fundamentally stable and for that reason have attracted foreign aid and investment; all have achieved high rates of growth since the mid-1970s and enjoy the highest standards of living in the region. Their very success, however, has created unexpected social and cultural changes. Prosperity, education, and increasing access to world media and popular culture have all given rise, for example, to various degrees of dissatisfaction with government-imposed limitations on freedom and to social and environmental criticism.

Particularly in Indonesia and Malaysia, there has been a noticeable trend toward introspection and discussion of national character, as well as a religious revival in the form of renewed interest in Islam. It appears that the comparatively small and unified middle class, including a generally bureaucratized military, is becoming larger, more complex, and less easily satisfied. That was undoubtedly not the intent of those who framed governmental policy, but it is a reality with which they must deal.

Reappearance of Regional Interests

After the end of the seventeenth century, the long-developed polities of Southeast Asia were pulled into a Western-dominated world economy, weakening regional trade networks and strengthening ties with distant colonial powers. In the early years of independence, these ties often remained strong enough to be called neocolonial by critics, but after the mid-1960s, these partnerships could no longer be controlled by former colonial masters, and the new Southeast Asian states sought to industrialize and diversify their markets. On the one hand, this meant a far greater role for Japan in Southeast Asia; that country is by far the most important trading partner of most Southeast Asian nations. On the other hand, it meant that many countries began to rediscover commonalities and examine possibilities within the region for support and markets.

Movements of National Liberation in Vietnam

The anticolonial movement in Vietnam can be said to have started with the establishment of French rule. Many local officials of Cochinchina refused to collaborate with the

French. Some led guerrilla groups, composed of the remnants of the defeated armies, in attacks on French outposts. A much broader resistance movement developed in Annam in 1885, led by the great scholar Phan Dinh Phung, whose rebellion collapsed only after his death in 1895.

The main characteristic of the national movement during this first phase of resistance, however, was its political orientation toward the past. Filled with ideas of precolonial Vietnam, its leaders wanted to be rid of the French in order to reestablish the old imperial order. Because this aspiration had little meaning for the generation that came to maturity after 1900, this first stage of anticolonial resistance did not survive the death of its leader.

Modern Nationalism

A new national movement arose in the early twentieth century. Its most prominent spokesman was Phan Boi Chau, with whose rise the old traditionalist opposition gave way to a modern nationalist leadership that rejected French rule but not Western ideas, science, and technology. In 1905, Chau went to Japan. His plan, mildly encouraged by some Japanese statesmen, was to free Vietnam with Japanese help. Chau smuggled hundreds of young Vietnamese into Japan, where they studied the sciences and underwent training for clandestine organization, political propaganda, and terrorist action. Inspired by Chau's writings, nationalist intellectuals in Hanoi opened the Free School of Tonkin in 1907, which soon became a centre of anti-French agitation and consequently was suppressed after a few months. Also, under the inspiration and guidance of Chau's followers, mass demonstrations demanding a reduction of high taxes took place in many cities in 1908. Hundreds of demonstrators and suspected organizers were arrested—some were condemned to death, while others were sent to Con Son

(Poulo Condore) Island in the South China Sea, which the French turned into a penal camp for Vietnamese nationalists.

Phan Boi Chau went to China in 1910, where a revolution had broken out against the Qing (Manchu) Dynasty. There, he set up a republican government-in-exile to attract the support of nationalist groups. After the French arranged his arrest and imprisonment in China (1914–17), however, his movement began to decline. In 1925, Chau was seized by French agents in Shanghai and brought back to Vietnam for trial; he died under house arrest in 1940.

After World War I, the movement for national liberation intensified. A number of prominent intellectuals sought to achieve reforms by obtaining political concessions from the colonial regime through collaboration with the French. The failure of such reformist efforts led to a revival of clandestine and revolutionary groups, especially in Annam and Tonkin. Among these was the Vietnamese Nationalist Party (Viet Nam Quoc Dan Dang, founded in 1927 and usually referred to as the VNQDD). The VNQDD preached terrorist action and penetrated the garrisons of indigenous troops with a plan to oust the French in a military uprising. On the night of Feb. 9–10, 1930, the troops of one garrison in Tonkin killed their French officers, but they were overwhelmed a day later and summarily executed. A wave of repression followed that took hundreds of lives and sent thousands to prison camps. The VNQDD was virtually destroyed, and for the next fifteen years, it existed mainly as a group of exiles in China supported by the Chinese Nationalist Party (Kuomintang).

Vietnamese Communism

The year 1930 was important in the history of Vietnam for yet another reason. Five years earlier, a new figure, destined to become the most prominent leader in the national movement, had appeared on the scene as an expatriate revolutionary in South China. He was Nguyen Ai Quoc, better known by his later pseudonym of Ho Chi Minh. In June 1925, Ho Chi Minh had founded the Revolutionary Youth League of Vietnam, the predecessor of the Indochinese Communist Party.

Ho Chi Minh had left Vietnam as a young seaman in 1911 and traveled widely before settling in Paris in 1917. He joined the Communist Party of France in 1920 and later spent several years in Moscow and China in the service of the international communist movement. After making his Revolutionary Youth League the most influential of all clandestine resistance groups, he succeeded in early 1930 in forming the Vietnamese Communist Party—from late 1930 called the Indochinese Communist Party—from a number of competing communist organizations. In May of that year, the communists exploited conditions of near starvation over large areas of central Vietnam by staging a broad peasant uprising, during which numerous Vietnamese officials and many landlords were killed, and "Soviet" administrations were set up in several provinces of Annam. It took the French until the spring of 1931 to suppress this movement and, in an unparalleled wave of terror, to reestablish control.

Unlike the dispersed and disoriented leadership of the VNQDD and some smaller nationalist groups, the Indochinese Communist Party recovered quickly from the setback of 1931, relying on cadres trained in the Soviet Union and China. After 1936, when the French extended some political freedoms to the colonies, the party skillfully exploited all opportunities for the creation of legal front organizations, through which it extended its influence among intellectuals, workers, and peasants. When political freedoms were again curtailed at the outbreak of World War II, the Communist

Party, now a well-disciplined organization, was forced back into hiding.

World War II and Independence

For five years during World War II, Indochina was a French-administered possession of Japan. On Sept. 22, 1940, Jean Decoux, the French governor-general appointed by the Vichy government after the fall of France to the Nazis, concluded an agreement with the Japanese that permitted the stationing of thirty thousand Japanese troops in Indochina and the use of all major Vietnamese airports by the Japanese military. The agreement made Indochina the most important staging area for all Japanese military operations in Southeast Asia. The French administration cooperated with the Japanese occupation forces and was ousted only toward the end of the war (in March 1945), when the Japanese began to fear that the French forces might turn against them as defeat approached. After the French had been disarmed, Bao Dai, the last French-appointed emperor of Vietnam, was allowed to proclaim the independence of his country and appoint a Vietnamese national government at Hue. However, all real power remained in the hands of the Japanese military commanders.

Meanwhile, in May 1941, at Ho Chi Minh's urging, the Communist Party formed a broad nationalist alliance under its leadership called the League for the Independence of Vietnam, which subsequently became known as the Viet Minh. Ho, returning to China to seek assistance, was arrested and imprisoned there by the Nationalist government. After his release, he returned to Vietnam and began to cooperate with Allied forces by providing information on Japanese troop movements in Indochina. At the same time, he sought recognition of the Viet Minh as the legitimate representative of Vietnamese nationalist aspirations. When the Japanese surrendered in August 1945,

Ho Chi Minh

The son of a poor country scholar, Nguyen Sinh Huy, Ho Chi Minh was brought up in the village of Kim Lien. He had a wretched childhood, but between the ages of fourteen and eighteen, he was able to study at a grammar school in Hue. He is next known to have been a schoolmaster in Phan Thiet and then was apprenticed at a technical institute in Saigon.

In 1911, under the name of Ba, he found work as a cook on a French steamer. He was a seaman for more than three years, visiting various African ports and the American cities of Boston and New York. After living in London from 1915 to 1917, he moved to France, where he worked, in turn, as a gardener, sweeper, waiter, photo retoucher, and oven stoker.

During the six years that he spent in France (1917–23), he became an active socialist, under the name Nguyen Ai Quoc ("Nguyen the Patriot"). He organized a group of Vietnamese living there and in 1919 addressed an eight-point petition to the representatives of the great powers at the Versailles Peace Conference that concluded World War I. In the petition, Ho demanded that the French colonial power grant its subjects in Indochina equal rights with the rulers. This act brought no response from the peacemakers, but it made him a hero to many politically conscious Vietnamese. The following year, inspired by the success of the communist revolution in Russia and Vladimir Lenin's anti-imperialist doctrine, Ho joined the French Communists when they withdrew from the Socialist Party in December 1920.

After his years of militant activity in France, where he became acquainted with most of the French working-class leaders, Ho went to Moscow at the end of 1923. In January 1924, following the death of Lenin, he published a moving farewell to the founder of the Soviet Union in *Pravda*. Six months later, from June 17 to July 8, he took an active part in the 5th Congress of the Communist International, during which he criticized the French Communist Party for not opposing colonialism more vigorously. His statement to the congress is noteworthy because it contains the first formulation of his belief in the importance of the revolutionary role of oppressed peasants (as opposed to industrial workers).

In December 1924, under the assumed name of Ly Thuy, Ho went to Canton, a communist stronghold, where he recruited the first cadres of the Vietnamese nationalist movement, organizing them into the Vietnam Thanh Nien Cach Menh Dong Chi Hoi ("Vietnamese Revolutionary Youth Association"), which became famous under the name Thanh Nien. Almost all of its members had been exiled from Indochina because of their political beliefs and had gathered together in order to participate in the struggle against French rule over their country. Thus, Canton became the first home of Indochinese nationalism.

When Chiang Kai-shek, then commander of the Chinese army, expelled the Chinese communists from Canton in April 1927, Ho again sought refuge in the Soviet Union. In 1928, he went to Brussels and Paris and then to Siam (now Thailand), where he spent two years as a representative of the Communist International, the world organization of communist parties, in Southeast Asia. His followers, however, remained in South China.

Among twentieth-century revolutionaries, Ho waged the longest and most costly battle against the colonial system of the great powers. One of its effects was to cause a grave crisis in the national life of the mightiest of capitalist countries, the United States. As a Marxist, Ho stands with the Yugoslav leader Tito as one of the progenitors of the "national communism" that developed in the 1960s and (at least partially) with communist China's Mao Zedong in emphasizing the role of the peasantry in the revolutionary struggle.

the communist-led Viet Minh ordered a general uprising, and, with no one organized to oppose them, they were able to seize power in Hanoi. Bao Dai, the Vietnamese emperor, abdicated a few days later and declared his fealty to the newly proclaimed Democratic Republic of Vietnam.

The Communist Party had clearly gained the upper hand in its struggle to outmaneuver its disorganized rivals, such as the noncommunist VNQDD. The French, however, were determined to restore their colonial presence in Indochina and, with the aid of British occupation forces, seized control of Cochinchina. Thus, at the beginning of 1946, there were two Vietnams: a communist north and a noncommunist south.

The First Indochina War

Negotiations between the French and Ho Chi Minh led to an agreement in March 1946 that appeared to promise a peaceful solution. Under the agreement, France would recognize the Viet Minh government and give Vietnam the status of a free state within the French Union. French troops were to remain in Vietnam, but they would be withdrawn progressively over five years. For a period in early 1946, the French cooperated with Ho Chi Minh as he consolidated the Viet Minh's dominance over other nationalist groups, in particular those politicians who were backed by the Chinese Nationalist Party.

Despite tactical cooperation between the French and the Viet Minh, their policies were irreconcilable: the French aimed to reestablish colonial rule, while Hanoi wanted total independence. French intentions were revealed in the decision of Georges-Thierry d'Argenlieu, the high commissioner for Indochina, to proclaim Cochinchina an autonomous republic in June 1946. Further negotiations did not resolve the basic differences between the French and the Viet Minh. In late November 1946, French naval vessels bombarded Haiphong, causing several thousand civilian casualties. The subsequent Viet Minh attempt to overwhelm French troops in Hanoi in December is generally considered to be the beginning of the First Indochina War.

Ho Chi Minh sits in command at the Battle of Dien Bien Phu in Vietnam, May 1954. Collection Jean-Claude LABBE/Gamma-Rapho/Getty Images

Initially confident of victory, the French long ignored the real political cause of the war—the desire of the Vietnamese people, including their anticommunist leaders, to achieve unity and independence for their country. French efforts to deal with those issues were devious and ineffective. The French reunited Cochinchina with the rest of Vietnam in 1949, proclaiming the Associated State of Vietnam, and appointed the former emperor Bao Dai as chief of state. Most nationalists, however, denounced these maneuvers, and leadership in the struggle for independence from the French remained with the Viet Minh.

Meanwhile, the Viet Minh waged an increasingly successful guerrilla war, aided after 1949 by the new communist government of China. The United States, fearful of the spread of communism in Asia, sent large amounts of aid to the French. The French, however, were shaken by the fall of their garrison at Dien Bien Phu in May 1954 and agreed to negotiate an end to the war at an international conference in Geneva.

The Two Vietnams (1954–65)

The agreements concluded in Geneva between April and July 1954 (collectively called the Geneva Accords) were signed by French and Viet Minh representatives and provided for a cease-fire and temporary division of the country into two military zones at latitude 17 °N (popularly called the 17th parallel). All Viet Minh forces were to withdraw north of that line, and all French and Associated State of Vietnam troops were to remain south of it. Permission was granted for refugees to move from one zone to the other during a limited time period. An international commission was established, composed of Canadian, Polish, and Indian members under an Indian chairman, to supervise the execution of the agreement.

Following the signing of the Geneva Accords, Viet Minh soldiers have a victory parade through the streets of Hanoi, Vietnam, Oct. 9, 1954. © AP Images

This agreement left the Democratic Republic of Vietnam (henceforth called North Vietnam) in control of only the northern half of the country. The last of the Geneva Accords—called the Final Declaration—provided for elections, supervised by the commission, to be held throughout Vietnam in July 1956 in order to unify the country. Viet Minh leaders appeared certain to win these elections, and the United States and the leaders in the south would not approve or sign the Final Declaration; elections were never held.

In the midst of a mass migration of nearly one million people from the north to the south, the two Vietnams began to reconstruct their war-ravaged land. With assistance from the Soviet Union and China, the Hanoi government in the north embarked on an ambitious program of socialist industrialization; it also began to collectivize agriculture in earnest in 1958. In the south, a new government appointed by Bao Dai began to build a new country. Ngo Dinh Diem, a Roman Catholic, was named prime minister and succeeded with American support in stabilizing the anticommunist regime in Saigon. He eliminated pro-French elements in the military and abolished the local autonomy of several religious-political groups. Then, in a government-controlled referendum in October 1955, Diem removed Bao Dai as chief of state and made himself president of the Republic of Vietnam (South Vietnam).

Diem's early success in consolidating power did not result in concrete political and economic achievements. Plans for land reform were sabotaged by entrenched interests. With the financial backing of the United States, the regime's chief energies were directed toward building up the military and a variety of intelligence and security forces to counter the still-influential Viet Minh. Totalitarian methods were directed against all who were regarded as opponents, and the favouritism shown to Roman Catholics alienated the majority Buddhist population. Loyalty to the president and his family was made a paramount duty, and Diem's brother, Ngo Dinh Nhu, founded an elitist underground organization to spy on officials, army officers, and prominent local citizens. Diem also refused to participate in the all-Vietnamese elections described in the Final Declaration. With support from the north, communist-led forces—popularly called the Viet Cong—launched an insurgency movement to seize power and reunify the country. The insurrection appeared close to succeeding when Diem's army overthrew him in November 1963. Diem and his brother Nhu were killed in the coup.

The Second Indochina War

The government that seized power after Diem's ouster, however, was no more effective than its predecessor. A period of political instability followed, until the military firmly seized control in June 1965 under Nguyen Cao Ky. Militant Buddhists who had helped overthrow Diem strongly opposed Ky's government, but he was able to break their resistance. Civil liberties were restricted, political opponents—denounced as neutralists or pro-communists—were imprisoned, and political parties were allowed to operate only if they did not openly criticize government policy. The character of the regime remained largely unchanged after the presidential elections in September 1967, which led to the election of Gen. Nguyen Van Thieu as president.

No less evident than the oppressive nature of the Saigon regime was its inability to cope with the Viet Cong. The insurgent movement, aided by a steady infiltration of weapons and advisers from the north, steadily built its fighting strength from about 30,000 men in 1963 to about 150,000 in 1965 when, in the opinion of many American intelligence analysts, the survival of the Saigon regime was seriously threatened. In addition, the political opposition in the south to Saigon became much more organized. The National Front for the Liberation of the South, popularly called the National Liberation Front (NLF), had been organized in late 1960 and within four years had a huge following.

Growing U.S. Involvement in the War

Until 1960, the United States had supported the Saigon regime and its army only with military equipment, financial aid, and, as permitted by the Geneva Accords, seven hundred advisers for training the army. The number of advisers had increased to seventeen thousand by the end of 1963, and they were joined by an increasing number of American helicopter pilots. All of this assistance, however, proved insufficient to halt the advance of the Viet Cong, and in February 1965,

U.S. Marines are briefed prior to a mission in DaNang, South Vietnam, 1965. Larry Burrows/Time & Life Pictures/Getty Images

U.S. Pres. Lyndon B. Johnson ordered the bombing of North Vietnam, hoping to prevent further infiltration of arms and troops into the south. Four weeks after the bombing began, the United States started sending troops into the south. By July, the number of U.S. troops had reached seventy-five thousand; it continued to climb until it stood at more than five hundred thousand early in 1968. Fighting beside the Americans were some six hundred thousand regular South Vietnamese troops and regional and self-defense forces, as well as smaller contingents from South Korea, Thailand, Australia, and New Zealand.

Three years of intensive bombing of the north and fighting in the south, however, did not weaken the will and strength of the Viet Cong and their allies from the north. Infiltration of personnel and supplies down the famous Ho

Chi Minh Trail continued at a high level, and regular troops from the north—now estimated at more than one hundred thousand—played a growing role in the war. The continuing strength of the insurgent forces became evident in the so-called Tet Offensive that began in late January 1968, during which the Viet Cong and North Vietnamese attacked more than one hundred cities and military bases, holding on to some for several weeks. After that, a growing conviction in the U.S. government that continuing the war at current levels was no longer politically acceptable led President Johnson to order a reduction of the bombing in the north. This decision opened the way for U.S. negotiations with Hanoi, which began in Paris in May 1968. After the bombing was halted over the entire north in November 1968, the Paris talks were enlarged to include representatives of the NLF and the Saigon regime.

The war continued under a new U.S. president, Richard M. Nixon, who began gradually to withdraw U.S. troops. Public opposition to the war, however, escalated after Nixon ordered attacks on the Ho Chi Minh Trail in Laos and on Viet Cong sanctuaries inside Cambodia. In the meantime, the peace talks went on in Paris.

Withdrawal of U.S. Troops

Finally, in January 1973 a peace treaty was signed by the United States and all three Vietnamese parties (North Vietnam, South Vietnam, and the Viet Cong). It provided for the complete withdrawal of U.S. troops within sixty days and created a political process for the peaceful resolution of the conflict in the south. Nothing was said, however, about the presence of more than one hundred thousand North Vietnamese troops in South Vietnam. The signing of the Paris Agreement did not bring an end to the fighting in Vietnam. The Saigon regime made a determined effort to eliminate the communist forces remaining in the south, while northern leaders continued to strengthen their military forces in preparation for a possible future confrontation. By late 1974, Hanoi had decided that victory could be achieved only through armed struggle, and early the next year North Vietnamese troops launched a major offensive against the south. Saigon's forces retreated in panic and disorder, and President Thieu ordered the abandonment of several northern provinces. Thieu's effort to stabilize the situation was too late, however, and on April 30, 1975, the communists entered Saigon in triumph. The Second Indochina War was finally at an end.

Reunification and Early Challenges

Following the communist victory, Vietnam remained theoretically divided (although reunified in concept) until July 2, 1976, when the Socialist Republic of Vietnam was officially proclaimed, with its capital at Hanoi. Vietnam at peace faced formidable problems. In the south alone, millions of people had been made homeless by the war, and more than one-seventh of the population had been killed or wounded; the costs in the north were probably as high or higher. Plans to reconstruct the country called for the expansion of industry in the north and of agriculture in the south. Within two years of the communist victory, however, it became clear that Vietnam would face major difficulties in realizing its goals.

Hanoi had been at war for more than a generation—indeed, Ho Chi Minh had died in 1969—and the bureaucracy was poorly trained to deal with the problems of peacetime economic recovery. The government encountered considerable resistance to its policies, particularly in the huge metropolis of Saigon (renamed Ho Chi Minh City in 1976), where members of the commercial sector—many of whom were ethnic Chinese—sought to avoid cooperating in the new socialist economic measures and resisted assignment to "new economic zones" in the countryside. During the late 1970s, the country also suffered major floods and drought that severely reduced food production. When the regime suddenly announced a program calling for the socialization of industry and agriculture in the south in early 1978, hundreds of thousands of people (mainly ethnic Chinese) fled the country on foot or by boat.

These internal difficulties were compounded by problems in foreign affairs. Perhaps unrealistically, the regime decided to pursue plans to form a close alliance with new revolutionary governments in neighbouring Laos and Cambodia (Kampuchea). Such plans risked incurring not only the hostility of the United States but also that of China, which had its own interests in those countries. As Sino-Vietnamese relations soured, Hanoi turned to Moscow and signed a treaty of friendship and cooperation with the Soviet Union. In the meantime, relations with the revolutionary Democratic Kampuchea (Khmer Rouge) government in Cambodia rapidly deteriorated when it refused Hanoi's offer of a close relationship among the three countries that once formed French Indochina. Savage border fighting culminated in a Vietnamese invasion of Cambodia in December 1978. The Khmer Rouge were dislodged from power, and a pro-Vietnamese government was installed in Phnom Penh.

Khmer Rouge forces now took refuge in isolated areas of the country and began a guerrilla war of resistance against the new government, the latter backed by some two hundred thousand Vietnamese troops. In the meantime, China launched a brief but fierce punitive invasion along the Sino-Vietnamese border in early 1979 in response to Vietnamese actions in Cambodia. During the month-long war, the Chinese destroyed major Vietnamese towns and inflicted heavy damage in the frontier zone, but they also suffered heavy casualties from the Vietnamese defenders.

Vietnam was now nearly isolated in the world. Apart from the protégé regime in Phnom Penh and the government of Laos, which also depended heavily on Vietnamese aid for its survival, the country was at odds with the rest of its regional neighbours. The member states of the Association of Southeast Asian Nations (ASEAN) opposed the Vietnamese occupation of Cambodia and joined with China in supporting guerrilla resistance forces represented by the Khmer Rouge and various noncommunist Cambodian groups. An economic trade embargo was imposed on Vietnam by the United States and most other Western countries. Only the Soviet Union and its allies in Eastern Europe stood by Vietnam.

Under such severe external pressure, Vietnam suffered continuing economic difficulties. The cost of stationing troops in Cambodia and of maintaining a strong defensive position along the Chinese border was especially heavy. To make matters worse, the regime encountered continuing problems in integrating the southern provinces into a social-ist economy. In the early 1980s, the government announced a number of reforms to spur the economy. Then, following the death of veteran party chief Le Duan in 1986 (Le Duan had succeeded Ho Chi Minh as party chief in 1960) and his succession by the pro-reform Nguyen Van Linh, the party launched a program of sweeping economic and institutional renovation (*doi moi*). Actual implementation, however, did not begin until 1988, when a deepening economic crisis and declining support from the Soviet Union compelled the gov-ernment to slash spending, court foreign investment, and liberalize trade. Other policies essentially legalized free-market activities that the government had previously tried to limit or suppress.

Vietnam Since *c.* 1990

These measures stabilized the economy, but the sudden collapse of communist rule in Eastern Europe and disintegration of the Soviet Union left Vietnam completely isolated. Having begun removing its armed forces from Cambodia in 1985, Vietnam completed withdrawal in September 1989 and intensified efforts to improve relations with its neighbours. A peace conference in Paris formally ended the Cambodian conflict in 1991 and provided United Nations supervision until elections could be held in 1993. The Cambodian settlement removed a key obstacle to normalizing relations with China, Japan, and Europe. The Vietnamese agreement to help the United States determine the fate of Americans missing in action encouraged the United States to lift the embargo in 1994 and establish diplomatic relations with Hanoi in 1995. Admission to membership in ASEAN in July 1995 symbolized Vietnam's full acceptance into the family of nations.

The return of peace and stability to the region allowed Vietnam to concentrate on the economic reforms begun in the late 1980s. The government took a pragmatic approach, responding flexibly to domestic realities while seeking ideas from diverse international sources. Major components of reform included instituting a relatively liberal foreign investment law, decollectivizing agriculture, ending fixed prices and subsidies, and significantly reducing the number of state-owned enterprises. Results were on the whole favourable. The output of food staples per capita, after a half century of decline, increased sufficiently for Vietnam to become a sizeable exporter of rice in 1989. Job creation in the private sector made up for job losses in the public sector. Foreign investment spurred growth in crude oil production, light manufacturing, and tourism. Vietnam also redirected its trade in a remarkably short period of time from ex-communist countries to such new partners as Hong Kong, Singapore, South Korea, Taiwan, and Japan. Growth in the gross domestic product (GDP) averaged nearly 8 percent annually through the 1990s.

With success, however, came a weakening of commitment to further change and renewed concern about preserving Vietnam's "socialist orientation." One consequence was the continued prominence in the economy of state-owned enterprises, fewer than half of which were profitable but which accounted for nearly one-third of GDP. Leaders also worried that the corruption, inequality, and materialism associated with the new market economy could undermine support for the party. In 1991, Nguyen Van Linh yielded the party's chairmanship to Do Muoi, a cautious, consensus-seeking politician. Although a new constitution enacted in 1992 was seen as a step toward loosening party control of the government, the party remained unwilling to share power with non-communist elements. Muoi's replacement, Le Kha Phieu, chosen in 1997 after months of bitter factional infighting, lacked both the power and the determination to accelerate the pace of reform. Internal opposition to further liberalization caused Vietnam in 1999 to decide, after years of negotiation, not to sign a trade agreement with the United States that would have also secured membership in the World Trade Organization (WTO). In the face of relentless globalization, Vietnam was threatened by paralysis on account of its reluctance to reform its political institutions.

Impatience with government corruption and slowing economic growth (exacerbated by the Asian economic crisis of the late 1990s) catalyzed large-scale demonstrations early in the twenty-first century. The demonstrations, in turn, ultimately contributed to the senior party leaders' decision to replace Le Kha Phieu with Nong Duc Manh in April 2001. The new party leader immediately took steps to curb corruption and integrate Vietnam more fully into the global economy. Once again the country's GDP experienced a surge of growth. Trade negotiations with the United States were rekindled, and an accord was signed later that year. At the end of 2006, Vietnam ratified the accession agreement to become the WTO's 150th member in January 2007. Nguyen Phu Trong was chosen as the party's new leader in January 2011, replacing a retiring Nong Duc Manh.

Communism in Cambodia

At the end of the nineteenth century, Cambodia found itself under French rule, a political and economic strategy with aims to garner more money for French nationals. The French took the country by force, thus leaving Cambodians happy to embrace the Japanese when they occupied during the Pacific War. Though like other Southeast Asian countries, their alliance with the Japanese did not last.

French Rule

French control over Cambodia was an offshoot of French involvement in the neighbouring provinces of Vietnam. France's decision to advance into Cambodia came only when it feared that British and Siamese expansion might threaten its access to the largely unmapped Mekong River, which it assumed (incorrectly) would provide access to central China. In 1863, French naval officers from Vietnam persuaded the Cambodian King, Norodom, to sign a treaty that gave France control of Cambodia's foreign affairs. The effect of the treaty was to weaken Siamese protection. A French admiral participated in Norodom's coronation, with Siamese acquiescence, in 1864.

For the next fifteen years or so, the French were not especially demanding, and Norodom benefited from French military help in putting down a series of rebellions. By the late 1870s, however, French officials in Cambodia were pressing for greater control over internal affairs. Shocked by what they regarded as the ineptitude and barbarity of Norodom's court and anxious to turn a profit in Cambodia, they sought to introduce fiscal and judicial reforms. In doing this, the French knew that Norodom's half brother, Sisowath, who had ambitions for the throne, would cooperate with them. Norodom, however, resisted the reforms, which he correctly perceived as infringements on his power. Exasperated by his intransigence, the French in 1884 forced him at gunpoint to sign a document that virtually transformed Cambodia into a colony. Soon thereafter, provincial officials, feeling threatened, raised guerrilla armies to confront the French.

The rebellion, which lasted until mid-1886, was the only anti-French movement in the kingdom until after World War II. The French succeeded in suppressing it after agreeing to some concessions to the king, but Norodom's apparent victory was hollow. What the French had been unable to achieve by the convention of 1884, they proceeded to gain through piecemeal action. As Norodom's health declined and as senior Cambodian officials came to see their interests increasingly linked with French power, the way was opened for greater French control. In 1897, the French representative in Phnom Penh assumed executive authority, reducing the king's power to a minimum. Norodom died, embittered and overtaken by events, in 1904.

The first forty years of the French protectorate—whatever French motives may have been—had guaranteed the survival of the Cambodian state and saved the kingdom from being divided between its two powerful neighbours. Norodom's successor, Sisowath (ruled 1904–27), was more cooperative with the French and presided benignly over the partial modernization of the kingdom. The northwestern provinces of Bătdâmbâng and Siĕmréab were returned to Cambodia by the Siamese in 1907. By the time Sisowath died, twenty years later, hundreds of miles of paved roads had been built, and thousands of acres of rubber plantations had been established by the French. Resistance to French rule, in sharp contrast to what was happening in neighbouring Vietnam, was almost nonexistent.

Sisowath's eldest son, Monivong, who reigned until 1941, was even more of a figurehead than his father had been. During the 1930s, a railway opened between Phnom Penh and the Siamese (Thai) border, while the first Cambodian-language newspaper, *Nagara Vatta* ("Angkor Wat"), affiliated with the Buddhist Institute in Phnom Penh, conveyed a mildly nationalistic message to its readers.

World War II and Its Aftermath

When Monivong died in 1941, Japanese forces had already occupied the component states of French Indochina, while leaving the French in administrative control. In these difficult circumstances, the French governor-general, Jean Decoux, placed Monivong's grandson, Prince Norodom Sihanouk, on the Cambodian throne. Decoux was guided by the expectation that Sihanouk, then only eighteen years old, could be easily controlled. In the long run, the French underestimated Sihanouk's political skills. But for the remainder of World War II, he was a pliable instrument in their hands.

The effect of the Japanese occupation was less profound in Cambodia than it was elsewhere in Southeast Asia, but the overthrow of the French administration by the Japanese in March 1945, when the war was nearing its end, provided Cambodians with some opportunities for greater political autonomy. Pressed by the Japanese to do so, Sihanouk declared his country's independence, and for several months the government was led by Son Ngoc Thanh, a former editor of *Nagara Vatta*, who had been forced into exile in Japan in 1942.

In October 1945, after the war was over, the French returned to Indochina, arrested Son Ngoc Thanh, and reestablished their control. Cambodia soon became an "autonomous state within the French Union," with its own constitution and a handful of political parties, but real power remained in French hands. There were, however, several significant political developments between 1945 and the achievement of complete independence in 1953, the most important of which was the confrontation between Sihanouk and his advisers on the one hand and the leaders of the pro-independence Democratic Party, which dominated the National Assembly, on the other. Cambodia was poorly prepared for parliamentary democracy, and the French were unwilling to give the National Assembly genuine power. The Democrats, for their part, suffered from internal dissension. The death in 1947 of their leader, Prince Yuthevong, was a severe blow, exacerbated by the assassination of Yuthevong's heir apparent, Ieu Koeuss, in early 1950. Outside Parliament, Son Ngoc Thanh, released from exile in France in 1951, formed a dissident movement, the Khmer Serei ("Free Khmer"), which opposed both Sihanouk and the French.

In June 1952, Sihanouk assumed control of the government. Many Cambodian students in France, among them Saloth Sar (who would become the future communist dictator Pol Pot), objected to Sihanouk's move, but inside Cambodia the king remained extremely popular. His self-styled "Royal Crusade," consisting of a tour of several countries to elicit their support, wrested political independence from the French, who by the end of 1953 were anxious to compromise. Sihanouk's success discredited the communist-dominated guerrilla movement in Cambodia—associated with the Viet Minh of Vietnam—and Son Ngoc Thanh's anticommunist Khmer Serei.

Prime Minister Pol Pot and ministers lead members of the Cambodian army, May 1979. Kurita Kaku/Gamma-Rapho/Getty Images

Independence

Sihanouk's government was recognized as the sole legitimate authority within Cambodia at the Geneva Conference convened in 1954 to reach a political settlement to the First Indochina War. This decision prevented the Viet Minh from gaining any regional power in Cambodia, as they did in Laos.

While Democrats and communists alike recognized Sihanouk's role in gaining Cambodia's independence, they opposed his increasing authoritarianism. Sihanouk abdicated the throne in March 1955 in favour of his father, Norodom Suramarit, and formed a mass political movement, the Sangkum Reastr Niyum ("People's Socialist Community"), whose members were forbidden to belong to other political parties. The effect of the move was to draw thousands of people away from the Democrats, who had expected to win the national elections scheduled for later in the year. When the elections took place, amid widely reported abuses by Sihanouk's police, the Sangkum won every seat in the National Assembly. Sihanouk became the central figure in Cambodian politics from then until his overthrow in 1970, as prime minister and—after his father's death in 1960, when no new monarch was named—as head of state. Overt political life was strictly controlled by the prince, his colleagues, and the police. Cambodian communists, a marginal group of fewer than a thousand members, operated clandestinely and enjoyed little success. In 1963, Saloth Sar, a schoolteacher who was also secretary of the Communist Party, fled Phnom Penh and took refuge in the forests along the Vietnamese border; from there he built the organization that later would be known as the Khmer Rouge.

Sihanouk was widely revered in Cambodia until the late 1960s, when opposition to his rule intensified. He saw Thailand and what was then South Vietnam as the greatest threats to Cambodia's survival. Those two countries were allied with the United States, which the prince disliked. At the same time, Sihanouk feared the eventual success of the Vietnamese communists in their war against South Vietnam and the United States, and he dreaded the prospect of a unified Vietnam under communist control. To gain some freedom to maneuver, he proclaimed a policy of neutrality in international affairs. Sihanouk broke off relations with the United States in 1965, convinced of American involvement in two South Vietnamese-backed plots against the Cambodian state in 1959 and encouraged in his anti-Americanism by the French president, Charles de Gaulle, whom he idolized. Soon afterward, he concluded secret agreements with the Vietnamese communists, who were allowed to station troops on Cambodian territory in outlying districts as long as they did not interfere with Cambodian civilians. The secret agreement protected Sihanouk's army from attacks by the Vietnamese but compromised his neutralist policies. After 1965, when the war in Vietnam intensified, he also edged toward an alliance with China.

Cambodia's internal politics after 1965 developed in a complex fashion. Elections in 1966, the first since 1951 not to be stage-managed by the prince, brought in a majority of National Assembly members who owed little or nothing to Sihanouk himself. Although the prince was still a revered figure among the rural populace, he became increasingly unpopular with the educated elite. Conservatives resented his break with the United States and his seemingly procommunist foreign policy, while Cambodian radicals opposed his internal policies, which were economically conservative and intolerant of dissent. A rebellion in Bătdâmbâng province in 1967, manipulated by local communists, convinced the prince that the greatest threat to his regime came from the radical sector. Without hesitation, he began using severe measures—including imprisonment without trial, assassinations, and the burning of villages—to impose his will.

By 1969, Sihanouk's grip on Cambodian politics had loosened, and conflict between his army and communist guerrillas, especially in the northeast, had increased. Some anticommunist ministers led by Prince Sirik Matak and Gen. Lon Nol plotted to depose Sihanouk, whose credibility with radicals had evaporated following his renewal of diplomatic relations with the United States. Sihanouk's elaborate policy of juggling major powers against each other had failed. Matak and Lon Nol worked closely with anticommunists in South Vietnam, including Son Ngoc Thanh, whose Khmer Serei movement had gained recruits among the Khmer-speaking minority in Vietnam.

Civil War

In March 1970, while Prince Sihanouk was visiting the Soviet Union, the National Assembly voted to remove him from office as head of state. Lon Nol subsequently took control of the government. Confused and hurt, Sihanouk traveled to Beijing and accepted Chinese advice to resist the coup by taking charge of a united front government-in-exile. This government was to be allied with China and North Vietnam and use the Cambodian communist forces led by Saloth Sar, which only a few days before had been fighting against Sihanouk's army.

In Phnom Penh, Lon Nol's new government was initially popular, particularly for his quixotic pledge to rid Cambodia of Vietnamese communist troops. In fact, the resulting confrontation dragged Cambodia fully into the Vietnam conflict. In May 1970, an American and South Vietnamese task force invaded eastern Cambodia, but communist forces had already retreated to the west. Two offensives launched by Lon Nol—named for the semi-mythical Cambodian kingdom of Chenla—were smashed by the Vietnamese, and thereafter his troops assumed a defensive stance. North Vietnamese support for the Cambodian communists diminished in 1973, following a cease-fire agreement reached in Paris with the Americans. The Cambodian communists, however, refused to adhere to the agreements, and in 1973, they were subjected to a massive American aerial bombardment, although the United States and Cambodia were not at war and no American troops were endangered by Cambodia. The bombing slowed communist attacks on Phnom Penh and wreaked havoc in the heavily populated countryside around the capital. The civil war lasted two more years, but already by the end of 1973 the Lon Nol government controlled only Phnom Penh, the northwest, and a handful of provincial towns.

In the meantime, Sihanouk declined in importance. By the end of 1973, the Cambodian communists dominated every element of the resistance, although they still claimed Sihanouk as a figurehead. Lon Nol's isolated regime in Phnom Penh continued to receive large infusions of American aid, increasing opportunities for corruption.

In April 1975, the Lon Nol government collapsed. Communist forces quickly entered Phnom Penh and immediately ordered its inhabitants to abandon the city and take up life in rural areas. Phnom Penh and other cities and towns throughout the country were emptied in less than a week. Thousands of city dwellers died on the forced marches, and in subsequent years conditions worsened.

Democratic Kampuchea

Over the next six months, following the directives of a still-concealed Communist Party of Kampuchea, Cambodia experienced the most rapid and radical social transformation in its history. Money, markets, and private property were abolished. Schools, hospitals, shops, offices, and monasteries were closed. Nothing was published, no one could travel without permission, and everyone was ordered to wear peasant work clothes. As in Mao Zedong's China, the poorest peasants were favoured at everyone else's expense. A handful of party leaders controlled everything in the country, but they remained in hiding and explained few of their decisions. Instead, they urged everyone to "build and defend" the country. In April 1976, Sihanouk resigned as head of state, soon after a new constitution had renamed the country Democratic Kampuchea. A soft-spoken and unknown figure named Pol Pot became prime minister, and more than a year passed before observers outside the country were able to identify him as Saloth Sar.

In 1976–77, the new regime, following the lead of Maoist China, sought to collectivize Cambodia totally, mobilizing its population into an unpaid labour force and seeking to double the average prerevolutionary yields of rice immediately and on a national scale. The human costs of this ill-conceived experiment were enormous, and the Khmer Rouge were widely condemned by the international community once the magnitude of their crimes became known, most notably through the release in 1984 of *The Killing Fields*, a film adaptation of the Khmer Rouge story. Conservative estimates are that between April 1975 and early 1979, when the regime was overthrown, at least 1.5 million Cambodians—about 20 percent of the total population—died from overwork, starvation, disease, or execution. Parallels have been drawn between these events and Joseph Stalin's collectivization of Ukrainian agriculture in the Soviet Union in the 1930s, the Nazi Holocaust of World War II, Mao's Great Leap Forward in China in the late 1950s, and the massacres in Rwanda in the mid-1990s. The Soviet and Chinese experiments appear to have been models for the Khmer Rouge, although the proportion of the population killed in Cambodia under the Khmer Rouge was greater than it had been in China or the Soviet Union. The number of deaths stemmed from the literalism with which plans were carried out (Pol Pot's supporters were told to "smash" the enemy), the cruelty of the inexperienced communist cadres, and—as far as executions were concerned—the suspicions of the leadership that the failure of their experiment could be traced to "traitors" in the pay of foreign powers. The Communist Party's interrogation centre in Phnom Penh, a prison code-named "S-21," was the site of more than fifteen thousand such executions. Those tortured and put to death included men and women who had served the party faithfully for years—victims of the extreme paranoia of Pol Pot and his colleagues.

Vietnamese Intervention

The Khmer Rouge initially had been trained by the Vietnamese, but from the early 1970s, they had been resentful and suspicious of Vietnam and Vietnamese intentions. Scattered skirmishes between the two sides in 1975 had escalated into open warfare by the end of 1977. The Cambodians were no match for the Vietnamese forces, despite continuing infusions of Chinese aid. In December 1978, a large Vietnamese army moved into Cambodia, brushing aside the Democratic Kampuchean forces. Within two weeks, the government had fled Phnom Penh for Thailand, and the Vietnamese had installed a puppet regime—called the People's Republic of Kampuchea—consisting largely of Cambodian communists who had deserted Pol Pot in 1977–78.

Over the next decade, under the relatively benign tutelage of the Vietnamese, Cambodia struggled back to its feet. Private property was restored, schools reopened and some Buddhist practices were reintroduced, cities were repopulated, and, with freedom of movement, internal trade flourished. At the same time, at least five hundred thousand Cambodians, including some one hundred thousand associated with the communists, fled to Thailand in the aftermath of Democratic Kampuchea's fall and because of the hardship, uncertainty, and disorder that accompanied the installation of the new regime. Of these, perhaps two hundred thousand people, including most of the surviving members of Cambodia's educated elite, sought refuge in other countries, while the rest came under the control of three resistance groups camped along the Thai-Cambodian border: Norodom Sihanouk and his followers, the Khmer Rouge, and the noncommunist Khmer People's National Liberation Front (renamed the Buddhist Liberal Democratic Party in 1992) under the leadership of Son Sann (a former prime minister). These groups were supported financially by foreign powers, including the United States, that were anxious to oppose Vietnam. Thousands of Cambodians continued to enter Thailand in the 1980s; by the end of the decade, those in refugee camps were thought to exceed three hundred thousand.

In 1982, an uneasy alliance was reached among the three groups opposing the Vietnamese-backed regime in Phnom Penh, and a government-in-exile was established with Sihanouk as president and Son Sann as prime minister. This government, despite UN recognition, received little support from Cambodians inside the country and was largely ineffectual. The member groups of the coalition continued independently to resist the Phnom Penh regime, the larger and better-equipped forces of the Khmer Rouge being the most effective.

Cambodia Since 1990

The political stalemate that developed among the four groups vying for power was broken in the late 1980s, when international political pressure, an economic boycott of Cambodia led by the United States, and a reduction in aid from the Soviet Union contributed to Vietnam's decision to withdraw its forces from Cambodia, which was completed in 1989. Freed from Vietnamese tutelage, the Phnom Penh government took two initiatives that sharply increased its popularity. It legalized property ownership, which created a real estate boom in Phnom Penh. More significantly, it openly encouraged the practice of Buddhism, and hundreds of Buddhist monasteries were restored, often with funds provided by Cambodians living overseas. One result of the resurgence of Buddhism was that thousands of young Cambodian males became Buddhist monks, even if only for a brief time, as in most cases. The withdrawal of the

Vietnamese also allowed the resistance factions to seek through negotiation the political objectives that they had been unable to obtain by military action against the Phnom Penh government; they were encouraged in this endeavour by their foreign patrons.

These negotiations, which had been conducted for some time and had intensified after 1989, led in 1991 to two significant results. The first was the creation of a largely ceremonial coalition government under a Supreme National Council (SNC) chaired by Sihanouk and composed of representatives of the government and the three factions. Although the SNC was recognized by the United Nations, effective control in most of Cambodia remained in the hands of the Phnom Penh regime. The second and more important result was the conclusion of a peace agreement among the factions that also provided for a popularly elected government. The UN Security Council, with the backing of the factions, endorsed this treaty and agreed to establish in the country a peacekeeping operation consisting of both soldiers and civil servants under the control of a United Nations Transitional Authority in Cambodia that would monitor progress toward conducting elections, temporarily run several government ministries, and safeguard human rights.

The operation, inaugurated in January 1992, was difficult to implement, notably because the Khmer Rouge refused to disarm and cooperate, the UN machinery for such an innovative mission was cumbersome, and the ruling party in Phnom Penh was unwilling to cede day-to-day political power to the UN. Nonetheless, more than three hundred thousand refugees were repatriated from Thailand under UN auspices in 1992–93, and in July 1993, national elections were held under UN supervision. These were arguably the first free and fair elections in Cambodian history. More than 90 percent of the registered voters went to the polls, and by a clear majority they chose candidates from a royalist political faction sponsored by Prince Sihanouk, who had returned home in 1992 after twelve years of residence in China and North Korea. The incumbent Cambodian People's Party (CPP) and the former prime minister, Hun Sen, refused to accept the results of the election. In a deal brokered by Prince Sihanouk and approved by the UN, the victorious royalists, led by Sihanouk's son, Prince Norodom Ranariddh, agreed to form a coalition with the CPP, with Ranariddh as first prime minister and Hun Sen as second prime minister. Under the new constitution, Cambodia became a kingdom again, and Sihanouk became its monarch for the second time.

Because the CPP controlled the army, judiciary, and police, it soon dominated the coalition, and Prince Rana-riddh, despite his position, was unable to influence events. The Khmer Rouge movement collapsed in the mid-1990s, as it lost foreign backing, its leaders quarreled among themselves, and thousands of supporters defected to the government and were offered positions in the Cambodian army. In 1997, Hun Sen staged a coup against his coalition partners and tightened his control over the country. The brutality of the coup alarmed foreign donors and delayed Cambodia's entry into ASEAN (Association of Southeast Asian Nations).

By 1998, Pol Pot was dead, the Khmer Rouge movement had fallen apart, and for the first time in thirty years Cambodia was at peace. In July, after internationally monitored elections that were relatively free and fair, Hun Sen returned as prime minister to form a second coalition government; Rana-riddh became chairman of the National Assembly. Cambodia continued to face enormous problems: a runaway birth rate, an AIDS epidemic, a stagnant economy, widespread deforestation, a climate of violence exacerbated by the ruling party's unwillingness to abide by the rule of law, impatience among donors at the government's slowness in introducing reforms, and human rights abuses often traceable to members of the ruling party.

Over the next few years, the country began to stabilize. Cambodia was officially admitted to ASEAN in 1999, which meant that it was constructively linked, perhaps for the first time in its history, to the rest of Southeast Asia. By the early twenty-first century, Cambodia had joined the WTO (2004), begun to bring a serious AIDS epidemic under control, reined in the country's birth rate to approach the world average, reduced its dependence on logging, begun to realize the economic benefits of strong garment-manufacturing and tourist sectors, and regained the confidence of foreign investors and aid organizations. Sihanouk resigned as king in 2004, and his youngest son, Norodom Sihamoni, became king in his place.

In 2009, after years of delay, the first trial of the Khmer Rouge Tribunal (officially the Extraordinary Chambers in the Courts of Cambodia) got under way in Phnom Penh. The defendant, Kaing Guek Eav (better known as Duch), who had been in custody for some ten years, had been in charge of the notorious S-21 prison during the Khmer Rouge regime. He was convicted in 2010 and sentenced to an additional nineteen years of imprisonment.

CHAPTER 7

COMMUNISM IN LATIN AMERICA

Latin America in the first half of the twentieth century was feeling the impact of outside events not only on its economy but also politically, by the spread of imported ideologies

President Franklin Roosevelt's New Deal was an economic policy that aimed to stabilize industry in the wake of the Great Depression. It also helped to develop organized labour in the United States. FPG/Archive Photos/ Getty Images

and through the examples of President Franklin D. Roosevelt's New Deal in the United States and emerging totalitarianisms of the left and right in Europe. The European anarcho-syndicalism that had provided a model for many of Latin America's earliest radical cadres declined sharply in importance after World War I. Henceforth, the left consisted of socialist parties of generally moderate bent, inspired in large part by European social democracy; breakaway socialists who admired the Russian Revolution of 1917 and proceeded to found communist parties in their own countries; and, not least, such strictly

Latin American expressions as the Mexican agrarian reform movement. Socialist parties were strongest in the Southern Cone, the Chilean briefly gaining a share of national power as a member of a Popular Front government elected in 1938. The communists were also strong in Chile but first entered a national administration in Cuba, after Fulgencio Batista had been elected president with their support in 1940. Once the Soviet Union entered World War II in 1941, communist parties in several other countries, including Brazil and Nicaragua, formed alliances with local strongmen, but they nowhere became a true mass party, and an exaggerated fear of Bolshevism on the part of Latin American elites meant that the communist parties were subject to widespread repression except during the war itself.

Some other political organizations were frankly influenced by European fascism, but in most countries their membership was numerically insignificant. The chief exception was Brazil, whose green-shirted Integralistas (Ação Integralista Brasileira) emerged as the largest single national party in the mid-1930s until involvement in a foolhardy coup attempt led to their suppression. Hence, the influence of fascism was more often exercised through homegrown authoritarians who were attracted to certain aspects of it but carefully avoided any open embrace. Getúlio Vargas was one such leader, who, after suppressing the Integralistas, put the finishing touches on his own dictatorial regime, officially dubbed *Estado Novo*, or "New State."

Good Neighbor Policy and World War II

One reason Latin American nations avoided an overly close association with fascism was a desire not to offend the dominant power of the hemisphere, the United States. During the 1920s, it had already begun a retreat from the policy of active intervention in Latin America. This policy, adopted in the aftermath of the Spanish-American War and the United States' open support of Panamanian secession from Colombia, had featured the creation of formal and informal protectorates over many Caribbean and Central American states. Franklin D. Roosevelt completed the shift. His domestic policies were much admired in Latin America and in some cases copied by moderate reformists, but his Good Neighbor Policy won the warm approval of almost all Latin American rulers, since it entailed formal renunciation of the right of intervention in favour of peaceful cajoling and assorted economic, military, and technical aid programs. These programs were launched on the eve of World War II to help hemispheric neighbours prepare for the emergency. They were expanded after the start of the conflict, whose economic impact on Latin America was generally comparable to that of World War I but more intense because of the earlier and deeper involvement of the United States. The war emergency naturally gave still further impetus to the development of national industries to replace scarce imports.

The Good Neighbor approach proved far more effective in promoting U.S. hegemony than the occasional dispatch of gunboats. In 1938, Roosevelt calmly accepted Mexico's expropriation of the petroleum installations of U.S. and British companies, and he was rewarded several times over when Mexico loyally cooperated with the United States in World War II, even sending an air force squadron to serve in the Philippines. The one other Latin American country to send forces overseas was Brazil, which put an expeditionary force in Italy. In general, Latin America's wartime collaboration left little to be desired. In the end, all countries not only broke relations with the Axis powers but declared war, though Argentina took the latter step only at the last possible moment, in March 1945.

In Latin America as elsewhere, the close of World War II was accompanied by expectations, only partly fulfilled, of steady economic development and democratic consolidation. Economies grew, but at a slower rate than in most of Europe or East Asia so that Latin America's relative share of world production and trade declined and the gap in personal income per capita separating it from the leading industrial democracies increased. Popular education also increased, as did exposure to the mass media and mass culture—which in light of the economic lag served to feed dissatisfaction. Military dictatorships and Marxist revolution were among the solutions put forward, but none were truly successful.

Economic Agenda and Patterns of Growth

The economic shocks delivered by the depression and two world wars, in combination with the strength of nationalism, tilted economic policy after 1945 strongly toward internal development as against the outward orientation that had predominated since independence. The outward policy had been partially undermined by the trade controls and industrial promotion schemes adopted essentially as defensive measures in the aftermath of the depression and during World War II. Now, however, a reorientation of policy was explicitly called for by some of Latin America's most influential figures, such as the Argentine economist Raúl Prebisch, head of the United Nations Economic Commission for Latin America. Prebisch and his followers insisted that the terms of trade and investment in the contemporary world were stacked in favour of the developed industrial nations of the "centre" as against the developing nations of the "periphery." Their strategy therefore included emphasis on economic diversification and import substitution industrialization (ISI) for the sake of greater economic autonomy. They called for economic integration among the Latin American countries themselves, with a view to attaining economies of scale. They recommended internal structural reforms to improve the economic performance of their countries, including land reform both to eliminate underutilized latifundios and lessen the stark inequality of income distribution that was an obstacle to growth of the domestic market.

In the small Caribbean and Central American republics, and some of the smaller and poorer South American nations, the prospects for ISI were sorely limited by market size and other constraints, and governments still hesitated to promote manufacturing at the expense of traditional primary commodities. But in countries accounting for a disproportionate share of Latin America's population and GDP, the new approach

Raúl Prebisch of Argentina, secretary general of the United Nations Conference on Trade and Development (UNCTAD), speaks at the UN Conference on Trade and Development, Feb. 5, 1968. © AP Images

received full play through protective tariffs, subsidies, and official preferences. Overvalued exchange rates, which hurt traditional exports, made it easier to import industrial machinery and equipment. Manufacturing costs generally remained high, and factories were overly dependent on imported inputs of all kinds (including foreign capital), but advances were not limited to consumer goods production. In all major countries, the output of intermediate and capital goods rose appreciably, too. For example, in Argentina the state undertook construction of a steel industry, and in numerous other ways national governments further expanded their economic role. Brazil nationalized its incipient oil industry in 1953, creating the state firm Petrobrás that eventually ranked alongside Mexico's PEMEX (outcome of the 1938 oil expropriation) and Venezuela's PETROVEN (1975) as one of Latin America's three largest economic enterprises, all state-run.

Starting in 1960 with agreements fostering economic union, such as the Latin American Free Trade Association and Central American Common Market, and continuing with the Andean Pact of 1969, some progress was made toward regional economic integration, but the commitment to eliminate trade barriers was not as strong as in postwar Europe. Intra-Latin American trade increased, but probably not much more than would have happened without special agreements. In any case, quantitative economic growth was visible almost everywhere. It was evident even when expressed as per capita GDP—that is, factoring in a population growth that in most countries was accelerating because death rates had finally begun to fall sharply while birth rates remained high. (In the 1960s in much of Latin America the annual rate of population increase came to exceed 3 percent.) But there were clear differences in economic performance among countries. Brazil, with a diversified economic base and the largest internal market, and Panama, with its canal-based service economy, posted the best records, their GDP per capita doubling between 1950 and 1970. Mexico and Venezuela did almost as well, as did Costa Rica. But the Argentine economy seemed to stagnate, and few countries scored significant gains. Moreover, the conviction eventually grew in countries where ISI had been vigorously pushed that the easy gains in replacement of imports were coming to an end and that, to maintain adequate growth, it would be necessary to renew emphasis on exports as well. World market conditions were favourable for a revival of export promotion. Indeed, international trade had begun a rapid expansion at the very time that inward-directed growth was gaining converts in Latin America.

The promotion of industrial exports was slow to appear. Brazil was the most successful, selling automobiles and automotive parts mainly to other less developed countries but at times even to the industrial world. A slightly less satisfactory alternative was the setting up of plants to assemble imported parts or semifinished materials into consumer goods that were immediately exported, thus taking advantage of Latin America's low labour costs, particularly for women workers. Such plants proliferated along Mexico's northern border (where they were known as *maquiladoras*) but sprang up also in Central America and around the Caribbean.

In other instances, Latin Americans tried to develop new, nontraditional primary commodity exports. Colombian cut flowers were a highly successful example, promoted from the late 1960s through special incentives such as tax rebates; Colombia became the world's second leading flower exporter. It also assumed a leading role in the illicit narcotics trade. It enjoyed a brief boom of marijuana exports in the 1970s and in the following decade became the world's leading supplier of cocaine, which was processed in clandestine Colombian laboratories from leaf paste that at first came mostly from

Bolivia and Peru, though eventually Colombia displaced them as producers of the raw material.

Developments in Social Policy

Continued advances in public health were the principal basis for the explosion of population growth, which in turn made more difficult the provision of other social services. Nevertheless, educational coverage continued to expand, and state schools increased their share of students at the expense of private (often church-affiliated) institutions. Social security systems were introduced in countries that previously had none and expanded where they already existed. Yet such benefits chiefly went to organized urban workers and members of the middle sectors so that the net effect was often to increase, rather than lessen, social inequality.

Moreover, structural land reform received more lip service than actual implementation. Extensive land distribution did occur in Bolivia following that country's 1952 revolution, and in Cuba large private estates were eliminated after 1959; but Mexico, which had been the leader in this area, now tended to favour capitalist agribusinesses rather than peasant communities. The poor were also hurt by the high inflation that in the 1950s and after became endemic in Brazil and the Southern Cone and was intermittently a problem elsewhere, resulting in considerable part from an inability or unwillingness to generate by taxation the fiscal resources needed for economic and social development programs.

The United States and Latin America in the Cold War Era

Whatever policies Latin American countries adopted in the postwar era, they had to take into account the probable reaction of the United States, now more than ever the dominant power in the hemisphere. It was the principal trading partner and source of loans, grants, and private investment for almost all countries, and Latin American leaders considered its favour worth having. Policy makers in Washington, on their part, were unenthusiastic about ISI and state-owned enterprises, but as long as North American investors were not hindered in their own activities, the inward-directed policy orientation did not pose major problems. Moreover, as the Cold War developed between the United States and the Soviet Union, the great majority of Latin American governments sided willingly with the former, even though they complained of being neglected by Washington's preoccupation with the threat of communism in Europe and Asia.

A threat developed in Central America when the Guatemalan government of Jacobo Arbenz (1951–54), which frankly accepted the support of local communists, attacked the holdings of the United Fruit Company as part of an ambitious though ultimately abortive land reform. This combined political and economic challenge caused the United States to assist Guatemalan counter-revolutionaries and neighbouring Central American rulers in overthrowing Arbenz. The reversion to intervention-ist tactics featured use of the Central Intelligence Agency (CIA) rather than landing of military forces. But it fore-shadowed later CIA assistance to the Chilean military in ousting their country's Marxist president, Salvador Allende, in 1973, not to mention the U.S. vendetta against the Sandinista revolutionary government that took power in Nicaragua in 1979, only to be worn down by covert action and economic harassment to the point that it peace-fully accepted defeat in a free election in 1990.

Impact of the Cuban Revolution

By most social and economic indicators, Cuba by mid-century was among Latin America's most highly developed countries. However, in the postwar period it was afflicted with lacklustre economic growth and a corrupt political dictatorship set up in 1952 by the same Batista who earlier had helped put his country on a seemingly democratic path. It was also a country whose long history of economic and other dependence on the United States had fed nationalist resentment, although control of the sugar industry and other economic sectors by U.S. interests was gradually declining. While conditions for revolutionary change were thus present, the particular direction that Cuba took owed much to the idiosyncratic genius of Fidel Castro, who, after ousting Batista at the beginning of 1959, proceeded by stages to turn the island into the hemisphere's first communist state, in close alliance with the Soviet Union.

The Cuban Revolution achieved major advances in health and education, though frankly sacrificing economic efficiency to social objectives. Expropriation of most private enterprise together with Castro's highly personalistic dicta-torship drove many members of the middle and upper classes into exile, but a serious decline in productivity was offset for a time by Soviet subsidies. At the same time, thanks to its successful defiance of the United States—which tried and failed to overthrow it by backing a Cuban exiles' invasion in April 1961—and its evident social advances, Castro's Cuba was looked to as a model throughout Latin America, not only by established leftist parties but also by disaffected students and intellectuals of mainly middle-class origin.

Over the following years, much of Latin America saw an upsurge of rural guerrilla conflict and urban terrorism in response to the persistence of stark social inequality and political repression. But this upsurge drew additional inspiration from the Cuban example, and in many cases Cuba provided training and material support to guerrillas. The response of Latin American establishments was twofold and eagerly supported by the United States. On one hand, governments strengthened their armed forces, with U.S. military aid preferentially geared to counter-guerrilla operations. On the other hand, emphasis was placed on land reform and other measures designed to eliminate the root causes of insurgency, all generously aided by the United States through the Alliance for Progress launched by President John F. Kennedy.

Even though much of the reactive social reformism was cosmetic or superficial, the counterrevolutionary thrust was nonetheless generally successful. A Marxist, Salvador Allende, became president of Chile in 1970, but he did so by democratic election, not violent revolution, and he was overthrown three years later. The only country that appeared to be following the Cuban pattern was Nicaragua under the Sandinista revolutionary government, which in the end could not withstand the onslaughts of its domestic and foreign foes. Moreover, the Cuban Revolution ultimately lost much of its lustre even in the eyes of the Latin American left once the collapse of the Soviet Union caused Cuba to lose its chief foreign ally. Although the U.S. trade embargo imposed on Cuba had been a handicap all along, shortages of all kinds became acute only as Russian aid was cut back, clearly revealing the dysfunctional nature of Castro's economic management.

Fidel Castro

Fidel Castro, in full Fidel Alejandro Castro Ruz (born Aug. 13, 1926, near Birán, Cuba), was the political leader of Cuba (1959–2008) who transformed his country into the first

Fidel Castro (pictured at a rally in 2002) *was the communist leader of Cuba from 1959 until he stepped down in 2008, though he remained active in politics.* Adalberto Roque/AFP/Getty Images

communist state in the Western Hemisphere. Castro became a symbol of communist revolution in Latin America. He held the title of premier until 1976 and then began a long tenure as president of the Council of State and the Council of Ministers. He handed over provisional power in July 2006 because of health problems and formally relinquished the presidency in February 2008.

Castro was born in southeastern Cuba. His father, Ángel Castro y Argiz, an immigrant from Spain, was a fairly prosperous sugarcane farmer in a locality that had long been dominated by estates of the U.S.-owned United Fruit Company. While married to his first wife, Ángel Castro began an affair with one of his servants, Lina Ruz González, whom he later also married. Together they had seven children; Fidel was one of them, and Raúl, who later became his brother's chief associate in Cuban affairs, was another.

Fidel Castro attended Roman Catholic boarding schools in Santiago de Cuba and then the Catholic high school Belén in Havana, where he proved an outstanding athlete. In 1945, he entered the School of Law of the University of Havana, where organized violent gangs sought to advance a mixture of romantic goals, political aims, and personal careers. Castro's main activity at the university was politics, and in 1947 he joined an abortive attempt by Dominican exiles and Cubans to invade the Dominican Republic and overthrow Gen. Rafael Trujillo. He then took part in urban riots that broke out in Bogotá, Colombia, in April 1948.

After his graduation in 1950, Castro began to practice law and became a member of the reformist Cuban People's Party (called Ortodoxos). He became their candidate for a seat in the House of Representatives from a Havana district in the elections scheduled for June 1952. In March of that year, however, the former Cuban president, Gen. Fulgencio Batista, overthrew the government of Pres. Carlos Prío Socarrás and canceled the elections.

After legal means failed to dislodge Batista's new dictatorship, Castro began to organize a rebel force for the task in 1953. On July 26, 1953, he led about 160 men in a suicidal attack on the Moncada military barracks in Santiago de Cuba in hopes of sparking a popular uprising. Most of the men were killed, and Castro himself was arrested. After a trial in which he conducted an impassioned defense, he was sentenced by the government to fifteen years' imprisonment. He and his brother Raúl were released in a political amnesty in 1955, and they went to Mexico to continue their campaign against the Batista regime. There Fidel Castro organized Cuban exiles into a revolutionary group called the 26th of July Movement.

On Dec. 2, 1956, Castro and an armed expedition of eighty-one men landed on the eastern coast of Cuba from the yacht *Granma*. All of them were killed or captured except Fidel and Raúl Castro, Ernesto ("Che") Guevara, and nine others, who retreated into the Sierra Maestra to wage guerrilla warfare against the Batista forces. With the help of growing numbers of revolutionary volunteers throughout the island, Fidel Castro's forces won a string of victories over the Batista government's demoralized and poorly led armed forces. Castro's propaganda efforts proved particularly effective, and as internal political support waned and military defeats multiplied, Batista fled the country on Jan. 1, 1959. Castro's force of eight hundred guerrillas had defeated the Cuban government's thirty-thousand-man professional army.

As the undisputed revolutionary leader, Castro became commander in chief of the armed forces in Cuba's new provisional government, which had Manuel Urrutia, a moderate liberal, as its president. In February 1959, Castro became premier and thus head of the government. By the time Urrutia was forced to resign in July 1959, he had taken effective political power into his own hands. Castro had come to power with the support of most Cuban city dwellers on the basis of his promises to restore the 1940 constitution, create an honest administration, reinstate full civil and political liberties, and undertake moderate reforms. But once established as Cuba's leader, he began to pursue more radical policies: Cuba's private commerce and industry were nationalized; sweeping land reforms were instituted; and American businesses and agricultural estates were expropriated. The United States was alienated by these policies and offended by Castro's fiery new anti-American rhetoric. His trade agreement with the Soviet Union in February 1960 further deepened American distrust. In 1960, most economic ties between Cuba and the United States were severed, and the United States broke diplomatic relations with the island country in January 1961. In April of that year, the U.S. government secretly equipped thousands of Cuban exiles to overthrow Castro's government; their landing at the Bay of Pigs in April 1961, however, was crushed by Castro's armed forces.

Cuba also began acquiring weapons from the Soviet Union, which soon became the country's chief supporter and trade partner. In 1962, the Soviet Union secretly stationed ballistic missiles in Cuba that could deliver nuclear warheads to American cities, and in the ensuing confrontation with the United States, the world came close to a nuclear war. The Cuban Missile Crisis ended when the Soviet Union agreed to withdraw its nuclear weapons from Cuba in exchange for a pledge that the United States would withdraw the nuclear-armed missiles it had stationed in Turkey and no longer seek to overthrow Castro's regime.

In the meantime, Castro created a one-party government to exercise dictatorial control over all aspects of Cuba's political, economic, and cultural life. All political dissent and opposition were ruthlessly suppressed. Many members of the Cuban upper and middle classes felt betrayed by these measures and chose to immigrate to the United States. At the same time, Castro vastly expanded the country's social services, extending them to all classes of society on an equal basis. Educational and health services were made available to Cubans free of charge, and every citizen was guaranteed employment. The Cuban economy, however, failed to achieve significant growth or reduce its dependence on the country's chief export, cane sugar. Economic decision-making power was concentrated in a centralized bureaucracy headed by Castro, who proved to be an inept economic manager. With inefficient industries and a stagnant agriculture, Cuba became increasingly dependent on favourable Soviet trade policies to maintain its modest standard of living in the face of the United States' continuing trade embargo.

Castro remained premier until 1976, when a new constitution created a National Assembly and Castro became president of that body's State Council. He retained the posts of commander in chief of the armed forces and secretary-general of the Communist Party of Cuba—the only legal political party—and he continued to exercise unquestioned and total control over the government. Castro's brother Raúl, minister of the armed forces, ranked second to him in all government and party posts.

Fidel Castro's early attempts to foment Marxist revolutions elsewhere in Latin America foundered, but Cuban troops did eventually serve as proxies for the Soviet Union in various conflicts in less developed countries. From 1975 to 1989, Cuban expeditionary forces fought in the Angolan civil war on the side of the communistic Popular Movement for the Liberation of Angola. In 1978, Cuban troops assisted Ethiopia in repelling an invasion by Somalia. In the 1980s, Castro emerged as one of the leaders of the less developed world and the nonaligned countries, despite his obvious ties to the Soviet Union. He continued to signify his willingness to renew diplomatic relations with the United States, provided that it end its trade embargo against Cuba. In 1980, Castro released a flood of immigrants to the United States when he opened the port of Mariel for five months. The 125,000 immigrants, including some criminals, strained the capacity of U.S. immigration and resettlement facilities.

In the late 1980s, when the Soviet Union under Mikhail Gorbachev began to undertake democratic reforms and Eastern European countries were allowed to slip out of the Soviet orbit, Castro retained a hardline stance, espousing the discipline of communism. The collapse of the Soviet Union in 1991 took him by surprise and meant the end of generous Soviet subsidies to Cuba. Castro countered the resulting economic decline and shortages of consumer goods by allowing some economic liberalization and free-market activities while retaining tight controls over the country's political life.

In late 1993, Castro's daughter sought asylum in the United States, where she openly criticized her father's rule. The following year, economic and social unrest led to antigovernment demonstrations, the size of which had not been seen in Cuba in some thirty-five years. Shortly there-after, Castro lifted restrictions on those wanting to leave the country, and thousands headed for the United States in the largest exodus since the 1980 Mariel "freedom flotilla." In 1998, Castro allowed Pope John Paul II to visit Cuba for the first time.

In 2003, the National Assembly confirmed Castro as president for another five-year term. During that year, the Cuban government arrested dozens of independent journalists and activists in a renewed government crackdown on dissidents, and some seventy-five activists were convicted for conspiring with the United States to subvert the revolution. The following year, Castro strengthened his alliance with Venezuelan Pres. Hugo Chávez by helping him bring to fruition the Bolivarian Alternative for the Americas (Alternativa Bolivariana para las Américas [ALBA]; Alternativa later changed to Alianza ("Alliance")]), a socialist initiative to promote regional commerce, through which Cuba provided health care professionals to Venezuela in exchange for discounted oil.

On July 31, 2006, Fidel Castro passed power on a provisional basis to his brother Raúl in order to recover from surgery for a serious intestinal illness. It was the first time since the 1959 revolution that he ceded control. In February 2008, just days before the National Assembly was to vote for the country's leader, Fidel Castro (who had not appeared in public for nineteen months) officially declared that he would not accept another term as president. His announcement that he was stepping down was made through a letter that was addressed to the country and posted on the website of the official Communist Party newspaper, *Granma*. In part, it read, "I do not bid you farewell. My only wish is to fight as a soldier of ideas."

In the succeeding months, official photos were released of Fidel Castro in private meetings, and in July 2010 he made a public visit to the National Centre for Scientific Research in Havana. In September, on the eve of the release of the first volume of his memoirs, *The Strategic Victory*, he remarked to a reporter from the United States that "the Cuban model doesn't even work for us anymore." Many took his comment as an admission of the failure of communism. However, Fidel Castro was quick to qualify his remarks in a speech that followed a few days later. Most analysts saw his remarks as offering support for Raúl's introduction of economic reforms that included a massive layoff of government employees as well as increased toleration of private enterprise. In 2011, Fidel stepped down as secretary-general of the Communist Party of Cuba and was succeeded by Raúl.

Hugo Chavez and New Socialism

Hugo Chávez, in full Hugo Rafael Chávez Frías (born July 28, 1954, Sabaneta, Barinas, Venezuela—died March 5, 2013, Caracas), was a Venezuelan politician who was president of Venezuela (1999–2013). Chávez styled himself as the leader of the "Bolivarian Revolution," a socialist political program for much of Latin America, named after Simón Bolívar, the South American independence hero. Although the focus of the revolution had been subject to change depending on Chavez's goals, its key elements included nationalism, a centralized economy, and a strong military actively engaged in public projects. His ideology became known to many as simply *chavismo*.

Chávez took office in February 1999. During his first year in office, his approval rating reached 80 percent, and his platform—which advocated an end to corruption, increased spending on social programs, and redistribution of the country's oil wealth—was widely applauded. Riding this wave of popularity, Chávez oversaw the drafting of a new constitution that gave him unprecedented control over the three branches of government. The new constitution required new elections for every elected official in the country. In this "mega-election" of 2000, Chávez was reelected to a six-year term. He also increased his power in the National Assembly, but his party fell short of the two-thirds majority needed for absolute control. Nevertheless, the pro-Chávez majority was large enough to pass an enabling law that allowed the president to implement certain laws by decree; the National Assembly also appointed all new (pro-Chávez) justices to the Supreme Court.

While many Venezuelans had supported Chávez as an alternative to the corrupt two-party system that had ruled since 1958, others were alienated by his increasingly radical agenda. He formed intimate ties with Castro and stated his intent to take Venezuela down a path similar to Cuba's. He continued to pass controversial laws by decree and moved to limit the independent press. He also alienated the United States and other countries in the West by forging close ties with Iraq, Iran, and Libya, as well as by openly criticizing the U.S. invasion of Afghanistan following the September 11 attacks of 2001. By early 2002, his approval rating had fallen to 30 percent, and anti-Chávez marches had become regular occurrences. Moreover, many of his allies, including some members of the military, began to turn against him.

On April 11, 2002, a rally estimated at close to a million people marched on the president's palace to demand Chávez's resignation. The rally was met with pro-Chávez gunmen and National Guard troops, and a gun battle erupted, leaving dead and wounded on both sides. The violence sparked a military revolt, and, in a move widely condemned as an illegal coup d'état, the military took Chávez into custody. The following day the military established an interim government, choosing Pedro Carmona, head of a national federation of private businesses and a Chávez opponent, to be the interim president. But Carmona caused an uproar when he immediately dissolved most of Venezuela's democratic institutions and suspended the constitution. The Venezuelan military, fearing a right-wing dictatorship, then withdrew its support for the new government and on April 13 recognized Chávez's vice president, Diosdado Cabello, as the rightful successor. Once sworn in, Cabello restored Chávez to power, and Chávez returned to the presidential palace on the morning of April 14.

The coup was the first of a string of conflicts between the Chávez government and the opposition—clashes that continued to polarize Venezuelan society into two bitterly opposed camps: Chávez supporters (*chavistas*) and opposition members (*escuálidos* ["scrawny ones"], a derisive term coined by Chávez but quickly and proudly embraced by the opposition). In December 2002, the opposition began a national strike designed to force Chávez to resign. At the centre of the strike was the state oil company, Petróleos de Venezuela (PDVSA), which accounted for 80 percent of Venezuela's export revenue. In response, Chávez fired the striking PDVSA workers—about half the company's thirty-eight thousand employees—and brought in nonunion workers and foreign oil crews to maintain oil production. By February 2003, the strike had collapsed, and Chávez had full control of PDVSA.

Throughout 2003 and the first half of 2004, the opposition focused on a recall referendum that would push the president out of office midway through his term, but Chávez—now with PDVSA revenues at his disposal and the global price of oil climbing—began spending lavishly on social programs, including literacy and health care initiatives. His approval rating rebounded and, despite allegations of fraud, Chávez defeated the recall referendum in August 2004. In December 2005, to protest what they felt was corruption in the Chávez-dominated National Election Council (the institution that oversees elections), the opposition candidates boycotted the country's legislative elections. But the elections proceeded without them, and Chávez's coalition gained complete control of the National Assembly. It seemed to some political analysts that the more the opposition attacked Chávez, the stronger he became.

In December 2006, Chávez was elected president for a third time, with 63 percent of the vote. Ensured another six years in power, he pushed ahead with plans for "twenty-first-century socialism" by nationalizing key industries, including electricity and telecommunications, as well as what remained of the private oil sector. He also became more vocal in his anti-American rhetoric, particularly in his attacks against Pres. George W. Bush, whom he called "the Devil" in front of the United Nations General Assembly. In 2007, Chávez sponsored a package of changes to the Venezuelan constitution. While analysts noted that the new provisions included certain "crowd pleasers," like a maximum six-hour workday, most of the changes would have increased the power of the executive branch, including giving it greater control over the Central Bank and allowing it to seize property without a legal ruling. The most controversial provision, however, would have allowed for the president's indefinite reelection. In December 2007, the package of amendments was narrowly defeated in a popular referendum by a margin of 51 to 49 percent—Chávez's first defeat at the polls.

In February 2009, a more moderate package of constitutional changes was approved in a popular referendum, clearing the way for Chávez's perpetual reelection. Bolstered by the victory, the government launched an aggressive program to stifle dissent, arresting key political opponents, closing dozens of opposition radio stations, and moving to close Globovisión—the only television station that remained critical of the government.

In June 2011, Chávez was operated on in Cuba to remove a cancerous tumour. The specific nature of his cancer was not revealed, but, after coming home to Venezuela in early July, he returned to Cuba twice (first in July and then in early August) for follow-up treatment that included chemotherapy. Although speculation grew as to whether he would be physically able to stand for reelection in 2012, Chávez mounted an aggressive campaign against challenger Henrique Capriles Radonski, the popular forty-year-old governor of Miranda state, who headed a united opposition made up of some thirty parties from across the political spectrum. The election in October 2012 was not as close as expected, though Chávez's margin of victory (about 10 percent) was considerably less than that in his triumph in 2006, when he captured almost two-thirds of the vote.

In December 2012, Chávez underwent his fourth cancer surgery in Cuba. He remained there into the new year to recuperate, ostensibly from a lung infection that was a consequence of the surgery. However, the government was criticized by the opposition for not being more forthcoming with details of the president's health. When Chávez was not well enough to return to Venezuela for his scheduled inauguration in January 2013, it became a constitutional issue. The National Assembly voted to allow the president's swearing-in to be delayed, and the Supreme Court confirmed the constitutionality of that action. Opposition leaders—who had called for the head of the National Assembly to be named temporary president in Chávez's absence—grudgingly accepted the court's decision. Chavez died two months later.

Movement Toward Democracy

The Latin American countries that did not opt for the Cuban model followed widely varying political paths. Mexico's unique system of limited democracy built around the Institutional Revolutionary Party was shaken by a wave of riots in the summer of 1968 on the eve of the Olympic Games held in Mexico City, but political stability was never seriously in doubt. A somewhat analogous regime was devised in Colombia as a means of restoring civilian constitutional rule after a brief relapse in the mid-1950s into military dictatorship: the dominant Liberal and Conservative parties chose to bury the hatchet, creating a bipartisan coalition (called the National Front) whereby they shared power equally between themselves while formally shutting out any minor parties. Once this arrangement expired in

1974, Colombia became again a more conventional political democracy, such as Costa Rica had been since before 1950 and Venezuela became in 1958 after the overthrow of its last military dictator.

In Latin America generally, the practice of democracy was somewhat sporadic, but wherever regular elections took place, they involved an enlarged electorate. The last Latin American countries adopted woman suffrage in the 1950s, and literacy test requirements continued to fall (as did illiteracy itself). Women also began to occupy high political office, including the presidency in Argentina (1974–76 and 2010–), Bolivia (1979–80), Chile (2006–10), Costa Rica (2010–), and Brazil (2011–). Moreover, Violeta Chamorro won the Nicaraguan vote of 1990 that put a temporary end to Sandinista rule (in 2006, the Sandinistas took power once again when former president Daniel Ortega was reelected).

CONCLUSION

Despite the difficulties and dislocations wrought by the transition to a capitalist market economy, Russia and the former Soviet republics are unlikely to reestablish communist rule. The Communist Party of the Russian Federation, the successor of the CPSU, attracts some followers, but its ideology is reformist rather than revolutionary; its chief aim appears to be that of smoothing the continuing and sometimes painful transition to a market economy and trying to mitigate its more blatantly inegalitarian aspects. In China, Maoism is given lip service but is no longer put into practice. Some large industries are still state-owned, but the trend is clearly toward increasing privatization and a decentralized market economy. China is now on the verge of having a full-fledged capitalist economy. This raises the question of whether free markets and democracy can be decoupled, or whether one implies the other. The CCP still brooks no opposition, as the suppression of pro-democracy student demonstrations in Tiananmen Square in 1989 made clear. But the views of a new generation of leaders that arose in the early twenty-first century were unknown, which makes the direction of Chinese policy difficult to predict.

Mao's version of Marxism-Leninism remains an active but ambiguous force elsewhere in Asia, most notably in Nepal. After a decade of armed struggle, Maoist insurgents there agreed in 2006 to lay down their arms and participate in national elections to choose an assembly to rewrite the Nepalese constitution. Claiming a commitment to multiparty democracy and a mixed economy, the Maoists emerged from the elections in 2008 as the largest party in the assembly—a party that now appears to resemble the pragmatic CCP of recent years more closely than it resembles Maoist revolutionaries of the twentieth century.

Meanwhile, North Korea, the last bastion of old Soviet-style communism, is an isolated and repressive regime. Long deprived of Soviet sponsorship and subsidies, Cuba and Vietnam have been reaching out diplomatically and seeking foreign investment in their increasingly market-oriented economies, but politically both remain single-party communist states.

Today, Soviet-style communism, with its command economy and top-down bureaucratic planning, is defunct. Whether that kind of regime was ever consistent with Marx's conception of communism is doubtful; whether anyone will lead a new movement to build a communist society on Marxist lines remains to be seen.

GLOSSARY

agrarian Related to lands, farming, or agriculture.

apparat The organization or system used for operating something.

bourgeoisie Members of the middle class.

bureaucrat A person who is part of a government or large company and does everything according to the rules or law.

capitalism An economic system where all things used, made, and transported are owned by individual people and companies, not government.

cartel A group of businesses that agree to fix prices so that they all will make more money.

centrifugal Moving away from a centre.

commonwealth A nation, state, or other political unit in which supreme authority is vested in the people.

communism A way of organizing a society in which the government owns the things that are used to make and transport products and nothing is owned privately.

coup The sudden, violent overthrow of an existing government by a small group.

democrat A person who believes in social equality.

dictatorship Rule by one person with total power.

doctrine A set of ideas or beliefs that are taught or believed to be true.

espousal The act of taking up or adopting a cause or belief.

exploitative Characterized by unfairly or cynically using another person or group for profit or advantage.

feudalism A European social system from the Middle Ages in which people worked and fought for nobles who gave them protection and use of the land in return.

guerrilla A person who engages in irregular warfare, especially as a member of an independent unit carrying out harassment and sabotage.

hegemony Influence or control over another country or group of people.

ideology The set of ideas and beliefs of a group or political party.

imperialist Describing a country that increases its power by gaining control over other areas of the world.

in absentia Without being present.

indigenous Produced, living, or existing naturally in a particular region or environment.

labourite A member of a group favoring the interests of labour.

nationalism Being loyal to and proud of one's country, often with the belief that it is better and more important than other countries.

nepotism The unfair practice of giving jobs and other favors to relatives.

occupation The possession, use, or settlement of land.

oppress To crush or burden by abuse of power or authority.

peasant A poor farmer or farm worker who has low social status.

philosophy A set of ideas about how to do something or how to live.

progressive Using or interested in new or modern ideas.

proletariat The laboring class; the lowest social or economic class of a community.

radical Describing extreme political or social views that are not shared by most people.

reformer A person who works to change and improve a society or government.

regionalism Interest in or loyalty to a particular region.

saboteur A person who destroys or damages something deliberately.

semifeudal Having some characteristics of feudalism, the European social system in which people worked and fought for a noble class.

socialism A way of organizing a society in which major industries are owned and controlled by the government, rather than by individual people and companies.

summit A meeting or series of meetings between leaders of two or more governments.

totalitarian Controlling the people of a country in a very strict way with complete power that cannot be opposed.

utopian Having the characteristics of an idealistic place of perfection in laws, government, and social conditions.

vanguard The group of people who are the leaders of an action or movement in society, politics, or art.

BIBLIOGRAPHY

Communism

Plato's communism is concisely discussed in George Klosko, "Platonic Politics," part 3 in his *The Development of Plato's Political Theory*, 2nd ed. (2006). The classic critique of Plato's communism is his pupil Aristotle's *Politics*, Book II. The origins and development of Thomas More's utopian communism are deftly traced in J.H. Hexter, *More's Utopia: The Biography of an Idea* (1952, reprinted 1976); and in Edward L. Surtz, *The Praise of Pleasure* (1957).

The ways in which Marx was interpreted, reinterpreted, and misinterpreted by Marxists of various stripes are delineated in Leszek Kołakowski, *Main Currents of Marxism*, 3 vol., trans. by P.S. Falla (1978, reissued 2005; originally published in Polish, 1976–78). Peter Gay, *The Dilemma of Democratic Socialism* (1952, reissued 1983), treats Bernstein and revisionism.

Socialism

Marx's life, times, and ideas are the subjects of several biographies, including Isaiah Berlin, *Karl Marx: His Life and Environment*, 4th ed. (1978, reissued 1996); and Peter Singer, *Marx* (1980, reissued 1996). His collaboration with Engels is portrayed in Terrell Carver, *Marx & Engels: The Intellectual Relationship* (1983), and *Engels* (1981, reissued 1991). The lives and ideas of Lenin, Stalin, and Trotsky are explored in Bertram D. Wolfe, *Three Who Made a Revolution* (1948, reissued 2001), a readable, stimulating history of Bolshevism in its formative years. Two other important figures are examined in Baruch Knei-Paz, *The Social and Political Thought of Leon Trotsky* (1978); and Stephen F. Cohen, *Bukharin and the Bolshevik Revolution* (1973, reissued 1980). Jonathan Spence, *Mao Zedong* (1999, reissued 2006); and John Bryan Starr, *Continuing the Revolution: The Political Thought of Mao* (1979), treat Mao Zedong's life and ideas.

Communism in Russia

For analysis of the political structure of Soviet society, see Aryeh L. Unger, *Constitutional Development in the USSR: A Guide to the Soviet Constitutions* (1981); Jerry F. Hough and Merle Fainsod, *How the Soviet Union Is Governed* (1979); and Mikhail Heller and Aleksandr Nekrich, *Utopia in Power: The History of the Soviet Union from 1917 to the Present* (1986; originally published in Russian, 1982).

Richard Pipes, *The Russian Revolution* (1990), covers the decline of tsarism from 1899 to the first year of the Bolshevik dictatorship. George Leggett, *The Cheka: Lenin's Political Police: The All-Russian Extraordinary Commission for Combating Counter-Revolution and Sabotage, December 1917 to February 1922* (1981), examines the special political institution that turned into a terror machine. John W. Wheeler-Bennett, *Brest-Litovsk: The Forgotten Peace*, March 1918 (1938, reissued 1971), remains the best account of the treaty that ended Russia's involvement in World War I. The 1941–45 war period and military matters in general are surveyed in John Erickson, *The Soviet High Command: A Military-Political History, 1918–1941* (1962, reprinted 1984), *German Rule in Russia, 1941–1945: A Study of Occupation Policies*, 2nd rev. ed. (1981); and Seweryn Bialer (ed.), *Stalin and His Generals: Soviet Military Memoirs of World War II* (1969, reprinted with a new preface, 1984). For the origins and development of the Cold War, see John Lukacs, *A New History of the Cold War*, 3rd ed., expanded (1966); Steven Merritt Miner, *Between Churchill and Stalin: The Soviet Union, Great Britain, and the Origins of the Grand Alliance* (1988); and for internal postwar events, Robert Conquest, *Power and Policy in the U.S.S.R.: The Study of Soviet Dynastics* (1961; published also as *Power and Policy in the U.S.S.R.: The Struggle for Stalin's Succession, 1945–1960*, 1967); On the Khrushchev era, see George W. Breslauer, *Khrushchev and Brezhnev as Leaders: Building Authority in Soviet Politics* (1982), a detailed examination of politics at the top. For an analysis of the Brezhnev era, see Archie Brown and Michael Kaser (eds.), *The Soviet Union Since the Fall of Khrushchev*, 2nd ed. (1978). The economic reforms of the period are examined in Anders Åslund, *Gorbachev's Struggle for Economic Reform*, updated and expanded ed. (1991); Padma Desai, *Perestroika in Perspective: The Design and Dilemmas of Soviet Reform*, updated ed. (1990); Abel Aganbegyan, *The Challenge: Economics of Perestroika* (1988); Marshall I. Goldman, *What Went Wrong with Perestroika* (1991).

Communism in the Eastern Bloc

Mike Dennis, *The Rise and Fall of the German Democratic Republic 1945–1990* (2000), provides a political history of the former East Germany. Communism and its collapse and aftermath are examined in these works: Jakub Karpinski, *Countdown: The Polish Upheavals of 1956, 1968, 1970, 1976, 1980*, trans. from Polish by Olga Amsterdamska and Gene M. Moore (1982); Jan Józef Lipski, *KOR: A History of the Workers' Defense Committee in Poland, 1976–1981*, trans. by Olga Amsterdamska and Gene M. Moore (1985; originally published in Polish, 1983); Michael Checinski, *Poland, Communism, Nationalism, Anti-Semitism*, trans. from Polish by Tadeusz Szafar (1982). Tad Szulc, *Pope*

John Paul II, The Biography (1995), which is especially valuable for perspectives on Karol Wojtyła's early development and accomplishments in Poland; George Weigel, *Witness to Hope: The Biography of Pope John Paul II* (1999). L.S. Stavrianos, *The Balkans Since 1453* (1958, reissued 1965); Charles Jelavich and Barbara Jelavich (eds.), *The Balkans in Transition: Essays on the Development of Balkan Life and Politics Since the Eighteenth Century* (1963, reprinted 1974), one of the few English sources dealing with the social structure of the Balkans in the Ottoman period.

Communism in China

C. Martin Wilbur and Julie Lien-ying How (eds.), *Documents on Communism, Nationalism, and Soviet Advisers in China, 1918–1927* (1956, reissued with corrections, 1972), discusses the Nationalist revolution. Chalmers A. Johnson, *Peasant Nationalism and Communist Power: The Emergence of Revolutionary China, 1937–45* (1962, reprinted 1971), broke new ground by proposing that wartime communist recruitment in northern China came from reaction to Japanese violence during the war and not mainly from endemic social problems. Mao Zedong (Mao Tse-tung), *Selected Works*, 4 vol. (1961–65), published by the Foreign Languages Press in Beijing, is the official translation of Mao's writings, and numerous other versions of his works have been published. More background is provided in Stuart R. Schram, *The Political Thought of Mao Tse-tung*, rev. ed. (1969); Stuart Schram (ed.), *Mao Tse-tung Unrehearsed: Talks and Letters: 1956–71* (1974; U.S. title, *Chairman Mao Talks to the People: Talks and Letters, 1956–1971*); and Frederic Wakeman, Jr., *History and Will: Philosophical Perspectives of Mao Tse-tung's Thought* (1973). Roderick MacFarquhar (ed.), *The Politics of China: The Eras of Mao and Deng*, 2nd ed.

(1997); Roderick MacFarquhar, *The Origins of the Cultural Revolution*, 3 vol. (1974–97); its continuation, Roderick MacFarquhar and Michael Shoenhals, *Mao's Last Revolution* (2006); and vols. 14 and 15 of *The Cambridge History of China*, both ed. by Roderick MacFarquhar and John K. Fairbank, respectively *The People's Republic, Part 1: The Emergence of Revolutionary China, 1949–1965* (1987), and *The People's Republic, Part 2: Revolutions Within the Chinese Revolution, 1966–1982* (1991), are all thorough treatments.

Communism in Southeast Asia

John Bastin and Harry J. Benda, *A History of Modern Southeast Asia: Colonialism, Nationalism, and Decolonization* (1968), although dated, is still worthy of careful attention. Syed Hussein Alatas, *The Myth of the Lazy Native: A Study of the Image of the Malays, Filipinos, and Javanese From the 16th to the 20th Century and Its Function in the Ideology of Colonial Capitalism* (1977), is a convincing attack by a Southeast Asian intellectual on colonialism and colonial scholarship in the region. Fred R. von der Mehden, *South-East Asia, 1930–1970: The Legacy of Colonialism and Nationalism* (1974), although dated, is a well-illustrated, useful introduction to the postwar region. Ronald D. Palmer and Thomas J. Reckford, *Building ASEAN* (1987), offers a basic introduction to the organization's first twenty years.

Communism in Latin America

Treatments of political topics that cross national boundaries include A.E. Van Niekerk, *Populism and Political Development in Latin America* (1974; originally published in Dutch, 1972); Edward J. Williams, *Latin American Christian Democratic Parties* (1967); and John A. Peeler, *Latin American*

Democracies: Colombia, Costa Rica, Venezuela (1985), assessing variants of liberal democracy. The impact of the Cuban Revolution and associated leftist currents is explored in Jorge G. Castañeda, *Utopia Unarmed: The Latin American Left After the Cold War* (1993), by a frustrated sympathizer; and William E. Ratliff, *Castroism and Communism in Latin America, 1959–1976: The Varieties of Marxist-Leninist Experience* (1976), a conservative perspective.

INDEX

World Trade Organization
(WTO), 180, 208, 209, 223
World War I, 18, 44, 53, 140, 191,
194, 224
World War II, 22, 47, 62–63,
119, 125, 128, 130, 192, 193,
195–196, 210, 211–212,
225–227
Wyszyński, Stefan, 121, 125

Y

Yakovlev, Aleksandr, 78, 81, 84, 85
Yalta Conference, 63, 120
Yanayev, Gennady, 83, 93

Yavlinsky, Grigory, 88
Yeltsin, Boris, 78, 79, 80, 82, 83,
85, 93, 94

Z

Zaikov, Lev, 78
Zaslavskaya, Tatyana, 79
Zhang Xueliang, 146
Zhang Zuolin, 146
Zhdanov, Andrey, 65
Zhivkov, Todor, 131
Zhou Enlai, 142, 152
Zhu De, 149, 158
Zinoviev, Grigory, 61